North Korea under Kim Chong-il

North Korea under Kim Chong-il

Power, Politics, and Prospects for Change

KEN E. GAUSE

Praeger Security International

AN IMPRINT OF ABC-CLIO, LLC
Santa Barbara, California • Denver, Colorado • Oxford, England

Library of Congress Cataloging-in-Publication Data

Gause, Ken E.
  North Korea under Kim Chong-il : power, politics, and prospects for change /
Ken E. Gause.
        p. cm. — (Praeger security international)
  Includes bibliographical references and index.
  ISBN 978-0-313-38175-1 (hardcopy : alk. paper) —
ISBN 978-0-313-38176-8 (ebook)
1. Korea (North)—Politics and government—1994– 2. Kim,
Chong-il, 1942– I. Title.
  DS935.774.G38 2011
  951.9305'1—dc23   2011017849

ISBN: 978-0-313-38175-1
EISBN: 978-0-313-38176-8

15 14 13 12   2 3 4 5

This book is also available on the World Wide Web as an eBook.
Visit www.abc-clio.com for details.

Praeger
An Imprint of ABC-CLIO, LLC

ABC-CLIO, LLC
130 Cremona Drive, P.O. Box 1911
Santa Barbara, California 93116-1911

This book is printed on acid-free paper ∞

Manufactured in the United States of America

Contents

Preface

Everybody is trying to sort of read the tea leaves [on North Korea] as to what is happening and what is likely to occur, and there is a lot of guessing going on. . . . But there is also an increasing amount of pressure because if there is a succession, even if it's a peaceful succession, that creates more uncertainty and it may also encourage behaviors that are even more provocative as a way to consolidate power within the society.

Hillary Clinton, Secretary of State,
in Seoul, February 19, 2009

I think we've said many times that the leadership and how decisions are made in North Korea is an opaque process. . . . Who's actually taking decisions is very opaque as well. We don't have any direct contact on the ground and are not able to well judge what we hear coming out of North Korea.

Gordon Duguid, State Department
Spokesman, February 19, 2009

One of the most vexing foreign policy problems facing the international community today is the case of North Korea. Since the late 1980s, successive leaders of the five Northeast Asian powers have confronted the challenge to little effect. Despite a variety of foreign policy strategies ranging from threats of military force to engagement to benign neglect to engagement within the context of the Six Party Talks, neither the United States, nor South Korea, nor China has succeeded in removing the problems North Korea poses for the international community. The U.S. intelligence community summarizes the North Korea problem in the following way:

- North Korea has a million man army and missile arsenals that threaten South Korean and U.S. forces along the Demilitarized Zone (DMZ).
- North Korea has a nuclear weapons program and is pursuing fissile material through two processes, plutonium separation and uranium enrichment.
- North Korea probably has active biological and chemical weapons programs and probably chemical and possibly biological weapons ready for use.
- North Korea has an aggressive ballistic missile program and is developing delivery systems capable of one day hitting the continental United States.
- North Korea generates hard currency by proliferating ballistic missiles and associated technology, as well as conventional weapons. It has sold ballistic missiles to other states, including Iran and Syria.
- North Korea has engaged in a range of illegal activities more typical of an organized crime entity than a nation state, including kidnapping, narcotrafficking, and counterfeiting U.S. currency.
- North Korea's leadership has impoverished the nation and created refugee flows. North Korean refugees are a minor problem for neighboring states at this time, but could precipitate a regional crisis if the North Korean regime were to someday fall.[1]

As the United States and its allies have tried to deal with these challenges, they have been met with a country whose security and foreign policies appear erratic and unpredictable. North Korea's lack of susceptibility to diplomatic pressure and willingness to engage in provocative actions as part of a brinksmanship strategy makes it a seemingly intractable problem. Policy makers face many questions with no apparent answers.

- What are the North Koreans trying to accomplish by developing nuclear weapons and engaging in provocations, such as the sinking of the *Cheonan* or the shelling Yeonpyeong Island?
- Does North Korea seriously contemplate attacking South Korea?
- How can the international community effectively deter North Korean aggression and encourage democratic reform?
- Would a grand bargain that ensures North Korean sovereignty and security in return for dismantling the nuclear program be attractive to Kim Chong-il and his likely successors?

The challenge of coming up with a workable North Korea policy is made worse by the opacity of the regime. No country provides a harder target for the world's intelligence communities than North Korea. With no history of diplomatic relations with North Korea, no presence in its capital, Pyongyang, and little success in cultivating informants, U.S. policy makers have difficulty understanding the intentions behind North Korea's troublesome actions. Ambassadors from countries that do have an embassy presence lament that being in the "Land of the Fatherly Leader" yields little more situational awareness. Virtually every aspect of the Pyongyang regime is mysterious and puzzling. In short, North Korea is difficult for outsiders to understand and analyze, including the nature of its political system and the focus of its leadership, namely Kim Chong-il.

As a consequence, foreign policy toward North Korea often resorts to a "Black Box" approach devised in a vacuum and based largely on assumptions of rationality with little regard to North Korean motivations. This approach risks mirror imaging, which lacks appreciation for a target country's unique culture and political dynamics. This can lead to failed policies and policy makers scratching their heads wondering why certain approaches lacked traction.

PURPOSE OF THIS BOOK

The purpose of this book is to provide the reader with an understanding of the political process and leadership environment in North Korea. The barriers to such an understanding are formidable. Most scholars are denied access to North Korea and those who are fortunate enough to tour the Hermit Kingdom are tightly controlled, seeing only what the regime wants to reveal and talking only to those presented to them by their minders. Therefore, scholars are compelled to study North Korean developments at a distance. In recent years, the thankless task of analyzing the tea leaves from official announcements and such has been made easier by several channels into the regime that have begun to present themselves to those intrepid Pyongyang watchers who seek to shed light on the North Korean leadership.

Today, there are numerous channels of information on internal North Korean affairs, which make their way to the outside world. Pockets of information reside in foreign governments and intelligence agencies, business and personal networks that extend throughout the region and beyond, as well as a growing pool of defectors, some of whom were once members of the North Korean elite. While some of this information may make it into intelligence reports and ultimately into briefing books for policy makers, much remains hidden, not because it is necessarily beyond reach, but simply because it is not easily exploitable. Much of the information resides with individuals and in articles and books that U.S. scholars cannot take advantage of because they lack access, language skills, time, and especially a methodology for piecing the information together.

This study makes use of a wide variety of sources. In addition to English sources, of which there are few, this book will exploit the rich literature found in Korean, Japanese, and Chinese scholarship on the North Korean leadership, much of which has not been translated into English. This literature includes several recently published defector monographs, which examine the North Korean regime from several angles.

The study also sifts through and gleans what is possible from the primary source literature. Information on the NK leadership is routinely obscured in the official media. Details regarding the regime's organizational structure and many key positions within the military and party apparatuses are not revealed. During the KCI period, this control of information has not diminished but become tighter. That said, some information is available through a close reading of the North Korean press, provided the reader has additional sources to verify it against. According to a study by the Foreign Broadcast Information Service, several generalizations can be made with regard to North Korean treatment of leadership information.[2]

- With the exception of defense-related ministries and committees, North Korean media appears to be somewhat open concerning the names and official positions of most senior government officials, such as Cabinet ministers and vice ministers, and deputies to the Supreme People's Assembly (SPA). Positions within the party apparatus are also identified, but the nature of a cadre's portfolio is normally obscured. Dismissals/appointments of Cabinet ministers and other high-ranking officials are often announced by SPA Presidium decrees, which are publicized by the media. Sometimes, however, changes are made public indirectly, through the reporting of a person's attendance at an official function.

- Changes within the high command are made public through Supreme Commander's orders. Party appointments/dismissals are normally not made public. Biographical information on individuals is rarely found, although it sometimes appears in funeral notices. A rare exception to this rule occurred in the reporting surrounding the Third Party Conference when profiles of the Politburo appeared in the media.

- A reading of funeral lists can provide insights into North Korean pecking order and seniority of officials. An interesting insight gleaned over the last decade was the shift in the lineup as members of the National Defense Commission after 1998 began to be placed before the members of the Politburo. This was one of the first indications of how the Military-First Policy impacted the North Korean leadership.

- There are also discernable patterns related to the seating order on leadership rostrums.

- On occasion, the North Korean media resorts to the use of code words in order to convey information to domestic (elite) audiences.[3]

Finally, this study benefits from numerous interviews with key defectors and people with links into the regime, as well as discussions with over 100 Pyongyang watchers in the region. Before his death in October 2010, the author met with the most senior defector, Hwang Chang-yop, for several hours to discuss day-to-day operations of the regime. He was able to talk in detail about simple, often mundane, issues that are crucial to understanding how a totalitarian regime operates. Who talks to whom? Who is related to whom? How is a Politburo agenda set?[4]

If this study differs from the books that have come before it, it is in terms of the lens through which the material is examined. Unlike many studies that focus on North Korea as a state actor, this study examines Pyongyang's wider leadership and leadership environment. The book draws much of its inspiration from one of the fathers of leadership analysis in the United States, Merle Fainsod, who in his *How Russia Is Ruled* (1953) wrestled with many of the same problems facing today's Pyongyang watcher. As with that classic study, this study seeks to illuminate an opaque regime and the leadership that runs it. Unlike many studies that focus on Kim Chong-il and his colorful personality, this study focuses on the North Korean leadership environment. While it recognizes the importance of what B.R. Myers refers to in his groundbreaking work as the "paternal leader," it seeks to understand the court from which he rules.

A NOTE ABOUT TRANSLITERATION

This book uses a modified version of the McCune-Reischauer system. It eliminates apostrophes and other grammatical markings (other than in secondary citations) for ease of recognition by English speakers. It also resorts to some common spellings for names and words. The following examples will give the reader an understanding how certain rules are applied: Kim Il-sung (not Kim Il-song), Kim Chong-il (not Kim Jong-il), Ri Yong-ho (not Yi Yong-ho), Choe Tae-bok (not Choe Thae-bok or Choe Tae-pok), O Kuk-yol (not O Kuk-ryol), Cho Myong-nok (not Jo Myong-rok), Chang Song-taek (not Jang Song-thaek), U Tong-chuk (not U Dong-chuk), Choe Yong-rim (not Choe Yong-nim), Kim Myong-guk (not Kim Myong-kuk), *Chuche* (not *Juche*).

ACKNOWLEDGMENTS

This book is the beneficiary of a great deal of scholarship that has gone before. Several books are worth noting for their analysis of North Korean politics. The author benefitted from the analysis contained in their pages.

Adrian Buzo, *The Guerilla Dynasty: Politics and Leadership in North Korea* (Boulder, CO: Westview Press, 1999).

Andrei Lankov, *Crisis in North Korea: The Failure of De-Stalinization, 1956* (Honolulu: University Press of Hawaii, 2005).

Andrei Lankov, *From Stalin to Kim Il Sung: The Formation of North Korea, 1945–1960* (New Brunswick, NJ: Rutgers University Press, 2002).

Jae-Cheon Lim, *Kim Jong-il's Leadership of North Korea* (London: Routledge, 2009).

Bradley K. Martin, *Under the Loving Care of the Fatherly Leader: North Korea and the Kim Dynasty* (New York: St. Martin's Press, 2006).

Koon Woo Nam, *The North Korean Communist Leadership, 1945–1965: A Study of Factionalism and Political Consolidation* (Tuscaloosa: University of Alabama Press, 1974).

Dae-Sook Suh, *Kim Il-sung: The North Korean Leader* (New York: Columbia University Press, 1995).

Dae-Sook Suh, *Korean Communism 1945–1980: A Reference Guide to the Political System* (Honolulu: University Press of Hawaii, 1981).

The author would also like to acknowledge the tremendously important work being done by the Open Source Center. It is a vital source for any scholar and the insights its analysts glean from the world's media is without comparison.

Finally, the author would like to acknowledge the important contributions by a dedicated group of Pyongyang watchers in South Korea, China, Russia, and Japan, whose insights are reflected throughout this book. Although their names do not appear in these pages in order to protect their identities, their insights are nonetheless much appreciated.

PART I

Kim Chong-il as Leader

One of the unique characteristics of the succession from Kim Il-sung to Kim Chong-il was its drama. Kim Il-sung died on July 8, 1994, of a heart attack. He was 82. *Nodong Sinmun* reported the heart attack, blaming it on fatigue and heart disease.[1] It did not specifically mention that Kim had suffered from arterial sclerosis for years.[2]

Images of a shocked and grieving nation filled the North Korean media for weeks after Kim's death.[3] In fact, North Korean media explained the 11-day gap between Kim's death and the funeral on July 19 as resulting from the need to accommodate the great outpouring of grief and endless crowds that wished to pay their condolences. However, analysis of the funeral and memorial ceremony suggests another possible motive for the delay. This was political theater designed to send a message, one that probably took time to craft within the Korean Workers' Party (KWP's) Propaganda Department.

Television coverage of the funeral began with three hours of re-runs of coverage from the weeks before, showing the long lines of sobbing citizens and soldiers passing by Kim Il-sung's glass-covered funeral bier surrounded by flowers.[4] Part of this spectacle was Kim Chong-il greeting the mourners, silently mouthing greetings. In the later coverage of these events, the more important mourners were revealed on camera. The message the North Korean media apparently wanted to convey was that Kim Chong-il was a figure of authority, not just the dutiful son of the dead leader.

Even when Kim Chong-il was not on camera, his role within the regime was not forgotten. Images of family members of deceased first-generation partisan fighters were interspersed throughout the coverage. Almost on cue they loudly professed their regret for not working harder to fulfill Kim Il-sung's dreams for his country, then in the next breath just as loudly expressed their loyalty to Kim Chong-il.[5] Occasional interviews of these mourners yielded further exhortations of Kim Chong-il's considerable capabilities.[6]

The funeral itself was carried out with precision. The procession through the streets of Pyongyang began with several security vehicles, followed by a car carrying a huge photograph of Kim Il-sung, followed by a car carrying a floral wreath, followed by a phalanx of motorcycle police, followed by the limousine carrying Kim's flower-covered coffin, followed by several Mercedes sedans carrying high ranking North Korean figures and visiting dignitaries. The crowds lining the streets appeared to be in a state of complete shock and mourning, although some Korean analysts suggested that the grief was more an act than the real thing. Much of the coverage of the crowds focused on those at Kim Il-sung's statue. These crowds did not appear to be made up of random people, but mobilized groups (often wearing the same clothing or uniforms) gathered and organized for the cameras.

A curious aspect of the North Korean reporting of the event was references to Kim Chong-il as General Secretary and President. Mourners at the statue of Kim Il-sung pledged (in front of cameras) to "serve Kim Chong-il as the General Secretary of the Workers' Party of the Central Committee and the President of the state."[7]

For Pyongyang watchers, the memorial service the next day (July 20) was of particular interest. This was not so much a memorial service as another step in the coronation of Kim Chong-il as the new leader.[8] Kim himself did not speak, but left that to five selected VIPs representing different segments of North Korean society (a worker, a farmer, and three speakers representing the party, military, and Chosen Soren). Like the man-on-the-street interviews from the day before, they praised Kim Il-sung and then pledged loyalty to Kim Chong-il, "the Great Successor."[9] Two speakers, Foreign Minister Kim Yong-nam and Vice Minister of Defense Kim Kwang-chin, not only voiced support for the hereditary succession, but made it clear that no major shifts in policy would be forthcoming. Kim Il-sung's Ten Great Points and Three Great Principles (Self-Reliance, Peace, and Grand Solidarity of the Race) would continue to guide North Korean development. From a balcony high above the crowd, Kim was flanked by O Chin-u and Kang Song-san, the second- and third-ranking members of the leadership according to the state funeral committee list published on July 9.

Farther to Kim's right was his uncle, Kim Yong-chu, and next to him was Kim's mother-in-law, Kang Song-ae. Pyongyang watchers did not know what to make of Kang's role in the funeral given the rumors of the tensions between her and her son-in-law. The fact that she had catapulted to the rank of 14th at the funeral service and 7th at the memorial rally after having been ranked 104th on the July 9 273-member State Funeral Committee list led many to speculate that her power might be rising. A more likely explanation for the elevation in her ranking was that it was a matter of protocol given her status as the widow of Kim Il-sung. Her sons, Kim Pyong-il and Kim Yong-il, did not participate in the services, suggesting that Kim Chong-il had succeeded in "cutting the extra branch (*kyot-kaji*) that supported the Kang Song-ae part of the family."

Contrary to what many Pyongyang watchers expected, Kim Il-sung's death gave way to a smooth transfer of power, absent the purges and rampant factionalism that often accompany leadership turnover in totalitarian governments. Kim Chong-il's power consolidation strategy, while increasingly reliant on military-first politics, was not exclusionary. As one Pyongyang watcher noted, the politics Kim Chong-il practiced in the years following his father's death were characterized by inclusion, honor sharing agreements, and divide-and-rule tactics. This allowed him to mitigate the potential cleavages within the regime and build a ruling circle that would usher in a new ruling system in 1998.[10]

CHAPTER 1

Establishing the Kim Chong-il System

After the funeral, Kim Chong-il issued the edict that his father's body was to be preserved for eternity at Kumsusan Memorial Palace on the outskirts of Pyongyang. This was the first of several moves Kim made to preserve the legacy of Kim Il-sung. What role the preservation of Kim Il-sung's legacy played in Kim Chong-il's power consolidation was not immediately clear. As the weeks and months passed, outside commentators wondered when Kim would begin to place his stamp on the regime. When would the personnel changes come? When would Kim assume the top offices of party and state? The fact that he delayed these actions led many Pyongyang watchers to speculate that a system of checks and balances existed inside Pyongyang that placed limits on Kim's power and authority. This view, however, was at odds with the consistent emphasis by the North Korean media of Kim's virtue and authority, referring to him as the "Supreme Leader of the Party, State, and Army."[1]

In later years, it became clear that Kim Chong-il took a very deliberate path to securing his power. Observing a traditional Confucian respect for the dead, he paid tribute to his father for three years before assuming the formal mantle of power. Upon examination of the circumstances in which Kim found himself in July 1994, such a strategy makes sense. But embedded in the politics Kim was about to unfold were the potential seeds of the regime's demise.

LEADERSHIP ENVIRONMENT

Because of the two-man rule that had preceded Kim Il-sung's death, the leadership structure was populated with a variety of cleavages, divided loyalties, and potential factions. This extended to the Kim family itself. Although the efficient conduct of the funeral suggested at least temporary cohesion within the family, nepotism in Kim Il-sung's last years created the possibility for internecine power struggles in the future.[2] Kang Song-ae maintained a position within the regime, as did Kim Yong-chu.[3] This suggested at least two centers of power within the family that could eventually challenge Kim Chong-il's role as the rightful successor. They could even challenge his basic hereditary claim to power. In the case of Kang, she could point to her son, Kim Pyong-il, who allegedly enjoyed a great deal of support within military circles, as someone who understood the Korean People's Army (KPA) and could ensure its increasing involvement in politics. As for Kim Yong-chu, his ties to the first generation of partisan supporters of Kim Il-sung went back decades. He after all was the presumed heir apparent until he was supplanted by his nephew in the early 1970s.

Even though he had begun building a patronage system within the military in the early 1990s, Kim Chong-il still faced a high command that was divided between those who had served alongside Kim Il-sung in the guerrilla struggle against Japan and later during the Korean War and an upcoming second generation who had matured during the 1960s when the military actively pursued a political agenda. As had been evidenced in the O Kuk-yol affair in the 1980s,[4] this lack of a shared history sometimes bred distrust and suspicion. Kim Chong-il had taken steps to build relations with the first generation, especially through the support of O Chin-u and Choe Kwang. Despite this support, resentment toward Kim Chong-il and the dynastic succession still lingered.

The generational split was, of course, not confined to the military. The two-man rule had created two semi-independent hierarchies of authority throughout the regime. The first-generation partisans remained in key positions in the party and government apparatuses. Although some had been demoted and dismissed in the 1980s, many had returned to the central leadership as the succession process gathered speed. There was little in common between these old guard and the younger elites of Kim Chong-il's generation. Instead of a bond forged in combat, this part of the Kim patronage network was divided into many parts. Some were Kim's classmates, graduates of the Namsan School, Manyongdae Revolutionary Academy, and Kim Il-sung University. Others, such as members of the Three Revolution Movement squads of the 1970s, had helped him secure his position as heir apparent. Though many were the children of respected revolutionaries, none had taken part in the Kim Il-sung–led revolution and thus did not share the ethos of the so-called guerrilla generation.

This leadership landscape was potentially treacherous and not conducive to a quick transfer of formal power. Kim Chong-il most likely sensed that if he moved too quickly to secure the reins across the party, military, and government apparatuses, he risked inflaming the fault lines within the regime. Particularly troublesome were the first-generation revolutionaries, such as O Chin-u, Paek Hak-rim, and Choe Kwang, who by virtue of their relationship with Kim Il-sung were virtually untouchable. Kim Chong-il was limited in his ability to issue orders and, instead, had to lobby for their support.

Given these circumstances, Kim did not move at all. In fact, he went into seclusion for 100 days, finally appearing in public on October 16 at a memorial service. On November 14, *Nodong Sinmun* (the party's official mouthpiece) carried an article by Kim titled "Socialism Is a Science," which was the longest he had ever written.[5] It was an article about socialism, a subject that was highly abstract. Nestled within the platitudes and discussion of ideology was the announcement that Kim would not assume the title of *"Suryong"* (Leader). He wrote that his nation "must have a political leader who has boundless love for people," and then added,

It is the unshakable will of our people that dear Comrade Kim Il-sung should be upheld high as the *suryong* of our party and our revolution for thousands and tens of thousands of years to come.[6]

He thus made it clear that the title of *"suryong"* was reserved for Kim Il-sung only. North Korea became a country led by a successor of an extinct leader, in other words, a *suryong*-led country without a *suryong*.[7] This meant the country had no other choice but to change its political system. But that would not happen formally for another four years. At this moment, the ghost of Kim Il-sung would serve another purpose, that of providing political cover as the new regime was about to enter into one of its darkest periods.

DEATH OF O CHIN-U

On February 25, 1995, the Minister of People's Armed Forces, O Chin-u,[8] died shortly after returning from France, where he had undergone treatment for cancer. O's death left Kim Chong-il as the lone remaining Politburo standing member. More important, it removed the most powerful military figure. This presented Kim with a particular challenge in how to fill the vacuum within the high command created by O's death without upsetting the delicate balance of power he had taken pains to maintain since Kim Il-sung's death.

In March, North Korean media coverage of conferences of military commanders and political guidance officers held in Pyongyang suggested some movement within the KWP Central Military Committee. Although the last list of the KWP CMC was published before Kim Il-sung's death, seating and speech protocols at the meetings suggested the promotion of some of Kim's key lieutenants into the body, including VMAR Kim Kwang-chin, VMAR Kim Pong-yul, Gen. Kim Myong-guk, and Gen. Pak Ki-so. Kim Kwang-chin and Kim Pong-yul came from the 1.5 and first generations, respectively. Both had risen through the ranks under O Chin-u, but had not gathered much attention until Kim Il-sung's death, when both became very active in promoting Kim Chong-il's credentials as a military leader. Generals Kim Myong-guk and Pak Ki-so had frequently accompanied Kim Chong-il on his inspections of military units. Their positions as chief of the General Staff's Operations Bureau and commander of the Pyongyang Defense Command placed them at the heart of regime protection.

The apparent rise of Kim's supporters led to much speculation that a massive turnover within the high command was fast approaching. Many Pyongyang watchers expected Kim Kwang-chin to succeed O Chin-u as Minister of People's Armed Forces or, if Choe Kwang were appointed to that position, to replace Choe as Chief of the General Staff.[9] Others expected that O Kuk-yol, who had been shifted to the party apparatus after his removal as chief of the General Staff in 1988, would return to the heights of the military chain of command.

Kim used the 50th anniversary of the founding of the party in October to conduct the first large-scale reshuffle of the military since the death of his father. Despite some prior speculation, it was a well-balanced reshuffle designed to appease the old guard, whose support was still indispensible, and reward, yet temper, the passions of the new guard, whose ties to Kim were beyond question. On October 8, Choe Kwang was appointed Minister of People's Armed Forces, filling the post O Chin-u's death had left vacant seven months before. Five days later, Vice Marshal Kim Yong-chun was appointed chief of the General Staff, replacing Choe; Air Force Commander Cho Myong-nok was appointed director of the General Political Bureau; and Vice Marshal Kim Kwang-chin was appointed first vice minister of the People's Armed Forces, a newly created post.

Several clues emerged from this reshuffle. It appeared that in the absence of assuming formal control of the regime, Kim intended to hold sway over the military by "distributing military power." He divided the O Chin-u portfolio between Choe Kwang and Cho Myong-nok. In addition, a more clear division of labor was established between the ministry and the General Staff, with the latter assuming more operational authority and the former handling administrative issues. In addition the General Staff and General Political Bureau were elevated in status to be on par with the Ministry of People's Armed Forces. This ensured that Choe would not assume the power and influence of his predecessor, something made very clear at the military parade that marked the party's anniversary.[10] On the reviewing stand, Choe moved up one spot, switching positions with deputy premier and Minister of Foreign Affairs Kim Yong-nam. But Choe's position fell far short of O Chin-u's position on leadership rostrums, which came second only to Kim Chong-il.

Table 1.1
Leadership Positions on the Reviewing Stand for the KWP 50th Anniversary Parade[a]

Rank	Name	Position
		Politburo Members
1	Kim Chong-il	NDC Chairman and Supreme Commander
2	Ri Chong-ok	Vice President
3	Pak Song-chol	Vice President
4	Kim Yong-chu	Vice President
5	Kang Song-san	Premier
6	Choe Kwang	Minister of People's Armed Forces
7	Kim Yong-nam	Deputy Premier, Minister of Foreign Affairs
8	Kye Unt-tae	KWP Secretary
9	Chon Pyong-ho	KWP Secretary
10	Han Song-yong	KWP Secretary
11	Sun Yong-sok	Chairman, South Pyongan Province KWP Executive Committee
		Politburo Candidate Members
12	Kim Chol-man	NDC Member
13	Choe Tae-Pok	KWP Secretary
14	Choe Yong-in	Deputy Premier
15	Hong Song-nam	Deputy Premier
16	Yang Hyong-sop	Speaker of the SPA
17	Hong Sok-Hyong	Chairman, National Planning Committee
18	Yon Hyong-muk	Chairman, Chagang Province KWP Executive Committee
		High Command
19	MAR Ri Ul-sol	Commander, General Guard Command
20	VMAR Paek Hak-rim	Minister of People's Security
21	VMAR Yu Tu-ik	CMC Member
22	VMAR Kim Kwang-chin	NDC Member and First Vice Minister of People's Armed Forces
23	Kim Ik-hyon	CMC Member

(*continued*)

Table 1.1 *(Continued)*

Rank	Name	Position
24	VMAR Cho Myong-nok	Commander, Air Force (later Director of the General Political Bureau)
25	VMAR Ri Ha-il	Director, KWP Military Department
26	VMAR Kim Yong-chun	Chief of the General Staff Department
		KWP Secretaries
27	Kim Ki-nam	KWP Secretary
28	Kim Kuk-tae	KWP Secretary
29	Hwang Chang-yop	KWP Secretary
30	Kim Chung-in	KWP Secretary
31	So Kwan-hui	KWP Secretary
32	Kim Yong-sun	KWP Secretary

[a] This table only covers the top 32 positions on the reviewing stand. It is important to remember, protocol order does not necessarily reflect actual power in North Korea. According to the protocol of the mid-1990s, officials were generally ranked in the following order: Politburo Members, Politburo Candidate Members, party Secretaries, Premier and vice premiers, Cabinet ministers. As the profile of the military began to rise, vice marshals often were seated among the KWP Secretaries, after the senior secretaries, but before lower-ranking secretaries.

The reshuffle also brought into focus the importance of some rising stars within the high command, all of whom had strong ties to Kim Chong-il. Of these, Kim Yong-chun was the most surprising. He had seemingly come from obscurity to the top of the military chain of command in a matter of months. Defector reports would later confirm that his rise was likely due to his service in helping uncover and put down a potential coup d'état in April.[11] On the reviewing stand, VMAR Kim Yong-chun was seated alongside other senior military leaders, including other newly minted officers (VMAR Ri Ha-il,[12] MAR Ri Ul-sol,[13] VMAR Cho Myong-nok[14]), between Politburo candidate members and lower-ranked party secretaries. Three other military officers who played notable roles in the parade were generals Kim Myong-guk (chief of the General Staff's Operations Bureau), Chang Song-u (commander of the Third Corps), and Won Ung-hui (director of the Military Security Command).[15]

The final observation is that although these appointments came on the occasion of the 50th anniversary of the party, ironically no accompanying appointments were mentioned for the party or the Administrative Council, the other two principle organizations in the North Korean power structure.

Since Kim Il-sung's death, the Central Committee had remained moribund, with change coming only through the deaths of elderly party leaders. The Supreme People's Assembly was not convened in 1995 and was formally postponed for the duration of the mourning period. For many Pyongyang watchers, this inactivity was a clear indication of the increasing power of the North Korean military.

BRUSH WITH REFORM

In the intervening months between O Chin-u's death and the party's 50th anniversary, some Pyongyang watchers detected what they believed was an attempt at reform to deal with the country's increasingly dismal economic predicament.[16] One should caution that the evidence of this shift in policy is thin and based on a close reading of writings by Kim Chong-il in the context of what appears to be an attempt by North Korea to engage the outside world.

Reacting to a North Korean inquiry to purchase cheap rice, Japan sent a delegation to Pyongyang in March 1995 to explore the possibility of a rapprochement in relations with its long-time enemy. Leveraging off of the U.S.–North Korean Agreed Framework, the United States took advantage of this opening to reach an agreement with North Korea in June that enabled the Korean Peninsula Energy Development Organization (KEDO) to provide light-water nuclear reactors, thus allowing the agreement to go forward on halting the North Korean nuclear program.[17] In South–North talks held on June 21, South Korea promised to provide 150,000 tons of rice in aid. On June 30, Japan, which had been waiting for this to happen, agreed to provide 300,000 tons—a volume that went far over the volume promised by South Korea to North Korea.[18]

These tentative experiments at engagement were followed on June 21 by a Kim Chong-il article titled "Giving Precedence to Ideological Activities Is a Must in Carrying Out the Great Socialist Task." While giving deference to *Chuche* ideology and the "anti-Japan guerrilla model" to carry the message of the revolution, the article seemed to indicate the desire not to be constrained by the past bastion state mentality. As one Pyongyang watcher noted, it made him wonder whether "North Korea could be on the way to moving from the stage of being a mono-ideological system and a guerrilla state to the stage of being a country based on the national socialism of normal sense."[19]

Kim Chong-il called for the development of socialist legal codes of conduct and regulations to enable "economic and cultural exchanges and cooperation with other countries of the world based on the principle of equality and reciprocity" albeit with "special care so that bourgeois ideology, culture and life style will not contaminate the country." These points suggested North Korea was entertaining a limited opening up to the outside world.[20]

If this analysis is correct, it suggests that a year into the new regime, policy debates still took place within the North Korean leadership. Although the rise of the military and the hardline proclivities of the old guard dominated outside discussions of the regime in Pyongyang, some defectors believed that reformers still existed within North Korea, mainly within the Administrative Council, including Premier Kang Song-san, Vice Premier and Minister of Foreign Affairs Kim Yong-nam, and former Premier Hong Yong-muk. These more pragmatic members of the leadership insisted that North Korea's broad policy strategy should adhere to Kim Il-sung's last instruction, which was eventual reconciliation with South Korea. Within this mandate, they might have argued, was an implied step of reaching an accommodation with the outside world in order to make reconciliation a reality, especially if it satisfied the near-term goal of feeding the country.

ARDUOUS MARCH

As the regime wrestled with consequences of engagement and reform, problems continued to grow for the country at-large. A little more than a year after Kim Il-sung's death, a series of great floods struck North Korea in July and August 1995. Pyongyang's own figures indicated that 5.2 million North Koreans were affected across 145 counties and 8 provinces.[21] The floods caused nearly 15 billion (USD) in damage and left nearly 500,000 people homeless.[22] In addition to the devastation wrought on the population, the floods propelled the economy into a free fall. Crops were destroyed and an already fragile food rationing system failed to stave off famine.[23] From a high of 5.4 million metric tons in 1989, grain production plummeted in 1995 to 3.4 million metric tons.[24] The agricultural base of the country was nearly destroyed and left vulnerable to more floods and droughts, which would follow over the next two years. For the first time since the Korean War, North Korea failed to announce its budget. In a major blow to its national pride, Pyongyang asked the international community for assistance in feeding its people, something that likely reinforced Kim's decision to go slow when it came to assuming the formal positions of authority.[25] As if this was not enough, U.S.–North Korean relations, which appeared to be headed for improvement following the "Agreed Framework," failed to produce much follow-up progress due to delays in negotiations. The momentum of 1994 was lost.

This catastrophe brought with it daunting challenges for the new regime. It also exposed cleavages that undermined the regime's ability to function. Pyongyang watchers debated the nature of these cleavages and their culpability in the regime's impotence to deal with the problem. Some believed Kim Chong-il was tied to the failed economic policies of the past by hardline elements within the government who refused to let North Korea open up.[26] They argued that the seizure of a South Korean rice aide ship in a North Korean port, for example, resulted from a confrontation within the regime, which was won by the hardliners. Hardliners used the incident to send a signal that they would not tolerate continued reliance on international assistance, which undermined the tenets of *Chuche.*

This theory of regime dynamics was probably true to a point. Certainly Kim was cautious in dealing with power centers within the regime. But most likely, his authority was not constrained. Kim's leadership style had been set as far back as the late 1970s and continued with few alterations after he succeeded his father. Kim used parallel channels to exercise control—one centered on the formal heads of agencies and the other an informal line of control based on his close aides. Each monitored the other to ensure that loyalty to Kim was maintained. This often resulted in competition for influence, something that stifled coordination and even resulted in contradictory guidance. This situation was exacerbated by Kim's tendency to ingratiate himself with powerful figures in the party, government, and military by giving them villas and other expensive items brought into North Korea from his personal procurement network.[27]

This leadership style may have been important for Kim to maintain his position within the regime, but it was ill suited to policy development. In April 1996, Kim confessed that the state was having trouble managing the economy. But instead of diagnosing the problem and announcing bold initiatives, he signaled his increasing frustration with the system's inability to carry out his will. Much of his criticism was aimed at the party for its inability to solve problems at the provincial and local levels and to carry out instructions from Pyongyang. At a commemoration meeting of the 50th anniversary of Kim Il-sung University in December, Kim noted, "The reason why people are loyal to the instructions of the Central Committee is not because of party organizations and workers, but because of my authority."[28] In the same speech, he foreshadowed a shift in economic control and maintenance by revealing that President Kim Il-sung had repeatedly told him while he was alive to never become involved in the economic work, for it would interfere with his ability to carry on the work of the party and military and could "bring about irretrievable consequences to the revolution and construction." Contained in this remark was Kim's decision to remove from the party its responsibilities for economic policy, leaving this task to the leading economic officials.[29]

Unlike the year before, Kim's speeches and articles were no longer laced with reform-minded language. His return to hardline rhetoric and the abandonment of personal responsibility for the economy signaled that whatever traction reform elements inside the regime once had within the circle of Kim's closest aides was gone. With the country's economic condition worsening, Kim apparently decided to stick by the policies of his father and do nothing more than call for austerity measures.

As if to drive home this hardline approach, on December 24, *Nodong Sinmun* published an article under Kim Chong-il's byline titled "It Is Revolutionaries' Sublime Moral Duty to Respect Senior Revolutionaries." In

Table 1.2
National Defense Commission/KWP Central Military Committee:
North Korea's Crisis Management System

Member	Body	Comments
	National Defense Commission	
Kim Chong-il	Chairman	
Choe Kwang	Vice Chairman	Minister of People's Armed Forces
Chon Pyong-ho	Member	KWP Secretary for Logistics
Kim Chol-man	Member	Chairman, Second Economic Committee
Ri Ul-sol	Member	Director, General Guard Bureau
Kim Pong-yul	Member	Vice Minister of People's Armed Forces (died in 1995)
Kim Kwang-chin	Member	Vice Minister of People's Armed Forces
Ri Ha-il	Member	Director, KWP Military Department
	KWP Central Military Committee[a]	
Kim Chong-il	Member	
Choe Kwang	Member	Minister of People's Armed Forces
Paek Hak-rim	Member	Minister of People's Security
Ri Ul-sol	Member	Director, General Guard Bureau
Ri Tu-ik	Member	Former Director, General Staff Operations Bureau
Ri Ha-il	Member	Director, KWP Military Department
Kim Ik-hyon	Member	Director, CC Civil Defense Department
Cho Myong-nok	Member	Director, General Political Bureau
Kim Il-chol	Member	Commander, KPA Navy
Ri Pong-won	Member	Vice Director, General Political Bureau
O Yong-pang	Member	Vice Minister of People's Armed Forces

(*continued*)

Table 1.2   (*Continued*)

Member	Body	Comments
O Kuk-yol	Member	Director, KWP Operations Department
Kim Kang-hwan	Member	Depurty Chief, General Staff Department
Chon Mun-sop	Member	Chairman, State Control Committee
Kim Chol-man	Member	Chairman, Second Economic Committee
Choe Sang-uk	Member	Director, Artillery Guidance Bureau

[a] The last formal list of the Central Military Committee appeared in association with the Third Plenum of the Central Committee in 1993.

the article, he praised old revolutionaries and urged people to respect them as "revolution forerunners." He also went on to warn against the perils of reform, noting that it was Gorbachev's *perestroika* that destroyed socialism in the Soviet Union.

Socialism began to come off its track and to disintegrate internally because of modern revisionists, and eventually collapsed as a result of "reform" and "restructuring" policies of turncoats who rejected all the historical achievements of socialism. Opportunists and turncoats abused top leaders of the workers' class, insulted the holy revolutionary struggles of revolution forerunners, destroyed socialism, and restored capitalism.[30]

The article urged people "to produce, to study, and to live daily lives in the way of the anti-Japan guerrillas."[31]

By the end of 1996, Kim Chong-il had apparently come to the conclusion that the party and state apparatus were inadequate and too weak to deal with the crisis. Only the military continued to function, especially at the lowest levels. Only the military could be depended on to ensure the regime's survival. Kim resolved to deal with the internal and external difficulties that faced the country by establishing a military-oriented crisis management system. It would be through this system that he would run the country using military-first policies.

Kim's conclusion was reflected in *Nodong Sinmun*'s New Year's Day article for 1997. The article declared, "The general march this year is the last charge to conclude the 'Arduous March' in a victory." As if describing a great battle, it pointed the way ahead, noting: "The firm resolve of us willing to die thousands or tens of thousands times to defend Korean-style socialism and to share our destinies with it; indomitable fighting spirit that makes us stand back up hundred times if we fall one hundred times." At the head of this battle-like charge would be the military.

The KPA is the pillar of Korean revolution, and the main force to complete the great work of *Chuche*. All the officers and men of the KPA must get prepared to fight as the first guards and as the first death-defying corps for the supreme commander. The KPA must prepare soldiers in terms of political ideology, and make all troops to overflow with the spirit of getting ready to die to defend the *suryong*, the spirit of becoming human bombs, and the spirit of suicidal attack.[32]

REMAKING THE SENIOR LEADERSHIP: ADDITION THROUGH SUBTRACTION

Early in 1997, the godfather of the *Chuche* philosophy, Hwang Chang-yop, defected to South Korea. On February 17, the international media reported news of the defection. According to reports, Hwang had been attending an international symposium on *Chuche* ideology in Japan. On his return trip, he escaped his handlers in Beijing and sought sanctuary in the South Korean Embassy. North Korea protested his defection as a case of abduction. After all, this was an unprecedented act by such a high official. As the party secretary in charge of international affairs and as chairman of the Association of Social Scientists, Hwang was the most senior official ever to defect from North Korea. After the defection, Kim Chong-il allegedly made the statement that he could no longer trust anyone.

Hwang's defection was quickly followed by two more incidents within the North Korean leadership. First Premier Kang Song-san was relieved of his position and replaced by Vice Premier and Candidate Politburo Member Hong Song-nam. Kang had been the sixth-ranking member in the leadership hierarchy, but he had not been seen in public for months, leading to speculation about his health.[33] Other reports suggested that he had been purged for embezzlement, which was discovered after an investigation following his son's defection to South Korea.[34]

Within days of this announcement, the North Korean media on February 21 reported the death of the seventh-ranking leader, Choe Kwang. For at least a year, there had been reports that he had been suffering from a "chronic illness" and was not particularly active.[35] Six days later, Kim Kwang-chin, first vice minister of the Ministry of People's Armed Forces, died suddenly on February 27, the day after he attended the funeral service for Choe Kwang.

The death of these two leading figures within the high command sparked rumors of a coming generational turnover. Although first (partisan) generation military leaders dominated Kim Kwang-chin's funeral committee (seven of the nine members were from this generation),[36] this was probably a formality. In April, North Korea conducted a massive re-shuffle of its key military officer corps.[37] Notably, Kim Chong-il's close associates were assigned to prominent positions and most frontline division commanders and divisional political officers were replaced by generals age 45 or below. Most of the newly appointed division and corps commanders were graduates from Mangyongdae Revolutionary Academy, further supporting the argument that with this reshuffle, Kim Chong-il firmly placed his stamp on the military. It should be noted, however, that Choe Kwang's post of minister of People's Armed Forces was left vacant.

By the summer of 1997, the indications were clear that Kim Chong-il had fundamentally restructured the leadership, giving the military the lead role. Though elders remained in many of the top positions, their positions seemed honorific. It was the military that Kim relied on as the engine for the regime.[38] In a speech celebrating Kim's 55th birthday, Vice Premier and Minister of Foreign Affairs Kim Yong-nam said, "Kim Chong-il has presented a creative idea that the revolutionary army is the core capability of the revolution, and the army is the people, the state, and the party." As one Pyongyang watcher noted, the North Korean regime had been transformed from a presidential system to a mobilization system.

END OF THE MOURNING PERIOD

On July 8, North Korea declared that the three-year mourning period for Kim Il-sung ended. *Nodong Sinmun* in its editorial asked the nation "to follow great teachings of Comrade Kim Il-sung and to complete the great work of our party." The editorial wrote:

The unshakable belief of the people is that, if they did not have their Dear Comrade Kim Chong-il, they would die without winning in the final war that decides whether they become slaves or self-reliant people. Assuring the peace and safety of Comrade Kim Chong-il indeed is the only way to win happiness for the people, prosperity for the fatherland, and victory for socialism. The Red Flag we hoist is the flag of defending the *suryong* to the death. The "Arduous March" we are making now is also a march to defend the *suryong* by all means.[39]

For nearly a year, the North Korean press had been laying the groundwork for Kim's formal assumption of power. *Nodong Sinmun,* in an editorial in July 1996 marking the second anniversary of Kim Il-sung's death, had urged the population to look upon Kim Chong-il as the embodiment of his father, stressing that,

The latest history of Great Leader Kim Il-sung's activities to achieve *Chuche*-oriented tasks coincides exactly with the 30 years of General Kim Chong-il's history of revolutionary guidance. . . . We strongly believe that the Great Leader

(Kim Il-sung) is the Respected Comrade Kim Chong-il, and the Great Leader's achievements are the General's (Kim Chong-il's) achievements.[40]

On October 8, 1997, the anniversary of the founding of the party, Kim Chong-il finally stepped up to the mantle his father left behind, assuming the position of General Secretary of the Korean Workers' Party.[41] In contravention of the party by-laws, Kim forwent the Central Committee plenum, which according to Article 24 of the party by-laws is supposed to select the general secretary. Instead, he was elected to the position in the joint names of the KWP Central Committee and Central Military Committee.[42] Moreover, General Secretary Kim Chong-il's promotion was announced not as the KWP Central Committee General Secretary, but as the KWP's General Secretary. There was much speculation as to why Kim chose to finalize the succession in this manner. The most likely explanation was that the post of general secretary of the party carried more authority and allowed Kim to exercise his power in a more efficient manner.

Many Pyongyang watchers, however, wondered why no leadership lineup was announced in connection with Kim's succession. This event, they argued, provided an opportunity to appoint new members to the senior bodies of the party, namely the Politburo, its Presidium, and the Secretariat. In hindsight, it is clear that there was no need to reinvigorate the party apparatus. Kim was now ruling through what has come to be known as "close aide politics."[43] As a result, there was no urgent need to fill posts as they became vacant because of the death or incapacitation of their elderly occupants. The decentralization of power between top veterans and close aides next in rank were commonly found in organs and departments critical to running the regime. Only in areas less important to regime management, or areas in which Kim wanted to avoid responsibility, such as economy and administration, were swift personnel appointments most often made. It should also be noted that as Kim oversaw the generational turnover within the elite, senior posts remained vacant due to the shortage of experienced figures among the new generation's elites, who also had secured Kim's trust. As a former North Korean bureaucrat explained:

As Kim Chong-il's establishment of the unitary guidance system saw its completion . . . and the range of policy guidance escaped the party's boundaries . . . , power that had been centered on the party Secretariat Office once again began to be decentralized to various areas. However, such decentralization of power materialized not through the revival of the Politburo's authority but in the form of Kim Chong-il's direct rule in each area, i.e. close aide political method. For example, from the early 1990's, the KWP International Affairs Department's political guidance on the Foreign Affairs Department [oekyobu] was suspended as of the early 1990's and changed to a form where Kim Chong-il provided direct guidance on the policies of Foreign Affairs Department through the First Vice Director Kang Sok-chu.[44]

Along with close aide politics, the party's crisis management system gave way to a military-based system centered on the National Defense Commission chairman. As for the party, Kim Chong-il guided the remaining departments, excluding the Organization and Guidance Department, through the Secretariat secretaries or in many cases, through Kim's direct instructions (either by phone or during close aide parties) to KWP Central Committee first vice department or vice department directors.[45]

According to an examination of Kim's appearances and guidance inspections, as well as official leadership rankings and the testimony of leading North Korean defectors, Kim had identifiable close aides across the regime.[46] Within the party, his closest aides were in the KWP Secretariat, including party secretaries Kye Ung-tae (public security), Kim Ki-nam (propaganda), Choe Tae-pok (education), Kim Kuk-tae (cadres), and Kim Yong-sun (policy toward the South). Chang Song-taek (first vice director of the Organization Guidance Department) and Choe Yong-hae (first secretary of the youth league) were leading figures within the Central Committee apparatus.

As noted above, Kim's aides within the military had been reshuffled several times with the deaths of many key figures within the high command. Ri Ul-sol, Ri Ha-il, and O Kuk-yol remained close to Kim, but they for the most part kept out of the limelight. In 1997, the North Korean media tended to focus on Cho Myong-nok, director of the General Political Bureau, and Kim Yong-chun, chief of the General Staff. The coverage of Cho in particular led many to speculate that he was the likely candidate to fill the position of minister of People's Armed Forces left vacant by Choe Kwang. Other close aides included Pak Ki-so, commander of the Pyongyang Defense Command, and Chon Chae-son, commander of the First Army Corps, both of whom were promoted to vice marshal in April. Pak Chae-kyong, deputy chief of the Propaganda Department of the KPA General Political Bureau, was another of the people who most frequently accompanied Kim on his inspection activities. Along with Hyon Chol-hae, deputy chief of the Organization Department of the KPA General Political Bureau, Pak Chae-kyong was assessed to be one of the rising stars within the General Political Bureau.[47]

Those considered as influential in the Administration Council were Hong Song-nam, acting premier; Kang Sok-chu, vice foreign minister; and Kim Chong-u, vice chairman of the External Economic Affairs Committee. Hong Song-nam had been acting premier since February, when Premier Kang Song-san was dismissed. Kang Sok-chu was for all intents and purposes the acting foreign minister, reporting directly to Kim Chong-il, not to Foreign Minister Kim Yong-nam. Kim Chong-u, who supervised North Korea's overall external economic affairs, was a key economic advisor. He had become one of the chief advocates for engaging the outside world since the dismissal of Kim Tal-hyon, former vice premier who supported openness.

PURGES AND POLICY DEBATES

Rumors of changes in the power structure in North Korea filled the Asian media in the early months of 1998. In January, it was learned that Ri Il-hwan had replaced Choe Yong-hae as head of the Kim Il-sung Socialist Youth League (KSYL). Following on the news that was just leaking out of North Korea about the executions of Gen. Ri Pong-won (vice director of the General Political Bureau) and So Kwan-hui (KWP Secretary for Agriculture), Choe's removal took on an ominous tone.[48] Although the North Korean media stated that the reshuffle was for health reasons, the fact that Choe Yong-hae was regarded as one of Kim Chong-il's close aides led to widespread speculation that this was part of a larger purge going on within the leadership for reasons that were as yet unclear.[49]

The long absences of other key leaders—such as chairman of the External Economics Committee Kim Chong-u (a first cousin to Kim Il-sung) and chief of the General Staff Kim Yong-chun—from public view contributed to a sense that all might not be calm within the highest circles of power. There were even rumors that Chang Song-taek, Kim Chong-il's brother-in-law, might have been purged.[50]

In March, the rumor mill reached a crescendo as reports began to surface through diplomatic channels that a firefight had taken place in Pyongyang between elements of the Ministry of People's Security and the Ministry of People's Armed Forces.[51] According to South Korean media, the North Korean military had placed guards around important public buildings and Pyongyang was under a high state of alert. Foreigners were refused entry into the country. Intelligence agencies scrambled to figure out whether a coup d'état had occurred. But, according to South Korean government sources, there were no indications of a change in North Korean leadership.[52]

It was not clear whether these stories coming out of North Korea were linked, but in April, the direction of the rumors shifted from coups and assassination plots to an all-out power struggle between two of Kim's chief aides. Defector reports often discussed the squabbles within the Kim family. Two of the more colorful figures at the center of this drama were Kim Yong-sun and Chang Song-taek. Both were powerful figures within the party apparatus, running the day-to-day operations of two important Central Committee departments. Kim Yong-sun oversaw the KWP United Front Department, which oversaw operations aimed at the South. Chang Song-taek, who was married to Kim Chong-il's sister, Kim Kyong-hui, was the first vice director of the KWP Organization Guidance Department, the party's surveillance organ.

Policy toward South Korea had apparently been a source of frequent clashes between Kim and Chang in the past. In early April, evidence of another clash came, with replacement of Kim Chong-u by his deputy

Kim Mun-song. As Chairman of the External Economic Affairs Commission, Kim Chong-u was responsible for securing South Korean business investment through such special economic zones as Najin-Songbong, a high-profile North Korean operation that had by 1997 come under intense criticism because of the slow pace of investment. If the reshuffle had stopped with the lead agent for external economic development, rumors of a power struggle would have probably ceased, but during that time, another high-profile interlocutor with the South lost his job—An Pyong-su, vice chairman of the Committee for the Peaceful Unification of the Fatherland. The fact that two senior cadre with ties to South Korea had been removed in such a short span of time suggested that Kim Yong-chun's United Front apparatus was being targeted. As the story unfolded in the South Korean press, it seemed that Kim had overseen the purge that followed the Hwang Chang-yop defection, which investigated several officials attached to Chang Song-taek's patronage network. If this was true, Chang may have seized on Kim Chong-il's frustrations with the pace of investment in Najin-Songbong to return the favor.

It is possible that these power struggles were linked to Kim Chong-il's focus on the future direction of the North Korean economic and foreign policy, especially as it related to South Korea. As soon as it had to be self-reliant following the end of the Cold War, North Korea's *Chuche* ideology had failed. As if by providence, the new South Korean government of Kim Dae-chung emerged on the scene, reaching out to North Korea as part of a new "Sunshine Policy," which separated politics from economics.[53] In practice, this meant that the South loosened restrictions on its private sector to invest in North Korea, limiting its own involvement essentially to humanitarian aid.[54] By taking the South's offer, North Korea could begin to solve its food problem and get a grip on the famine that ravaged the country. But, by doing so, Pyongyang could also undermine *Chuche*, and thus Kim's own legitimacy.

A close reading of the North Korean press suggests that Kim may have wrestled with this decision through the summer. In an open letter reportedly penned by Kim Chong-il, titled "Let Us Reunify the Country Independently and Peacefully through the Great Unity of the Entire Nation,"[55] he suggested the possibility of cautiously reengaging South Korea, something he had steadfastly refused to consider in the aftermath of Kim Il-sung's death. The letter was less defensive in tone than the last authoritative statement on the subject issued in Kim Chong-il's name the previous August, which described inter-Korean relations as "more strained and acute than ever before" with a "danger of war breaking out at any minute."[56] It did not resort to standard formulations deriding the state of inter-Korean relations and blaming Seoul for increasing the level of tension and danger on the peninsula. Possibly reflecting an ongoing debate within Pyongyang, the letter noted that North Korea momentarily preferred non-official exchanges to government-to-government contacts. It contained no new initiatives or responses to overtures from Kim Dae-chung on areas such as separated families and exchanges of envoys.

Regardless of whether economic policy was still under debate, North Korea continued operations against the South. For many outside observers, the letter was nothing more than tactical maneuvering by North Korea to encourage the continued flow of South Koreans without any serious intention of engagement. These suspicions appeared to be confirmed in June with the ROK Navy's capture of a 70-ton Yugo-class North Korean submarine off the east coast of South Korea. As one South Korean government official argued,

The party-government-military balance of power of the past is long gone; it is meaningless to argue about which is more powerful. . . . We cannot overlook the absolute position and role of the military in North Korea if we are to understand the North's attitudes toward internal and external affairs. . . . We must consider the fact that the military holds in its hands the life of the present North Korean regime, and that secretary general Kim Chong-il stands at its head. . . . With the activity of the military increasing recently, driven by a competition to display loyalty, provocations such as the recent mini submarine infiltration could occur at any time.[57]

Despite the occasional soothing signals Kim sent to South Korea, it seemed by the summer of 1998 that little had changed in terms of regime dynamics. Kim had established a crisis management system, with the military as the support structure of the existing "party-centered system." This system allowed the regime to cope with the situation following President Kim Il-sung's death, represented by the North's diplomatic isolation, the acute economic crunch and the food crisis, an increase in deviant social behavior, and the prolonged absence of a legitimate supreme leader due to the delay in the official inauguration of the Kim Chong-il system. It did not easily allow shifts from existing policy. The party and state bodies, vital to any opening up to the outside world, continued to lie dormant.[58]

KIM CHONG-IL'S NEW RULING STRUCTURE

At the end of the summer, following a dramatic test of the new Taepodong missile, the 10th Supreme People's Assembly convened in Pyongyang on September 5. It had three items on its agenda: revise the North Korean Constitution, re-elect Kim Chong-il chairman of the National Defense Commission, and appoint officials to posts throughout the government. Although not described as such, the meeting was the ushering in of the Kim Chong-il ruling structure.

The revised constitution made Kim Il-sung the "eternal president" (*chusok*) of North Korea,[59] ending speculation on when his son would succeed him to the top state post. Instead, Kim Chong-il chose to continue the pattern begun in 1992 of concentrating authority in the National Defense

Commission. The new structure left little doubt that the NDC was Kim's organizational base from which to implement military-first politics. The NDC was elevated to the highest organ of state, and the position of NDC chairman to the highest position in government.[60] Its membership was increased from 5 to 10, with Cho Myong-nok as first vice chairman and newly appointed minister of People's Armed Forces Kim Il-chol as vice chairman.[61] Other new members included Ri Yong-mu and Yon Hyong-muk, both of whom were brought back into Pyongyang politics, and Paek Hak-rim. Though the new constitution did not specifically increase the NDC's powers beyond the defense sector, it did refer to the NDC as "the overall national defense management organ," stipulating that its chairman guides the "entirety of national defense work." This semantic addition allowed the interpretation of the chairman's powers to cover all aspects of political, economic, and sociocultural life.

The constitutional revisions also eliminated several posts, redistributed powers, and changed nomenclature. The changes to the national government structure, however, made no real break with the practices of Kim Il-sung's regime, but merely revived many of the power and government

Table 1.3
National Defense Commission in 1998

Name	NDC Position	Other Posts
Kim Chong-il	Chairman	KWP General Secretary
Cho Myong-nok	First Vice Chairman	Director, General Political Bureau
Kim Il-chol	Vice Chairman	Minister of People's Armed Forces
Ri Yong-mu	Member	
Kim Yong-chun	Member	Chief of the General Staff Department
Ri Ul-sol	Member	Director of the General Guard Command
Paek Hak-rim	Member	Minister of People's Security
Yon Hyong-muk	Member	Chagang Province Party Secretary
Chon Pyong-ho	Member	KWP Secretary for Munitions
Kim Chol-man	Member	KWP CMC Member, Chairman of Second Economic Committee

administrative structures in existence before the 1970s. The new constitution granted the Cabinet (the former Administrative Council) more autonomy by eliminating the presidency and the Central People's Committee.[62]
The Cabinet and its apparatus now had more direct authority over economic issues as the party oversight responsibilities were curbed if not
eliminated outright.[63]

The new Cabinet was composed of technocrats, many of whom brought
years of experience to their new positions. Premier Hong Song-nam was
an economist well known outside North Korea. Vice Premier Cho Chang-
tok was a professional geologist and had been a career bureaucrat in North
Korea's mining and extraction sectors. Vice Premier Kwak Pom-ki had
extensive experience in the machine industry field. As for the ministers,
Foreign Minister Paek Nam-sun had served as ambassador to Poland and
was the president of a foreign-language publishing company, a job that
allowed him to travel extensively abroad in support of the distribution
of foreign-language public relations materials for Kim Il-sung and Kim
Chong-il. Minister of Foreign Trade Kang Chong-mo was an experienced
trade councilor, having spent much of his career in Eastern Europe. He
was rumored to be an advocate of a more open trade policy. State Planning
Committee Chairman Pak Nam-gi's career history had been marked by
major successes and failures, but he apparently was recognized by Kim
Chong-il for his skill in the field of economics.

The new constitution fundamentally reoriented the relationship of the
party to the governing apparatus. Formally, the Cabinet and military no
longer reported to party officials. More than ever before, a tripartite relationship between the party, military, and government formed the foundation of the regime. However, it would be a mistake to assume that the
elevation in status of the NDC and increased autonomy of the Cabinet
somehow diminished the role of the party. In fact, the constitutional revisions only represented a restructuring of government, administrative,
and economic institutions, all of which were still subordinate organs of
the Korean Workers' Party. Kim Chong-il still held the post of General
Secretary and, probably more important, he also exerted direct authority
over the powerful KWP Organization and Guidance Department, which
exercised control and guidance in all areas, including control of the party
organization; execution and control of party decisions; personnel actions;
military and judicatory supervision; and control of intelligence organizations and economic affairs. It is through the party apparatus that Kim was
able to maintain control over the military and the population in the era
of military-first politics.

CONCLUSION

In the 1990s, Kim Chong-il and the North Korean leadership discovered
how ill equipped the regime was to stand on its own. The fall of the Soviet

Union forced Pyongyang to put *Chuche* to the test. When that failed, the regime was faced with numerous economic and security choices, all of which forced the regime to deal with the outside world. The regime's coping mechanisms, which were largely designed to promote the Kim family and protect the regime, were ill equipped to diagnose the evolving problems and find timely solutions. Its decision-making processes time and again proved shortsighted, with domestic policy initiatives being undone or derailed by security considerations. To make matters worse, the accumulation of structural problems over the previous five decades crippled the North Korean economy. The net outcome was the collapse of the economy, which led to the unprecedented massive famine in North Korea in the mid-1990s.

Faced with these problems, it is not surprising that Kim fell back on the one institution that his father trusted most, the military. Even though Kim Il-sung had tangled with the high command, especially in the 1960s, his closest relationships were with those he commanded on the battlefield. In 1995, Kim Chong-il unleashed military-first politics in an effort to tie himself more closely to the high command. Military-first politics was basically politics for crisis management, drawing on the power of the military to stabilize the situation. It also allowed Kim to create a ruling structure that played to his strengths of micromanagement and close aide politics, while limiting his exposure to the public other than his constant guidance inspections.

In what would turn out to be an ironic twist, it was only after Kim had created a system that was incapable of doing anything other than ensuring the survival of the regime that he appeared to embark on one of the most dramatic attempts at meaningful reform in North Korean history. An ongoing debate continues within the Pyongyang watching community over whether this attempt was real or nothing more than posturing. The answer to this question is at the heart of whether North Korea is capable of change, even if its survival depends on it.

CHAPTER 2

Crisis Management: Experimenting with Reform

Any expectations that Kim Chong-il's consolidation of power would lead to policy reform were quickly put to rest in the months following the 10th SPA. If anything, North Korea emerged from the Supreme People's Assembly in a more hardline posture. Although Pyongyang had apparently not given up hope on the Agreed Framework, it had become frustrated with the protracted negotiation process and Washington's stated inability to accept compensated one-time, one-site inspections. Reflecting this increased frustration with the process, Kim Chong-il lashed out at the United States, calling for heightened "anti-U.S. consciousness" across all sectors of North Korean society. Building on this rhetoric, on December 2 on the eve of bilateral talks on North Korea's suspected underground nuclear facilities, a spokesman for the KPA General Staff issued a strongly worded statement charging that the United States had "turned away from dialogue" and was using the suspected underground facilities issue as a pretext to "ignite the fuse of war."

The New Year's Joint Editorial for 1999 continued this theme. Devoid of any new initiatives in the foreign and domestic arenas, it called for heightened ideological and military vigilance against any external threats and sacrifice on the part of the population.[1] It also insisted on fundamental change in the South before serious North–South reengagement could take place.

In terms of Kim's leadership style, the Joint Editorial had replaced the New Year's speech as the preferred method of communicating the regime's vision.[2] For Pyongyang watchers, this shift in approach was puzzling. Some felt that Kim preferred the joint editorial because it contributed to the shroud of mystery surrounding North Korea's new leader. Others believed that it might be attributable to Kim's reticence to either speak in public or be directly linked with any public policy pronouncements. Regardless of the reason, Kim's reticence as a potential strong proponent of a particular policy line suggested that, at least in the economic realm, policies would likely be piecemeal, and done without extensive fanfare. In its foreign relations, Pyongyang would continue to portray itself as being under siege from outside forces seeking the collapse of the regime, while using the media to prepare its populace for a protracted period of strained relations with Washington and Seoul.

This was the prevalent view from the Pyongyang watching community in 1999. There was little hint of the changes and policy vacillations that North Korea would embark on over the next few years. From the visit of former U.S. Secretary of Defense William Perry to the summits with Kim Tae-chung and Junichiro Koizumi to the July 2002 economic reforms, North Korea was about to embark down policy paths it had never pursued before. All would end in failure. But embedded in these failures are insights into the North Korean policy process, its shortcomings and limitations.

REGIME DYNAMICS STILL SETTLING

Not four months after the announcement of the Kim Chong-il regime, South Korea's Ministry of Unification issued a report titled "The List of North Korea's Power Structure." Although it reflected the changes known to have occurred at the 10th SPA, it also announced some changes that until then had not been made public, most notably that the State Security Department had been placed under the direct control of the National Defense Commission.[3] The report also confirmed that North Korea had still not reorganized its party structure, leaving vacant the Secretariat posts, which had been occupied by Hwang Chang-yop (International Affairs) and Suh Kwan-hui (Agricultural Affairs). The identity of the chief of the United Front Department was also not yet known.[4]

This report was followed by an article by Hwang Chang-yop in which he described power struggles within the internal security apparatus and measures the regime was taking to root out corruption and ensure stability.[5] He pointed to Gen. Won Ung-hui and the Military Security Command as the lead agency behind a major purge of party, administration, and military cadres.[6] According to Hwang:

Kim Chong-il has turned the People's Armed Forces Ministry into a power outfit within the regime, even making the ministry take hold of the State Security Department and the Public Security Ministry (police). Military officers who in the past feared most party officials like political guidance officials have come to now regard the Security Command as the most fearful being, something that can determine their political fates. . . . Kim Chong-il has reached the point where he cannot rule North Korea without help from the military, with the People's Armed Forces Ministry having become Kim Chong-il's trouble-shooter.[7]

The Supreme People's Assembly, which convened on April 7 in Pyongyang for the first time since Kim Chong-il was officially confirmed as the new leader, showed an unusually large number of members absent. Of the 687 representatives elected the previous July, 50 members did not appear at the Assembly meeting. This was in contrast to the 7 absences for the September 1998 session. For many Pyongyang watchers, this was confirmation that a shake-up had occurred in North Korea's political arena, as Assembly regulations stipulate attendance is mandatory unless "an individual is abroad or seriously ill."[8]

Aside from the missing SPA delegates, the leadership rostrum also indicated a major change in North Korea's power lineup. Kim Il-sung's once sacrosanct leadership order, whereby the party took the top spots in the power ranking, no longer applied.[9] The ranking changed after the September 1998 SPA session, with the Politburo members still at the top of the ranking order, but they were followed by the members of the NDC, candidate Politburo members, and Central Committee secretaries, in that order.[10] Now military figures stood atop the new leadership hierarchy. VMAR Cho Myong-nok, who had ranked 24th on the second anniversary of Kim Il-sung's death, had jumped to 3rd. The rostrum list for the second session of the 10th SPA was as follows: Kim Chong-il, "de facto ruler" and chairman of National Defense Commission (NDC) and KWP General Secretary; Kim Yong-nam, "the head of state" and President of SPA Presidium; and Cho Myong-nok, "the first in the military lineup," director of the KPA General Political Bureau and first vice chairman of the NDC. Cho Myong-nok was listed before Premier Hong Song-nam in accordance with the fact that the revised constitution passed in September 1998 gave the NDC a higher status than the Cabinet. Other highly ranked officers included MAR Ri Ul-sol, director of the General Guard Command (5th); VMAR Paek Hak-rim, Minister of People's Security (10th); and VMAR Kim Yong-chun, Chief of the General Staff (11th). An examination of the SPA events suggested that 15 of the 30 top North Korean leaders were military figures.

Following the SPA meeting on April 13, the North Korean media announced the promotion of 78 officers to the rank of colonel general and lieutenant general.[11] This was the eighth list of flag officer promotions since Kim Chong-il became Supreme Commander in 1991. According to a South Korean assessment, 70 percent of the high command (1,023 or 1,400 general officers) had been turned over in these eight sets of promotions.[12] There was little doubt that by the end of the decade, the military leadership was of Kim's making.

The only other significant personnel move within the high command to take place in 1999 was the appointment of Col. Gen. Yo Chun-sok as vice minister of the People's Armed Forces.[13] An officer with a strong operational background, Yo had served as the commander of the Fourth, Fifth, Seventh, and Ninth corps. The fact that Yo was chosen personally by Kim

Il-sung to head the new Ninth Corps in 1980 was a reflection of the esteem with which he was held in Pyongyang.

Despite Kim's efforts to reshuffle the regime and build direct lines of loyalty within the high command, he continued his strategy of inter-generational balancing to assure regime stability in this time of change. This strategy was on display at a central memorial service held at the Kum-susan Memorial Palace in Pyongyang on July 8 to mark the fifth anniversary of the death of North Korean President Kim Il-sung. The only noticeable change to the North Korean power hierarchy was the elevation in rank of the veterans of the first generation of the revolution who fought alongside Kim Il-sung against the Japanese. In contrast to recent rostrum placement, Kim Chol-man (Chairman of the Second Economic Committee) and Paek Hak-rim (Minister of People's Security) were introduced before Kim Yong-chun (Chief of General Staff) and Kim Il-chol (Minister of People's Armed Forces), and Ri Yong-mu (vice chairman of the National Defense Commission), a sign that Kim Chong-il had taken account of their special relationship with his father.[14]

Table 2.1
Rostrum List for Central Memorial Service Commemorating Fifth Anniversary of Kim Il-sung's Death[a]

Rank	Person	Position
1	Kim Chong-il	KWP General Secretary and Chairman of the National Defense Commission (NDC)
2	Kim Yong-nam	Chairman of the SPA Standing Committee
3	VMAR Cho Myong-nok	Director of the KPA General Political Bureau and First Vice Chairman of the NDC
4	Hong Song-nam	Premier
5	MAR Ri Ul-sol	Director of the General Guard Command
6	Chon Pyong-ho	Secretary of the KWP Central Committee
7	Han Song-yong	Secretary of the KWP Central Committee
8	Kim Chol-man	Chairman of the Second Economic Committee and member of the NDC (anti-Japanese partisan)
9	VMAR Paek Hak-rim	Minister of People's Security and the member of the NDC (anti-Japanese partisan)
10	VMAR Kim Yong-chun	Chief of the KPA General Staff and member of the NDC
11	VMAR Kim Il-chol	Minister of the People's Armed Forces and Vice Chairman of the NDC
12	VMAR Ri Yong-mu	Vice Chairman of the NDC

(continued)

Table 2.1 *(Continued)*

Rank	Person	Position
13	Choe Tae-pok	Secretary of the KWP Central Committee and Chairman of the SPA
14	Yang Hyong-sop	Vice Chairman of the SPA Standing Committee
15	Choe Yong-rim	Prosecutor of the Central Public Prosecutor's Office
16	Kim Kuk-tae	Secretary of the KWP Central Committee
17	Kim Ki-nam	Secretary of the KWP Central Committee
18	Kim Chung-nin	Secretary of the KWP Central Committee
19	Kim Yong-sun	Secretary of the KWP Central Committee
20	Kim Ik-hyon	Director of the People's Defense Department of the party (anti-Japanese partisan)
21	Ri Chong-san	Director of the General Bureau of Munitions Mobilization (anti-Japanese partisan)
22	VMAR Kim Yong-yon	President of Mangyongdae Revolutionary Academy (anti-Japanese partisan)
23	VMAR Ri Ha-il	Director of the KWP Military Department
24	Pak Ki-so	Commander of the Pyongyang Defense Command
25	Cho Chang-tok	Vice Premier
26	Kwak Pom-ki	Vice Premier
27	Kim Yun-hyok	Secretary General of the SPA Standing Committee
28	Kim Yong-tae	Chairman of the Social Democratic Party
29	Yu Mi-yong	Chairman of the Chondoist Chongu Party

[a] "Hierarchy of Senior Cadres Who Were Anti-Japanese Partisans Goes Up in the Platform of the Ceremony Commemorating the Fifth Anniversary of Kim Il-sung's Death," *Yonhap*, 9 July 1999.

There was also a slight change in the power hierarchy even among the vice marshal group which had been sandwiched between the group of secretaries of the party Central Committee and that of cabinet vice premiers. The normal power hierarchy order of Kim Ik-hyon, Ri Ha-il, Pak Ki-so, Ri Chong-san, and Kim Yong-yon shifted to the order of Kim Ik-hyon, Ri Chong-san, Kim Yong-yon, Ri Ha-il, and Pak Ki-so. Partisan vice marshals Ri Chong-san and Kim Yong-yon vaulted over vice marshals Ri Ha-il and Pak Ki-so.

PERRY VISITS THE "BARRACKS STATE"

It was during the summer of 1999 that the international media began to refer to North Korea as a "barracks state."[15] Though it was generally accepted that the military's role in politics was nothing new and its roots could be traced back to the founding of the state, many Pyongyang watchers saw something different in the regime under Kim Chong-il. The presidential system that had existed under Kim Il-sung had been replaced by a "wartime system of military rule" in which the Supreme Commander had become, for all intents and purposes, the head of state. The majority of the deputies to the Supreme People's Assembly were high-ranking general officers. And though the official leadership ranking still paid some deference to party and government offices, many suspected that in reality the true positions of influence, outside of Kim himself and some of his close aides, belonged to the military.

Outside observers were troubled not so much by the military's role in politics, but by its predominant role. Kim Il-sung had managed to preserve a balance within the regime by keeping the party, military, and government in their spheres, minding their own affairs. Under the "military-first policy," the lines of demarcation between these three bodies had become blurred and the military (being the most critical to regime survival) had become first claimant on resources and, by extension, an entity that must be placated. Kim Chong-il continued to twist the nature of the party-military relationship by claiming that "The army is the only reliable guard of the party," but he allegedly also had a habit of saying, "It is the rifle butt that gives birth to and maintains the government."[16]

It is this "barracks state" that U.S. coordinator for North Korea William Perry entered on May 25. The highest-ranking U.S. representative to visit the country since former President Jimmy Carter visited Pyongyang in June 1994, Perry's brief by the Clinton administration was to determine the applicability of the new paradigm of the "comprehensive approach" for eliminating Cold War structures on the Korean Peninsula. During his four-day visit, Perry met with various North Korean officials, including Kim Yong-nam, head of the Presidium of the Supreme People's Assembly, Kim Kye-kwan, Minister of Foreign Affairs; and Ri Yong-chol, director of the North's powerful National Defense Commission. He did not meet with Kim Chong-il.

The Perry visit was the culmination of a several-month reassessment by the U.S. government of its North Korea policy. The 1994 U.S.–North Korean Agreed Framework under which North Korea agreed to freeze its nuclear program in return for the delivery of heavy-fuel oil and two 1,000MW light-water nuclear reactors was in trouble. In this time, it had also become clear to the outside world that North Korea was not on the verge of collapse. Instead of giving up its program, Pyongyang had come to regard its nuclear ambiguity and ballistic missile programs as bargaining chips in its negotiations with the United States and viewed them as essential tools to guarantee regime survival in the face of economic collapse and diplomatic isolation. In addition, South Korea's bold "Sunshine" engagement policy with North Korea increased the pressure on Washington to explore the prospects of normalizing economic and political relations with Pyongyang in order to achieve the twin U.S. foreign policy goals of regional stability and nonproliferation in Northeast Asia.[17]

In consultation with Japan and South Korea, the United States devised a two-path strategy focused on addressing North Korea's nuclear weapons- and missile-related activities. The first path involved a new, comprehensive approach to negotiations with Pyongyang whereby the international community would seek complete and verifiable assurances that North Korea did not have a nuclear weapons program. This path would seek the complete and verifiable cessation of testing, production, and deployment of missiles exceeding the parameters of the Missile Technology Control Regime, and the complete cessation of export sales of such missiles and the equipment and technology associated with them. If North Korea rejected this path, the second path involved containment and efforts to reduce, if not eliminate the threat. The United States and its allies would seek to keep the Agreed Framework intact and avoid, if possible, direct conflict. Moreover, the United States would take measures to isolate the Kim Chong-il regime to the point that it would collapse under the weight of its own economic and political contradictions.

In his meetings in Pyongyang, Perry proposed a comprehensive plan for engaging North Korea, including a package of economic and political incentives if North Korea abandoned its nuclear and missile programs. According to some reports, Perry's proposals included the possibility of normalizing U.S.–North Korean political-economic relations. Perry also allegedly informed Pyongyang of the disincentives if North Korea continued to be intransigent.

The North Korean media was subdued in its coverage of the Perry visit. It highlighted the meeting between Perry and Kim Yong-nam at Mansudae Assembly Hall in Pyongyang, where Perry passed Kim a personal letter from President Clinton to General Secretary Kim Chong-il.[18] International media speculation was mixed over how North Korea would respond. Some Pyongyang watchers were hopeful, given the fact that North Korea had accepted the Perry visit and allowed him to meet with Kim Yong-nam, the number two person in the regime. This, they suggested, was evidence that Pyongyang was "lending an ear to the new proposal by the United States and thereby relying on diplomatic negotiations to break through the difficult situation."[19] The fact that Kim Yong-nam followed the Perry visit with a visit to China was another encouraging sign.[20] His visit ended a five-year hiatus in high-level exchanges between the two countries. If North Korea was formulating a response to the U.S. initiative, some Pyongyang watchers argued, it would probably want to consult China.[21]

Others argued that given the North Korean leadership configuration, which included numerous members of the partisan generation who still harbored fear and resentment of the outside world, dating back to the Korean War, it was difficult to see Pyongyang opening up to the outside world or embracing economic reform. This speculation was bolstered by leaked information about what transpired during Perry's meetings.[22] According to these leaks:

- In response to Perry's call for a suspension of missile tests, North Korean interlocutors reportedly said, "We can launch a satellite again, any time it is necessary." They also allegedly reaffirmed Pyongyang's previous stance by stating that "missile exports could be discussed on the precondition of economic compensation, but [missile] development and production are matters concerning [North Korean] sovereignty, something the United States should not intervene in."[23]

- When the conversation turned to inter-Korean dialogue, Pyongyang's reaction became even more strident. Kim Yong-nam reacted "coldly" to Perry's recommendations for improving inter-Korean relations, refusing a request to relay a verbal message from President Kim Tae-chung to General Secretary Kim Chong-il. First Vice Foreign Minister Kang Sok-chu, who had met with Perry several times, flatly refused Perry's suggestion that North Korea open a dialogue with the South, maintaining that "inter-Korean relations are our nation's internal issue."[24]

Initial North Korean reaction to the Perry visit seemed to favor this latter line of reasoning. In the days following the visit, North Korea ratcheted up its anti-U.S. rhetoric in an apparent attempt to signal that the regime would not subordinate concerns about its survivability to improve its relationship with the United States and South Korea. Additionally, Pyongyang unleashed a media campaign to emphasize the need for a continued high state of military readiness toward the United States.[25] Touting North Korea's strong offensive military capability, including its inventory of missiles,[26] Pyongyang called on its people to remain vigilant and to firmly resist outside pressure to reform.[27]

In hindsight, it is likely that the North Korean leadership was caught off guard by the Perry message. As a consequence it adopted a confrontational posture both to highlight its concerns over regime survivability and ideological purity and, at the same time, buy time to figure out how to respond. This line of reasoning could shed light on why North Korea chose this moment to resurrect its complaints about the maritime military demarcation line (Northern Limit Line).[28] On June 9 and 15, North Korean patrol boats crossed the Northern Limit Line and clashed with vessels from the South Korean Navy in what has become known as the first battle of Yeonpyeong.[29] These incidents, which occurred just prior to the upcoming North–South vice ministerial–level talks slated for June 21 in Beijing, led North Korea observers to speculate that elements within the leadership, particularly within the high command, were getting nervous about losing maneuvering room if the dialogue went forth.[30] Others point to the fact that the incursions happened days after an inspection of the underground facility in Kumchang-ri (May 20–24) by U.S. inspectors, something that may have struck a raw nerve with the military. Whether Kim Chong-il sanctioned the incursion or permitted it to happen is not clear. But the event probably allowed him to co-opt the more hawkish elements within the regime as he mapped out the next steps North Korea would take toward the United States and South Korea.

IT'S ABOUT REPAIRING THE ECONOMY, NOT CHANGING THE SYSTEM

Although North Korea's belligerence on the security front was in part due to its confusion on how to handle initiatives from the international community, it also reflected an ongoing debate inside the regime regarding the need to reorient its relations with the outside world. Pragmatic elements within the regime, which had been sidelined in the early 1990s as Kim turned toward the military to consolidate his power, had been resurrected in 1998 with Kim's decision to grant Chong Chu-yong and the Hyundai Corporation permission to develop the Mt. Kumgang tourism project. Despite the sway that the isolationist faction still held within the party,[31] Kim allowing the Hyundai project to proceed gave space for the pragmatic position to take hold within North Korean policy-making circles.

As the months passed, the arguments of the pragmatic faction grew as Pyongyang internalized the potential benefits of the Sunshine Policy. The bold initiative of the Kim Tae-chung administration to reduce tensions on the peninsula was increasingly seen as an opportunity and a godsend for an impoverished North Korean economy.[32] North Korea's cold reaction to Perry's attempts to foster inter-Korean dialogue was not so much a rejection of the idea itself as a rejection of the U.S. attempt to interject itself into the process and force Pyongyang into a timeline not of its choosing.

The most visible aspect of the Kim Tae-chung government's North Korea policy was its adherence to the principle of separating political matters from economic matters when it came to inter-Korean relations. This meant that the relationship should not be held hostage to the ever-changing political currents in the region and that short-term feuds between the North and South should not get in the way of economic cooperation. According to one estimate, the Kim Tae-chung government, over the course of its 16-month-old Sunshine Policy, gave North Korea $48.97 million in the form of cash and commodities.[33] Included in this calculation was 50,000 tons of fertilizer (worth about 18 billion won) shipped to North Korea by the Korean Red Cross Society. It did not, however, include the 200,000 tons of fertilizer promised to North Korea as a condition for the vice-ministerial talks in Beijing. It also did not include the $150 million that the private corporation Hyundai paid to North Korea in exchange for the exclusive tourist rights to Mt. Kumgang ($25 million every month from December 1998 to May 1999). When combined, the total outlays of the South Korean government and private organizations to North Korea was $198.97 million, equivalent to 238.8 billion won, roughly 520 million won per day when averaged across the lifespan of the Kim Tae-chung administration (February 25, 1998, to June 1999).

Despite this aid, the North Korean economy continued to decline. A reading of the North Korean press revealed little, if any, mention of the foreign assistance. Instead it focused on yet another *chollima* movement.[34] Beginning in August 1999, *Nodong Sinmun* began carrying a number of commentaries on economic agitation.[35] These economy-related commentaries and reports conceded that North Korea had been trapped in the worst economic spiral of minus growth for nine straight years, since the turn of the 1990s, but stressed that the country had turned a corner. Pyongyang had set forth production normalization in all sectors of the people's economy and stabilization and betterment of people's living as the fundamental goals for 1999. In this connection, the media pointed to Kim's deep concern for the economy and highlighted his inspection tours in the economic sector.[36]

In typical North Korean fashion, within this rhetoric was embedded the suggestion of a policy shift.[37] In an August 15 *Nodong Sinmun* editorial marking the 54th anniversary of National Liberation was the following sentence: "The irrevocable determination and will of the General (Kim Chong-il) is to put our country to a road toward an **economically powerful state** at an early date by concentrating all energy on the construction of socialist economy." The revised constitution of 1998 had discussed the need for an ideologically, militarily, and economically powerful state. By 1999, Kim could argue that the first two objectives had been accomplished. The catch phrase "building up a prosperous [powerful] state" had replaced the "red flag idea," which had been the catch phrase of years of the "Arduous March." In other words, the editorial seemed to imply a strong determination on the part of the North Korean leadership to overcome the existing economic difficulty, even if it meant encroaching as never before on the foundations of *Chuche*.[38]

The 2000 New Year's Joint Editorial, while claiming that the year would be one of "decisive advancement in the construction of a powerful socialist state," provided few clues to how this would unfold. It did not give any indications of new policy direction or themes for the coming year on either foreign or domestic issues. In fact, some Pyongyang watchers did not expect much, given the emphasis the editorial put on ideological strength in the face of imperialism. That said, open criticism of South Korea was lower, although the phrases of basic independence and removal of foreign forces remained. Direct mention of scrapping of the national security law, disbanding of the NIS, and unification under the federal system was dropped. Criticism of the United States and Japanese imperialism was muted.[39]

In retrospect, the clue to North Korea's policy shift was buried in the New Year's Day editorial in *Nodong Sinmun,* which for the first time mentioned the importance of *silli* (practical benefit or profit) in economic activities.[40] This concept suggested a new embrace of pragmatism in pursuit of national interest and allowed for more latitude in Pyongyang's engagement with the outside world.

Despite the Cabinet's oversight role for economic affairs, the force behind this more pragmatic policy appears to have been the party, namely Kim Yong-sung, the KWP secretary for South Korean affairs. After having disappeared from the Politburo ranks in 1993, Kim's star had begun to rise again after the death of Kim Il-sung. He was appointed chairman of the newly established Asia-Pacific Peace Committee, which oversaw relations with South Korea, Japan, and the United States. It was within this committee that Kim brought together a coterie of pragmatic diplomats, who began laying the strategy for outreach. Chief among these were Song Ho-kyong and Chon Kum-chol. Song was vice director of the KWP United Front Department. He was close to Hyundai President Chong Mong-hon and had taken a leading role in pushing for Hyundai's Mt. Kumgang tourism project.[41] Chon was an expert on South Korean affairs and had been one of the leading members of the North Korean delegation that visited Seoul to negotiate rice donations.

Their engagement plan toward South Korea was set in motion in April with the announcement by the Korean Central Broadcasting Station that North Korea had accepted President Kim Tae-chung's request for a visit, noting that a summit between the two Koreas (the first to occur since the nation was divided) would take place in Pyongyang in June. Following a trip to China by Kim Chong-il at the end of May, ostensibly to coordinate positions with President Jiang Zemin and other Chinese leaders on the changing environment on the peninsula,[42] the summit commenced on June 13.

From the beginning, Pyongyang took extraordinary protocols to signal its interest in the meeting. In a move not seen since the Kim Il-sung era, Kim Chong-il and senior officials of the party, the government, and the military turned out at Pyongyang's Sunan Airport to welcome Kim Tae-chung and the visiting South Korean delegation. And in a move that shocked South Korean officials, Kim unexpectedly got into the Lincoln Continental brought for President Kim Tae-chung and accompanied him on the two-hour trip to Baekhwawon State Guest House.[43]

After two days of meetings, both sides signed the North-South Joint Declaration, which declared:

- The North and the South agreed to solve the question of the country's reunification independently by the concerted efforts of the Korean nation responsible for it.

- The North and the South, recognizing that the low-level federation proposed by the North and the commonwealth system proposed by the South for the reunification of the country have similarity, agreed to work together for the reunification in this direction in the future.[44]

- The North and the South agreed to settle humanitarian issues as early as possible, including the exchange of visiting groups of separated families and relatives and the issue of unconverted long-term prisoners, to mark August 15 this year.

- The North and the South agreed to promote the balanced development of the national economy through economic cooperation and build mutual confidence by activating cooperation and exchange in all fields, social, cultural, sports, public health, environmental and so on.

- The North and the South agreed to hold an authority-to-authority negotiation as soon as possible to put the above-mentioned agreed points into speedy operation.

Though the North was willing to agree to a broad set of agreements, the regime's strategy with regard to the inter-Korean dialogue was more narrowly focused. On one hand, the summit gave Kim a chance to shape his image on the international stage. While South Korean editorials lauded the summit and proclaimed it the dawn of a new era in inter-Korean relations, Pyongyang's coverage of the events was aimed at glorifying Kim Chong-il. He was portrayed as the outgoing, confident statesman, something that dovetailed well with recent themes in the North Korean media designed to build on Kim's growing personality cult.[45]

More important, the summit placed the inter-Korean relationship on a more stable footing, which allowed for a general expansion of economic engagement, social interaction, and political trust building. Of these three goals, economic engagement was the most important. As would later be revealed, the South Korean government had paid North Korea approximately $500 million to attend the summit. Viewed within this context, Kim Chong-il no doubt saw the summit as a means to an end. It allowed him to address the country's serious economic troubles and still maintain the balance within the regime between those who advocated reform and those who saw reform as a direct threat. After all, the reform he had put in place was not fundamental systemic reform, but a pragmatic step toward removing the international obstacles to North Korean economic development. According to one account of the summit, Kim revealed this cost-benefit calculation when he stated: "While the South wants to publicize this summit, we are satisfied to gain *silli* (practical benefit or profit) [from this summit]."[46]

PLACING THE MILITARY AT THE FOREFRONT OF DIPLOMACY

For North Korea to realize its goal of securing an economically powerful state, it had to move beyond just a warming in inter-Korean relations.

From Pyongyang's perspective, the United States, not South Korea, posed the real threat to the regime and its long-term aspirations. Normalization of ties with the United States not only would allow North Korea to address its deepest security concerns and escape international isolation, it was vital for reinforcing its economic cooperation and assistance from South Korea. The Sunshine Policy in essence would ultimately suffer if North Korea's relationship with the United States continued to drag behind its relationship with South Korea.

The dilemma for Kim was how to engage the United States while maintaining the balance he had struggled to develop within the North Korean leadership. After all, the military-first policy was predicated in part on maintaining a vigilant defense against "American imperialism." Any departure from the narrow bounds of North Korea's relations with the United States would have to come through military channels. The high command would have to carry the message.

Kim had recently become accustomed to using powerful military figures to push forward diplomatic initiatives. He compelled First Vice Chairman of the NDC Cho Myong-nok to deliver a luncheon speech (while wearing a suit instead of a military uniform) on the last day of the North–South summit talks. In September, Kim entrusted Cho's deputy, Pak Chae-kyong, who accompanied Kim Yong-sun to Seoul on the eve of *Chusok* (Korean thanksgiving), with a personal gift (songi mushrooms) for South Korean leaders. Later that month during a break in the first inter-Korean defense ministerial talks, Minister of People's Armed Forces Kim Il-chol paid a visit to Chongwadae (South Korea's presidential offices) to meet with President Kim Tae-chung.

In October, Kim once again turned to Cho Myong-nok to be his special envoy to meet with U.S. officials, including President Clinton. Cho was the logical choice. He was at the core of the military-first politics, and served as a link between Kim Chong-il and the military. He was the de facto second most powerful person in North Korea. The fact that such a figure would be visiting the United States signified, as least from North Korea's perspective, that it was willing to engage the United States in comprehensive negotiations on all military issues, including the future of U.S. forces on the Peninsula (the so-called USFK issue), as well as North Korea's missile program.[47]

At the end of the five-day visit, North Korea and the United States issued a Joint Communiqué in which they agreed to ease tensions on the Korean Peninsula through four-party talks and various other approaches. Both sides shared the view that the settlement of the missile issue would make an important contribution to fundamentally improved bilateral relations, as well as to peace and security in the Asia-Pacific region. North Korea informed the United States that it would not launch any long-range missiles while talks on the missile issue continued. The Communiqué also revealed a forthcoming trip to Pyongyang by Secretary of State

Madeleine Albright to prepare for President Bill Clinton's subsequent visit.[48]

On October 24, Secretary of State Madeleine Albright met for three hours with Kim Chong-il. During the meeting Albright gave Kim a letter from President Bill Clinton dealing with Clinton's expectations of how to further develop relations between the two countries. During their talks, Kim surprised Albright with his candor (admitting the sale of missiles to Iran and Syria for much-needed foreign currency) and his ability to delve into the details of Peninsula issues and North Korea's foreign and security policies. He laid out his vision of a way forward for U.S.–North Korea relations that included the presence of American troops on the Peninsula as a stabilizing force. However, as Albright later recorded in her memoirs, Kim confided that he was facing pressure from inside his military, which was divided in its view on North Korea's warming relations with the United States.[49] It was not the first and would not be the last time that Kim used the military as a convenient foil in his diplomacy with the outside world.

In addition to the diplomacy involving the United States, Kim looked to the military, be it divided or not, to take the lead on the inter-Korean dialogue. At the first inter-Korean defense ministers' talks held on Cheju Island in September, Kim Il-chol turned down South Korean National Defense Minister Cho Song-tae's request for a hotline between the two defense ministries. Kim's refusal indicated that North Korea saw this proposal as a useless step in the absence of a larger agreement that went beyond South Korea's capability to deliver. According to Kim, "Even if a hot line were installed between the North and South, it would be meaningless because the line has to pass through an area controlled by the United Nations Command (U.S. military)." He went on to add that "unless the Armistice Agreement is replaced with a peace agreement at an early date, confidence building in the military area between the North and South would be impossible."[50] Kim went on to criticize ROK–U.S. joint exercises and the South Korean military's definition of the North as its main enemy. However, it is noteworthy that he did not mention any issues related to the status of the U.S. forces on the Korean Peninsula or demand that they withdraw.[51]

Soon after Albright's visit, South Korean officials noted a dramatic change in the tone of statements attributed to the North Korean military. On October 26, Vice Unification Minister Yang Young-shik reported that in a notable shift from its earlier lukewarm attitude, the North Korean military was now supporting inter-Korean rapprochement. Yang ascribed this change to the military falling in line behind Kim's promises to President Kim Dae-chung. "The North Korean military has manifested its absolute allegiance to Defense Commission Chairman Kim Chong-il and pledged support for the implementation of the South-North Joint Declaration on June 15."[52]

Yang's assessment was probably accurate in a broad context. Most likely, the shift in the North Korean (military's) attitude was tied to Kim's courting of the United States. Not until that objective was secured could North Korea focus on its relationship with South Korea. According to one Pyongyang watcher,

North Korea usually wages a speed battle with all the force and resources concentrated on one goal once it decides to pursue that goal. At present, improving North Korea–U.S. relations is the top priority.[53]

Therefore, during this period, Kim, through the North Korean military, continued to reach out to South Korea, but only within the context of its larger strategic goals vis-à-vis the United States.

The Pyongyang watching community came away from the fall meetings between North Korea and its chief adversaries divided in its view over whether Kim was engaged in tactical maneuvers aimed at securing much-needed external aid or had come to the conclusion that a fundamental shift in policy was warranted. Madeleine Albright was convinced that Kim was serious about trading his missile program for economic assistance. Ultimately, the motive behind Pyongyang's diplomatic opening to the United States became moot as a new administration came to power in Washington, D.C.; one that was suspicious of Clinton's so-called accommodation of North Korea.

BUILDING AN ECONOMICALLY POWERFUL STATE

At the end of 2000, North Korea began to shows signs of a reorientation of its policy focus away from foreign affairs and toward the economy. Since the North–South summit in June, Kim's guidance inspection regime had changed. His inspection trips to military units declined dramatically in favor of economic facilities. Answering questions during the National Assembly Intelligence Committee's inspection of the National Intelligence Service (NIS) on November 3, NIS Director General Yim Tong-won said,

General Secretary Kim used to participate in military-related functions two or three times a month, which accounted for about 60 percent of all his public activities. However, since the North-South summit, his participation in military-related functions rapidly declined to 6 percent (a total of three times since the June summit), whereas his on-the-spot (*hyo'nji-eso'*) economic guidance increased to 17 percent (a total of eight trips since June).[54]

Other indications of this reorientation were personnel and organizational in nature. Successive replacements of high-level officials in the economic sector drew the attention of many Pyongyang watchers. On October 2, the Supreme People's Assembly suddenly announced that Minister of Finance Yim Kyong-suk had been replaced by Mun Il-pong, former trade representative to Russia, and long-time Central Bank of Korea Head Chong Song-taek had given way to Kim Wan-su, former vice finance minister. Two months later, on December 28, the SPA Presidium issued a decree replacing the Minister of Foreign Trade Kang Chong-mo with Ri Kwang-kun, the former president of the Korea General Equipment Export and Import Corporation. These changes not only represented new faces in positions of importance to North Korean economic policy making, but highlighted a generational change. For example, Ri Kwang-kun, at age 46, was 20 years younger than his predecessor.[55]

During this period, reports began to seep out of North Korea that 2002 was the target year for a great transformation of the country from its dire economic situation.[56] Toward this end, Kim had made the decision that despite the country's *Chuche* underpinnings, which emphasized self-sufficiency, North Korea would look outside its borders for solutions to its economic condition. Without fanfare, he authorized the establishment of the Research Institute on the Capitalist System within the Ministry of Foreign Trade, which had a mandate "to master capitalism's survival strategy and management capability of big enterprises."[57] In addition, North Korea applied to join the Asian Development Bank (ADB) and put out feelers about joining such international financial institutions as the International Monetary Fund (IMF) and the Asia-Pacific Economic Cooperation (APEC).

This revelation was coupled with signals coming from Pyongyang that it was ready to begin sending delegations abroad to seek economic lessons.[58] Stories began to appear in the South Korean press of an imminent delegation to Seoul in October 2000, which would be led by Kim Kyong-hui, 54, the director of the KWP Light Industry Department and Kim Chong-il's sister.[59] According to some sources, the delegation was also to include Kim Kyong-hui's husband, Chang Song-taek, who had assumed a higher profile in North Korean economic affairs.[60] The delegation was perceived in Seoul as being a preview of an eventual visit by Kim Chong-il, which had been discussed at the June summit. But, as quickly as the rumors began, they faded, as weeks passed and the trip never materialized.[61] At the end of the month, South Korean Unification Minister Pak Chae-kyu revealed that Pyongyang had informed Seoul (through Chon Kum-chin, responsible councilor in the Cabinet) that due to a manpower shortage following the moves toward establishing diplomatic relations with the United States and Japan, "it needs to slow down the speed for the next one or two months but will speed it up from spring of next year."[62]

In its 2001 New Year's Joint Editorial, Pyongyang signaled that the previous year's diplomatic efforts had been necessary to lay the foundation for significant things to come on the domestic (economic) front. The editorial touted the gains North Korea had made on the diplomatic front, namely its perceived breakthroughs (on its own terms) in relations with South Korea and the United States. This was followed by a bold statement that the country was nearing the end of its Arduous March and now needed to turn to the central task of "building up the economy ... by forging ahead with the work to reconstruct the overall people's economy with modern technology while revamping the existing economic basis,"[63] an apparent tacit admission that the system was not simply in need of repair but of an overhaul from the ground up. The editorial went on to say, this "reconstruction of the people's economy" is a "pressing task that cannot afford to be delayed any longer." For many Pyongyang watchers, this editorial, combined with Kim's own article three days later in *Nodong Sinmun*,[64] which cautioned that "things are not what they used to be in the 1960s" and people should not follow old practices, hailed the implementation stage of "a new far-reaching reform policy, one that had probably been under formulation for years."[65]

Whether a significant policy reform effort had been in preparation for years is debatable given the constant turnover, the rewiring of the lines of authority within the economic sector, and the continued emphasis at the highest levels on military-first policy.[66] What is clear, however, is that North Korea traded on the gains it secured from its diplomatic outreach in 2000 to pave the way for a period of examination and study of foreign economic systems in search of lessons that could be applied at home.

As noted above, Pyongyang originally wanted to begin this economic outreach in Seoul. Kim had designated his sister to lead the delegation in order to receive an unvarnished report on the success of the South Korean economic model and whether anything could be learned from that experience. When this fell through, Kim took matters into his own hands, leading two delegations to China and Russia. His trip to China in January 2001 began with a tour of Shanghai's Pudong district—not only an embodiment of China's socialist market economic system and but also a crystallization of its reform and opening policy—instead of going straight to Beijing. The Shanghai of 2001 was a world away from the Shanghai that Kim Chong-il first saw in 1983. In his previous visit, he had not been impressed and had criticized his Chinese hosts as being "revisionists." Shanghai at that time was still a closed city and, laden with the problems and inefficiencies of a socialist planned economic system, was standing on the verge of collapse. Kim's tour of Pudong, now a production base of the Asia-Pacific region and an international financial center that is home to regional headquarters for more than half the world's top 100 multinationals, led him to exclaim that Shanghai had undergone "unbelievable change" and that North Korea should develop its own, similarly modeled city.[67]

Kim's trip to China provided insights into the evolving thinking in Pyongyang on how to structure its new economic policy.[68] First, Kim concentrated largely on the issue of finance during his visit to China. During the Shanghai portion of his trip, Kim visited advanced technology research facilities, such as software development research facilities and facilities related to urban planning and traffic as well as the Pudong area, but it was exclusively the Shanghai Stock Exchange that he visited twice. This indicated his growing interest in how finance worked and how it was tied to the international community. The fact that Premier Zhu Rongji, who was a prominent figure behind Chinese financial policy, accompanied him seemed to reinforce this point. Second, Kim's trip from China, instead of heading directly back to Pyongyang, detoured to the border city of Sinuju, where he made a guidance inspection of a cosmetic factory, an enameled ironware factory, and a basic food commodities plant. This led some Pyongyang watchers to correctly forecast that the framework of the economic development strategy that North Korea had conceived was in large part tied to designating a few core special economic zones and fostering a specialized industrial sector.[69]

In the wake of Kim's trip, North Korean economic delegations visited Malaysia and the United States. A delegation headed by a vice minister of electronic industry toured the Samsung Electronic Industrial Complex in Malaysia. This was followed in February by a delegation headed by Vice Foreign Minister Kim Kye-kwan, which visited several U.S. cities to examine how finance and banking was conducted in the heart of the capitalist market economy.

In July, Kim again took to the road, taking a 24-day train ride across Russia to examine how the country had dealt with the economic consequences of the collapse of communism.[70] Whereas his trip to China had focused on issues of finance, his trip to Russia revolved around more practical applications at the factory level. Upon his return, Kim demanded new economic thinking from North Korean bureaucrats and in an "economic management guideline" promulgated in October in Pyongyang, he urged that North Korea should pursue "practical benefits" while maintaining socialist principles.

Taken separately, these economic delegations revealed little about North Korea's evolving economic strategy. Defector reports, however, began to place the regime's activities in context. Kim was seeking a path of development in which North Korea could interact with the outside world on its own terms. This meant not directly competing with China or South Korea, a competition that North Korea would end up losing. Instead, "new economic thinking" was centered on aggressively developing potential merchandising areas in places where they themselves possessed the national technology. Given the increasing importance of the Internet in driving science and technology at the end of the 20th century, Kim Chong-il increasingly focused on this as being the lynchpin for North Korea's economic development. In October 1999, North Korea launched its first website, the Choson Infobank (dprkorea.com).[71] The next year, Kim oversaw the creation of the Korea Advanced Technology Center, which was dedicated to developing the country's IT industry. According to some reports, he put his oldest son, Kim Chong-nam, in charge of this venture and tasked him with figuring out how to anchor the country's economic development to this growth industry.[72]

The problems that North Korea faced going forward with this economic strategy were many. In addition to the basic issues of how to merchandise these applied technologies and manage enterprises, Pyongyang had much to learn about marketing and luring capital. For answers to these problems, North Korea looked abroad, especially to China, which had proven its ability to attract foreign capital while defending its economic system from the predatory international capital markets.

LEADERSHIP TURNOVER

In an ironic twist of fate, Kim Tal-hyon, the North Korean leadership's chief proponent for economic reform, died of heart disease in January 2001. He was 60 years old. A former vice premier and chairman of the State Planning Commission, Kim Tal-hyon had spent the last 8 years in political exile as the manager of the February 8 Vinalon Complex in Hamhung, South Hamgyong Province.[73]

Kim's passing was not the only leadership event to take place in 2001. During the summer, reports began to surface in the South Korean press of a rising generation of cadres to fill the ranks of the party and government. Many of these rising stars were protégés of Kim Chong-il, who had either attended Kim Il-sung University with him in the early 1960s or worked alongside him in the KWP's Organization Guidance Department in the mid-1960s. As most of these people were in their late 50s or early 60s, they were on the leading edge of a generational turnover in North Korea's political landscape.

Within the party, four names caught the attention of Pyongyang watchers. Ri Che-kang and Kim Hi-taek were appointed first vice directors of the KWP Organization Department, joining Ri Yong-chol and Chang Song-taek. Chu Kyu-chang, party vice director who once served as the director of the Second Academy of Natural Sciences (devoted to military research and development), was appointed to be the KWP Munitions Industry Department's first vice director. Hong Sok-hyong was picked to be chief secretary of the Party Committee of North Hamgyong Province in the middle of July. The grandson of Hong Myong-hui, who defected to the North in 1948 and served as first Cabinet vice premier, Hong had risen through the ranks to be an alternate member of the Politburo (14th in the party hierarchy).[74] In September, Chong Ha-chol, who had been appointed director of the KWP Propaganda and Agitation Department in 2000, was made a secretary of the Central Committee.[75]

A feature of this reshuffle, especially on the government side, was the large number of highly educated technocrats with deep economic knowledge frontally deployed throughout the apparatus. In the Cabinet, ministers were replaced by persons in their 40s and 50s. The Agriculture and Light Industry ministries saw significant turnover. Vice agriculture minister Kim Chang-sik was promoted to agriculture minister in March 2001 and vice light industry minister Ri Chu-o was promoted to light industry minister in May 2001. Both were rising economic bureaucrats. Light industry minister Ri had attracted attention the previous May when he contributed an essay to *Kulloja,* the party's theoretical journal, calling for the modernization of the light industry sector and improving the quality of light industry products.[76]

By the end of the year, Kim had put into place a leadership configuration that would have to take on the daunting task of implementing, explaining, and safeguarding reforms that were out of character with the North Korean experience. North Korea's reliance on the "mosquito net-type" reform strategy of putting priority on the regime's defense was failing. State-operated industry and the central distribution system had for all intents and purposes collapsed and markets had appeared across the country to fill in the breach. Kim could no longer ignore that "de-Stalinization was taking place from below" or maintain that a China-type reform strategy did not fit with North Korea's reality in terms of the regime's security.[77] Step-by-step Kim had put a new generation with new ideas in place. The only thing left to do was issue the order.

THE JULY ECONOMIC REFORMS

After a flurry of activity in 2001, North Korea appeared to step back from its embrace of reform at the beginning of 2002. The New Year's Joint Editorial laid out modest goals focused more on regime stability than economic recovery, emphasizing the importance of the North's political and military system and moving away from the previous year's talk of a new year of "new advances and great change." Repackaging some of the most frequent subjects of media propaganda as the "four firsts," the editorial stressed that the "great revolutionary advance" for 2002 would be to "glorify the dignity and honor of the Kim Il-sung nation by thoroughly realizing the idea of putting our leader, our ideology, our military, and our system first." The editorial did continue to stress that the country should focus its efforts on technological development and information technology. What was not mentioned, however, was the increasing momentum forming behind the scenes for a fundamental reworking of the country's economic system in a last-ditch effort to deal with the failing economy.

In October 2001, Kim Chong-il had issued a secret, economy-related order to officials in the party and government to begin to lay the groundwork for significant reforms in 2002. The order, titled "On Improving and Reinforcing the Management of the Socialist Economy Based on the Requirements to Create a Powerful Nation," pointed out that the economy was "not on track and there [is] major confusion in the management of the socialist economy and [social] order." As a specific policy, it argued that "uniformity in terms of distribution must be thoroughly abolished and those who produce volume and high quality labor should receive credit accordingly in materialistic and political terms." Even on the rationing system that is the foundation of the North Korean society, it said that a drastic review was necessary, including partial abolishment on grounds that "there is much waste in the economic life. This must be sorted out, and free supplies and national security should be reviewed, and what should be abolished must be abolished." It said that "commodity prices and living expenses must be corrected overall," and signaled substantial hikes in prices in order to alleviate the price differences in fixed prices and those of the black market.[78]

The reforms entailed removing government-set controls on prices to allow them to rise to a point that reflected the reality of the markets.[79] Wages were to be increased twentyfold to keep up with the inflation in prices. Just as dramatically, Kim ordered a significant reworking of the planning system, transferring authority for production management planning from the central government to lower echelons. This top-down decision was allegedly driven by Kim's recent trips to China and Russia and represented a growing realization that North Korea's centrally planned economy was dysfunctional. It also represented an effort on the part of Kim and his economic advisers to come to grips with the reality of the markets that had emerged during the 1990s, something that the regime could not eradicate.

Prime Minister Hong Song-nam made reference to "dramatic" measures in a speech in March 2002, and on July 1, the reforms were made public. The "July 1st reform measures" included the following:

- Abolition of the existing food and commodity rationing system. Accordingly, factories and firms were no longer given subsidies for carrying out production or distribution activities. Instead, the price was to be calculated in accordance with the actual cost.
- The new wage system raised the basic payment for ordinary workers from 110 won to 2,000 won a month. For some particularly demanding jobs, such as miners, the wage was raised to 6,000 won. Previously, all workers in the same job classifications had received the same payment.
- The currency was devalued from 2.15 won to 150 won to the U.S. dollar in order to force foreign exchange hidden in the private economic sector into the open economy.[80]

Signs of change were not confined to changes inside North Korea. Over the next few months, Pyongyang engaged in inter-Korean economic talks on a range of topics, including linking of inter-Korean railroads and highways, construction plans for the Kaesong industrial complex and Imjin River flood prevention measures. The first North Korean delegation traveled to Seoul in August. It was headed by Pak Chang-ryon, first vice chairman of the State Planning Commission, and included Pak Chong-song, director of the external railways cooperation department under the Ministry of Railways; Pak Song-hui, Ministry of Power and Coal Industries (Electric Technology) Department director; Choe Hyon-ku, Samch'olli

Table 2.2
Changes in North Korea's Economic Planning Model[a]

	Revised Planning System	Previous Planning System
Principles of Improvement	–Secure large actual benefits within the range of adhering to socialist principles –Boldly change what has to be changed and actively create what has to be created –Ministries and central government organs will be held responsible before the party and the state	–Socialist ownership system –Centrally planned economy based on the principle of building a self-reliant national economy
Production Management Plan	–Large-scale transfer of planning authority to local governments and lower-echelon organs –The State Planning Committee handles only the indices of strategic and national importance –Except for major indices, such as each province's total industrial output and the amount of investment in basic construction, the provinces, cities, and counties plan the detailed indices befitting their situations	–The State Planning Committee was in charge according to the principles of streamlined and detailed planning
Price Setting	–Local factories decide on the goods produced by local industries –The state prepares only financial principles and standards	–The State Price Assessment Bureau set the prices according to the principle of streamlined prices
Economic Life	–Reduction of free supply, compensations by the state, and other sectors' benefits, with the exception of education, medical treatment, and social insurance –Workers pay for food and rent out of their income	–The state provided the components of residents' life, including food, clothing, and shelter

[a] This table was adapted from one that appeared in "North Undertakes Major Overhaul of Order-Type Planned Economy," *Chungang Ilbo*, 1 August 2002.

General Corporation president; and Cho Hyon-chu, councilor to the National Economic Cooperation Federation.

This delegation was followed in October by a more high-profile delegation led by the chairman of the State Planning Commission Pak Nam-gi. The most important person in the delegation, however, was Chang Song-taek, the first vice director of the KWP Organization Guidance Department and Kim Chong-il's brother-in-law. The rest of the delegation was rounded out by Kim Ki-taek, another first vice director of the KWP Organization Guidance Department, and Pak Pong-chu, the Minister of Chemical Industry and a rising star among Kim Chong-il's economic advisers.[81]

Although no hard agreements were reached, the nine-day tour of the South by North Korea's team of economic and commerce officials was hailed by the South Korean media as a potential breakthrough in inter-Korean economic relations. Pak Nam-gi and his delegation allegedly promised future trips to broaden the North's knowledge of capitalist development. After Seoul, the delegation spent another 20 days touring Southeast Asia, with stops in Indonesia, Singapore, and Malaysia.

Nestled between these fact-finding visits to Seoul was a summit in Pyongyang between Japanese Prime Minister Junichiro Koizumi and Kim Chong-il. For months, Japan had been sending signals that it was willing to increase its aid to North Korea in return for a resolution on the abduction issue. Unlike South Korea and the United States, where the nuclear issue essentially put on hold planned efforts at cooperation, Japan was willing to move aside issues of national security to put closure to cases involving the abduction of several Japanese citizens by North Korean special forces in the 1970s.

The North Korean Ministry of Foreign Affairs reportedly counseled Kim not to agree to the summit, arguing that the groundwork had not been properly prepared. Kim's economic advisers countered that for the July 1st Measures to be successful, North Korean enterprises, no longer tethered to the state, needed loans and assistance to allow them to operate until they became self sustaining.[82] If such aid was not forthcoming, they would go bankrupt and have to return to a state-run distribution system. This would essentially doom the reform effort. According to Russian sources, Kim's wife, Ko Yong-hui, who was born in Japan of Korean parents, weighed into the debate, counseling her husband to find a way to resolve the outstanding differences with her homeland.[83]

Whether Ko Yong-hui's growing influence played a role in Kim finally agreeing to the summit is not clear. What is clear is that Kim's strategy of denying complicity but admitting North Korea's guilt in the abductions and apologizing for "some members of a special agency carrying out rash actions or seeking heroism" backfired.[84] Although the Japanese government at first accepted the apology and announced that it would work toward normalization of ties with North Korea, in the weeks that followed, the anger in Japan forced the government to backpeddle and take an even more strident position, essentially closing yet another aid channel.

MILITARY-FIRST POLITICS IN THE
MIDST OF CHANGE

Amidst the fanfare surrounding the apparent changes going on inside North Korea, there were also signs that military-first politics remained the primary lens through which Pyongyang viewed the world. As noted above, the New Year's Joint Editorial had departed from recent themes of economic development. Instead, it placed primary emphasis on national defense, stressing that North Korea was in a "life-and-death showdown against the enemies." The people were urged to be "proud of the army," which received special mention in conjunction with commemorating the 70th anniversary of the founding of the Korean People's Army (KPA).

At the fifth session of the 10th Supreme People's Assembly (March 27), the rostrum ranking revealed the continuation of a trend of NDC membership ascendancy in leadership rankings. Ri Ul-sol and Paek Hak-rim joined Cho Myong-nok, Kim Yong-chun, Kim Il-chol, and Chon Pyong-ho at the top of the list before any of the Politburo members.[85] The year before, at the fourth session of the 10th SPA, Yon Hyong-muk, an alternate member of the Politburo was elevated over full members of the body. This reinforced the view among Pyongyang watchers that power within the regime now firmly resided along the axis of the military chain of command.

In the spring and summer, leading up to the July 1st Measures, Kim took steps to reinforce his control over the military. On April 14, in his capacity as Supreme Commander, Kim promoted 54 general grade officers (Order No. 00152). Gen. Chang Song-u, commander of the Third Corps and older brother of Chang Song-taek, was promoted to vice marshal, and colonel generals Kim Yun-sim (commander of the KPA Navy),[86] Kim Chong-gak (vice minister of the People's Armed Forces),[87] and Yo Chun-sok (vice minister of the People's Armed Forces) were made full generals.[88]

The promotion of Chang Song-u, a close confidante of Kim Chong-il, was particularly important given the changes going on inside the regime. Not only did it make him 1 of only 13 vice marshals in the North Korean high command, but given the previous year's promotions within the KWP's Organization Guidance Department, it highlighted Kim Chong-il's increasing concerns regarding regime stability.[89] As head of the Third Corps, which was deployed around Pyongyang, Chang was a key member of the "Praetorian Guard," thus making his position just as much political as military.[90]

In addition to the appointments, Kim also stepped up his guidance inspections of military units, paying particular attention to tactical training. According to South Korean sources, Kim's inspections had taken on a more urgent character.

Table 2.3
Leadership Rostrum Changes from 1998 to 2002

Rank	Session 1, 10th SPA (September 1998)	55th Anniversary of KWP (October 2000)	Session 4, 10th SPA (April 2001)	Session 5, 10th SPA (March 2002)
1	Kim Chong-il	Kim Chong-il	Kim Chong-il	Kim Chong-il
2	Kim Yong-nam	Kim Yong-nam	Kim Yong-nam	Kim Yong-nam
3	Hong Song-nam	Pak Song-chol	Cho Myong-nok	Cho Myong-nok
4	Ri Chong-ok	Kim Yong-chu	Hong Song-nam	Hong Song-nam
5	Pak Song-chol	Hong Song-nam	Kim Yong-chun	Kim Yong-chun
6	Kim Yong-chu	Kim Yong-chun	Kim Il-chol	Kim Il-chol
7	Cho Myong-nok	Kim Il-chol	Chon Pyong-ho	Ri Ul-sol
8	Ri Ul-sol	Ri Ul-sol	Yon Hyong-muk	Paek Hak-rim
9	Kim Il-chol	Paek Hak-rim	Ri Ul-sol	Chon Pyong-ho
10	Ri Yong-mu	Yon Hyong-muk	Yang Hyong-sop	Han Song-yong
11	Kye Ung-tae	Han Song-yong	Paek Hak-rim	Kye Ung-tae
12	Chon Pyong-ho	Kye Ung-tae	Ri Yong-mu	Kim Chol-man
13	Han Song-yong	Kim Chol-man	Kim Chol-man	Ri Yong-mu
14	Kim Yong-chun	Choe Tae-pok	Kye Ung-tae	Yang Hyong-sop
15	Yang Hyong-sop	Yang Hyong-sop	Han Song-yong	Choe Yong-rim
16	Choe Tae-pok	Choe Yong-rim	Choe Yong-rim	Kim Yun-hyok
17	Kim Chol-man	Kim Kuk-tae	Kim Yun-hyok	Kim Yong-tae
18	Yon Hyong-muk	Kim Chung-nin	Yu Mi-yong	Yu Mi-yong
19	Paek Hak-rim	Kim Yong-sun		
20	Chon Mun-sop	Ri Yong-mu		

(*continued*)

Table 2.3   (*Continued*)

Rank	Session 1, 10th SPA (September 1998)	55th Anniversary of KWP (October 2000)	Session 4, 10th SPA (April 2001)	Session 5, 10th SPA (March 2002)
21	Choe Yong-rim	Kim Ik-hyon		
22	Hong Sok-hyong	Cho Chang-tok		
23		Kwak Pom-ki		
24		Kim Yung-hyok		
25		Ri Ha-il		

Our analysis is that while NDC Chairman Kim Chong-il's style of on-the-spot guidance to military units in the past had a strong aspect of underscoring "concern for the military," such as for materials and support the military units required, lately he is putting emphasis on the combat readiness posture of the units. . . . This style follows the idea of military-first politics and has a strong aspect of aiming for a multi-purpose effect, in that the image of strengthening the KPA's combat readiness posture will encourage arming with ideology and improving performance in all fields outside of the military.[91]

On June 29, just three days before the July 1st Measures, in what had become a familiar *modus operandi* for North Korea just before taking seemingly important shifts in policy, North Korean patrol boats crossed the Northern Limit Line (NLL) and opened fire on a South Korean Navy ship.[92] Whether this was an orchestrated event to reiterate the continued importance of the military-first policy or just an unfortunate coincidence, Kim used the occasion to send an unmistakable signal. As had happened in June 1999 after a similar incident, Kim chose to visit a military unit for his first public activity since the West Sea clash, making clear that the military continued to play a commanding role in the life of the regime.[93]

CONCLUSION

The general relaxation begun in 2002 with the July 1st Measures would continue for another two years. Mobile phones, which made their appearance in North Korea during this period, grew to 20,000 by the end of 2003.[94] By 2004, as one Pyongyang watcher noted, many international observers believed that North Korea had turned a corner and "finally embarked on a reformist path."[95]

A simple reading of the New Year Joint Editorial for 2003 would have suggested that Pyongyang's policy agenda was not so cut and dried. It described 2002 as a historic year of victory won in all sectors of the revolution and construction even though the imperialist maneuvers to isolate and crush North Korea had intensified. The editorial asserted that North Korea's dignity and power were exhibited in 2002, and noted that new changes (July 1st Measures) were made in building a powerful state and new breakthroughs were also made in the economic sector. Then, it went on to call 2003 a year of bold offensive and great changes under the military-first banner. It pointed out that the struggle for 2003 was to fully embody the *Chuche*-oriented, military-first line in all sectors, such as politics and the economy. It urged people to push ahead with building a powerful state, calling for single-hearted unity, which was "a conclusive guarantee for a powerful state." Finally, it warned people against the ideological and cultural infiltration of imperialism.

Read against the backdrop of economic change occurring in North Korea, this editorial made clear that Pyongyang viewed these so-called reforms in a fundamentally different way than did the outside world. The overall goal was not to secure a bright future for the average North Korean. It was a tactical shift in support of a larger crisis management strategy designed to preserve the stability of the regime. Unlike China, the reforms had a shelf life and were not evolutionary. North Korea could never completely follow the Deng model. The circumstances between the two countries were fundamentally different. North Korea had to contend with the South Korea factor. If it were to undertake true economic reform, it would place itself in direct competition with South Korea, a competition it could not win. Dismantling the command economy would also mean opening the country up to foreign influence and relaxing the blockade on information, two things that would begin to erode the *Chuche* fortress that had taken the Kim regime 50 years to construct.

Viewed in this light, what the international community often described as North Korean irrationality and lack of policy consistency is more appropriately characterized as an ongoing tactical dance. In a country ruled largely by one individual, policy choices are often based on instinct and reaction to unfolding events, as well as internal and external pressures. The first decade of Kim Chong-il's rule suggested that brinksmanship and reform, both in limited measure, went hand-in-hand. Whenever the scales tipped too far in one direction, actions were taken to keep things in balance. In terms of dealing with North Korea's long-term problems, it was a disaster. In terms of crisis management, it preserved the thing that Kim cherished most, regime survival.

CHAPTER 3

Kim Family Politics

Two things happened with regard to the North Korean leadership at the beginning of 2003. Kim disappeared from public view and a cult began to form around his wife, Ko Yong-hui. Kim Chong-il's disappearance for nearly 50 days coincided with the run-up to the war in Iraq.[1] The issue drew public attention when Kim failed to attend the Sixth meeting of the 10th Supreme People's Assembly in March. His absence was unusual, as he had never skipped a parliamentary session since the first meeting of the 10th SPA in September 1998, which also was the first parliamentary session after the death of Kim Il-sung. High-ranking military leaders, including Cho Myong-nok, first vice chairman of the National Defense Commission, and Kim Yong-chun, chief of the General Staff, also failed to attend the SPA session, leading to speculation that the North Korean leadership had secured itself in a bunker awaiting the inevitable U.S. attack.

At the time of Kim's disappearance from public view, an even more important development appeared to be taking hold within the regime: a cult around Ko Yong-hui. According to an alleged internal document obtained by Kyodo News, an idolization campaign surrounding Ko first surfaced in the summer of 2002. The campaign touting the "respected mother" was indirect. It did not mention Ko Yong-hui by name, suggesting that Kim Chong-il had not yet built a consensus within the leadership by what appeared to be a new direction in his eventual succession plan. Even though Kim Chong-nam, the first son, had reportedly been disgraced with his failed attempt to enter Japan in 2001, Kim Chong-il had kept quiet on this incident's implications for the future of the regime.

By 2004, politics inside the regime began to intersect with politics inside the Kim family. The result was a year of indecision. The regime continued to flirt with economic reform, but in fits and starts. On the external front, apparent breakthroughs on the nuclear program and the abduction issue quickly gave way to a reimposed stalemate. Was this just a replay of normal North Korean policy half measures or something more? Was it the product of a mind divided?

THE HOUSE OF KIM

The saga of the Kim family has been one of drama for over 60 years. From Kim Il-sung's reliance on his brother and oldest son to fight off opponents in the 1950s and 1960s to Kim Chong-il's own struggles to consolidate his power against his uncle and so-called side branches within the family in the 1970s and 1980s, the history of the family has been intertwined with the politics of the nation. By the early 2000s, members of the family were sprinkled throughout the North Korean leadership. Some held formal posts in the regime, but many of the most influential figures resided in the much more powerful informal circles around Kim.

In the hours after Kim Il-sung died, Kim Chong-il reportedly had the body transported to Pyongyang, where an impromptu wake was held.[2] Only members of the Kim family were invited to the service in which Kim Chong-il passed on the wishes of his dead father. According to sources close to the family, Kim told the gathering that he was now the head of the family and he would carry on in the tradition of Kim Il-sung. He then swore the family to four commandments (or laws).

- The unity of the Kim family takes precedence over all else.
- All important affairs of the family should first receive Kim's approval in advance.
- All quarrels within the family should be settled in accordance with family rules.
- Kim Chong-il's orders are commands, not to be questioned.[3]

At a closed funeral for the family, every family member allegedly followed Kim's lead in bowing before the body of Kim Il-sung and laying flowers on the deceased. The order in which this occurred roughly corresponded to the pecking order within the family in 1994. Kim was followed by his sister, Kim Kyong-hui; Kim Il-sung's widow, Kang Song-ae; and Kim's first son, Kim Chong-nam. The final three members of the procession were Kim's two youngest sons, Kim Chong-chol and Kim Chong-un.[4]

Over the next 10 years, this arrangement unraveled as the House of Kim fell victim to infighting and alliance building. Though the fourth commandment continued to hold, the first three gave way to plotting with an eye toward Kim's own succession.

KIM KYONG-HUI AND CHANG SONG-TAEK

Within Kim's innermost circle, his relationship to his closest family members was changing. For nearly 30 years, his sister, Kim Kyong-hui, had occupied a trusted position that surpassed any other within the regime. Only she had unfettered access to her brother.[5] She also was a political figure in her own right. She began her official career in 1971 with a management position in the Korean Democratic Women's Union. In the mid-1970s, she became a vice director and then first vice director of the KWP International Department. From the 1980s onward, Kim Kyong-hui held several concurrent party management positions. She was a manger of the business operations of Office 35 (External Investigations), which involved tobacco, narcotics, and weapons trafficking to earn income to finance intelligence operations and tithed a portion of its revenue to the Kim family. Since late 1987, she has held the position of director of the KWP Light Industry Department. Some companies under the Light Industry Department are tied to North Korea's illicit business operations including narcotics, counterfeiting, and cigarette smuggling. In the early 1990s, she supervised the merger of the KWP Financial Planning and Light Industry departments into the Economic Policy Inspection Department. When her father passed away in July 1994, Kim Kyong-hui ranked 47th on the funeral committee. In 1997, she was again identified as director of the newly reconstituted Light Industry Department.[6]

Outside of her official duties, Kim Kyong-hui also served as an intermediary for her brother, monitoring loyalty throughout the regime. She had numerous personal and political connections among her brother's cohorts, including SPA President Kim Yong-nam, KWP secretaries Choe Thae-pok and Kim Ki-nam, Vice Foreign Minister Kang Sok-chu, and United Front Department Director Kim Yang-gon. She was also close to the late KWP International Affairs Secretary Kim Yong-sun. Within Kim Chong-il's retinue of close aides, she was particularly close to Kim Chang-son, the deputy director of Kim Chong-il's Personal Secretariat, and his late wife. For decades, she attended her brother's banquets and parties, a superficial indication of social and political prominence in Pyongyang. Actress Choi Eun-hee dined and attended parties with Kim Kyong-hui in the 1970s and 1980s. Kenji Fujimoto recalled the constant presence of Ms. Kim at such gatherings in the 1980s and 1990s, where she was a dominant figure.

Kim Kyong-hui is a small woman, about 150 centimeters tall. But she made her presence strongly felt. She was known as a heavy drinker. When she got drunk at parties, she poured liquor for high-ranking officials around her. When she poured liquor for them, any of them stood stiffly to attention and drank a whole glass of liquor without a pause. When Kim Chang-son, deputy department director of the Workers' Party of Korea Secretariat, held a wedding ceremony at Sinchon Guest

House in 1990, she barked at the bride and groom, "Do you say you cannot drink liquor I poured?" Then, she made them get extremely drunk.[7]

Kim Kyong-hui also acted as her brother's personal representative to extended members of the Kim and Kang families, as well as to elites from other favored Revolutionary families.[8] The nature of her relationships with individual personalities is not clear, and it is likely that they are not all cordial. She has also had the sensitive task of attending to her brother's personal life. She coordinated Kim Chong-nam's move to Switzerland in the early 1980s, and told his mother, Song Hye-rim, that she was to be exiled. According to Kenji Fujimoto, Kim Chong-il also owed a more personal debt to his sister. In the early 1980s, at her brother's behest, Kim Kyong-hui allegedly adopted a child born to Kim Chong-il and his mistress. Little is known about the child other than that Kim Kyong-hui raised it alongside her two own children, Chang Kum-song (daughter born in 1977) and Chang Kim-song (son born around 1979).[9]

Kim Kyong-hui's primary ally within the family was her husband, Chang Song-taek, the first vice director of the KWP Organization Guidance Department, a post he had held since the mid-1990s. As the vice director in charge of administrative affairs, Chang had oversight responsibility for North Korea's internal security apparatus, including the Ministry of People's Security and the State Security Department. His responsibilities also included a variety of revenue-generating enterprises that had ties to Office 39, the party office dedicated to securing hard currency and luxury goods for the Kim family.

As a couple, Kim and Chang controlled a powerful patronage and surveillance network that stretched throughout the regime and provided Kim Chong-il with a situational awareness he could not get through the formal mechanisms of power. Of particular importance were the Kim/ Chang ties to key figures within the high command, most of whom began to rapidly rise during the mid-1990s as Chang Song-taek consolidated his position within the Organization Guidance Department. Some of the more notable officers within this group included officers in charge of critical command and control nodes, such as Chief of the General Staff Kim Yong-chun and director of the General Staff's Operations Bureau Kim Myong-guk. Kim Yong-chun and Chang Song-taek reportedly collaborated on suppressing the Sixth Corps uprising in 1995, and Kim Myong-guk's tie to the Chang network probably ran through Chang's older brother Chang Song-u, the commander of the Third Corps.[10]

KO YONG-HUI

By the late 1990s and early 2000s, another powerful faction was emerging within the Kim family tied to his unofficial wife, Ko Yong-hui. An enigma to outsiders, Ko's background is the source of much dispute. For years, the story was that Ko Yong-hui was in fact Ko Chun-haeng, a native of Tsuruhashi, Osaka, Japan. Her father, Ko Tae-mun, was a famous judo master in Japan who came from Cheju Island. The family moved to North Korea in the early 1960s. However, in December 2006, the South Korean National Intelligence Service (NIS) issued a strong refutation of this biography, asserting that Ko Yong-hui and Ko Chun-haeng were different individuals. Regardless of this discrepancy, Pyongyang watchers agree that Ko began work as a dancer for the Mansudae Art Troupe in Pyongyang in the 1970s. She first met Kim Chong-il in the mid-1970s while attending a secret party he hosted. They began living together in 1975. Even though they never married, she gave birth to Kim's two youngest sons—Kim Chong-chol and Kim Chong-un—and daughter Kim Yo-chong.[11]

The Kim–Ko relationship was kept quiet, even within North Korean leadership circles. After all, Kim Chong-il was reportedly still married to Kim Yong-suk.[12] Despite her brother's discretion, Kim Kyong-hui reportedly objected to the relationship. For years, she had kept tabs on his love life. When Kim rebuilt his official residence at Mount Taesong San to allow for co-habitation, it became clear that Ko was not just another mistress.[13] She was a threat not only to Kim Kyong-hui's status, but to Kim Chong-nam's status as heir apparent, something his aunt apparently supported. As long as Kim Il-sung was alive, Kim Kyong-hui most likely used the threat of her father's disapproval to keep Ko under wraps as a political player within the regime. After his death, Ko remained an enigmatic figure, maybe in part to keep peace within the family.

Notwithstanding her low profile, the regime began a campaign in 1999 to publicize Ko Yong-hui within the armed forces, calling her "Pyongyang Mother." The General Political Bureau (GPB) of the Korean People's Army organized literature and art workers to compose "Dear Mother" and other songs to promote her virtues within the armed forces. After Kim's longtime mistress, Song Hye-rim, died in Moscow in 2002, the propaganda campaign surrounding Ko accelerated. This campaign was allegedly organized by a number of Cho Myong-nok's vice directors, including Hyon Chol-hae and Pak Chae-kyong, the latter being the head of the GPB's Propaganda Department.[14]

Ko's primary ally, however, was reportedly Ri Che-kang, Chang Song-taek's chief rival within the KWP Organization Guidance Department (OGD). A graduate of Kim Il-sung University, Ri began his career as a guidance official in the OGD in the early 1970s, becoming Kim Chong-il's chief subordinate when he took over the department in 1973. During this time, Ri and Kim worked closely together to prepare the Kim Il-sung succession. According to one prominent defector, "Ri possessed an exceptional memory and kept the status of party figures in his head at all times."[15] After supporting Kim's Pyongyang redevelopment project in the 1980s, Ri apparently joined a cadre of OGD officials within the heir apparent's personal secretariat, something that advanced his career. In 2001, he began to appear in official functions as first vice director of the OGD.

The ROK National Intelligence Service's biography of Ri Che-kang noted that he was in charge of examining internal documents on the life of party cadres.[16] He also controlled the flow of documents to Kim's personal secretariat.[17] This placed him in close contact with Kim's family and presumably Ko Yong-hui. In the late 1990s, Ri was at the forefront of the idolization campaign surrounding Ko, something that contributed to rumors of his ongoing rivalry with Chang Song-taek for control of the powerful department they both ran. It is questionable whether Ri's patronage system was as extensive as Chang's, but with his position as one of Kim Chong-il's primary gatekeepers, Ri's assay of the regime was probably just as clear.

SIDE BRANCHES[18]

Although Kim Chong-il had eliminated any serious opposition within the family to his leadership role by 1994, relatives remained, albeit in fewer numbers, throughout the regime. Kim Yong-chu, Kim Chong-il's uncle, served as an honorary vice president of the Supreme People's Assembly. He appeared at functions until April 2003, when he disappeared from the public scene for nearly four years.[19]

Outside the country, several relatives served in diplomatic posts. The most important such relative, and one of the least visible, was Kim Pyong-il, Kim Chong-il's half brother. Born in 1954 to Kim Il-sung and his personal secretary Kim Song-ae, Kim Pyong-il has been in virtual exile since the 1970s. Rumors that Kim Il-sung would transfer the three branches of power to his three sons (with Kim Chong-il controlling the party, Kim Pyong-il the military, and Kim Yong-il the government) did not come to pass as Kim Chong-il sidelined his half-siblings to ensure they could not interfere in politics. Kim Pyong-il was posted to the North Korean embassy in Yugoslavia in 1979. At about the same time, Kim Yong-il was posted to East Germany and his half-sister Kim Kyung-chin's husband Kim Kwang-sup was posted to Czechoslovakia (he is now the ambassador to Austria). Over the next 20 years, Kim Pyong-il served in a number of postings across Europe, being sent to Hungary in 1988 until Hungary recognized South Korea in December 1988, at which time Kim was sent to Sofia (Bulgaria). At that time, Berlin and Sofia were the only two non-Soviet European capitals with direct air links to North Korea. In 1998, he became the ambassador to Poland.

According to defector reporting out of Europe, Kim Pyong-il made two attempts in the 1990s to usurp his brother's power. As Kim Il-sung lay dying, his second son returned to Pyongyang to be by his bedside. The content of their conversation is not known. Some believe that the father may have apologized for not supporting his second son when he had a chance. Though he was too weak to make up for this mistake, Kim Il-sung did order the release of Kang Song-ae from informal house arrest and reinstated her to the post of Chairwoman of the Korean Union of Women, a move that guaranteed her several bodyguards and a fighting chance of not disappearing without a trace.[20] When Kim died, Kim Pyong-il's name did not appear on the funeral committee list, although he took part in the ceremony.

In the months after Kim Pyong-il returned to Europe to take up his new posting as ambassador to Finland, disturbances reportedly broke out in Pyongyang. According to South Korean sources, gunfire was exchanged behind the walls of a government complex between the secret police (presumably the State Security Department) and several military officers allied to Kim Pyong-il. Whether this was part of a larger coup attempt or an isolated act of violence has never been made public and the particulars of the incident have remained shrouded in mystery. A purge of several of Kim's protégés reportedly occurred in the weeks after the skirmish, but Kim Pyong-il himself remained at his post in Helsinki. By the early 2000s, he had faded from the memory of many Pyongyang watchers.[21]

RESPECTED MOTHER

Kim family politics went dormant in the late 1990s. Rumors of infighting and sibling-on-sibling rivalry disappeared from the international press. Speculation of Kim Chong-il's own succession appeared from time to time, usually focusing on Kim Chong-nam as the likely heir apparent. This ceased with his ill-fated trip to Japan.

Eight months after Kim Chong-nam was arrested at Narita Airport (May 2001) and six months after an article appeared in *Nodong Sinmun* titled "A Brilliant Succession" (July 21, 2001),[22] a three-part feature appeared in the party daily discussing the moral decay of capitalist society. The second article of this feature, titled "I Want to Live Like a Human Being, as a Woman," painted the sad picture of a poor woman who died in a fire. Quoting from the woman's diary, the author argues that this woman was "subjected to an abject life in capitalist society that forces women, who should be loved and protected by people as the flower of home and the flower of a country otherwise, to walk the path of an abject life 'just because' they were born into the wrong social system." The article uses this fundamental argument to support a lesson ascribed to Kim Chong-il, namely that "in capitalist society, people are increasingly enslaved by money and things with their political life oppressed."[23]

One might ask why such a rather pedestrian piece of North Korean propaganda should warrant any notice. The only reason is that one of the three authors on the article's byline was Ko Yong-hui. This was the first instance Ko's name had appeared in the North Korean media. While there was no indication that she had written the article, there was little doubt that the use of her name would have required approval at the highest levels. [24]

Over the next three months, the same author wrote two more articles aimed directly at the United States. The first, penned only three days after the rant against the moral chaos in capitalist society, dealt with nuclear weapons. It urged North Korea to keep a vigilant eye on the United States, which it described as harboring an "ambition to dominate the world through nuclear weapons."[25] The article also noted the Bush administration's announcement to reduce the number of nuclear warheads from the currently deployed 6,000 to 1,700–2,200 by 2012, something that gave the author another chance to evoke Kim Chong-il's lesson: "We should ban the test and production of nuclear weapons, reduce existent nuclear weapons, and, going a step further, completely abolish all nuclear weapons." Returning to the call for vigilance, the author concluded by arguing that any U.S. calls for nuclear reduction were a trap designed to ensure its dominance. With this article, Ko Yong-hui made what would become a regular foray over the next few years into the realm of foreign affairs.

The Ko Yong-hui article on March 12 tied the terror the United States experienced on September 11 to its obsession with global domination. Because of its desire to insinuate itself in the sovereign affairs of countries and regions far from its own shores, the article argued, the United States had neglected its own domestic national security. Although not explicitly warning the United States against military actions against North Korea, something that had clearly concerned the regime ever since President Bush's "axis of evil" speech on January 29,[26] the article suggested that the United States could relieve its own terror by refraining from "doing wicked acts against other people and to do only good things for mankind . . . [and] squarely look at sentiments of the world's people and the trend of the time, and to behave with discretion."[27]

In two articles, Ko Yong-hui had summed up North Korea's fears and distrust of the United States. As such, they were bellwether articles, reflecting the views of the North Korean leadership. Why the regime had chosen to tie these articles to Kim Chong-il's wife through their authorship is not clear. But, by having Ko's name attached to articles focusing on ideology and national security, probably two of the most important responsibilities of a future leader, might have been the regime providing a clue to the wider North Korean leadership that a new succession architecture not centered on Kim Chong-nam, but on the Ko Yong-hui matrilineal line, was being constructed.

Later that year, in August, the regime appeared to further elevate Ko by issuing a military "lecture document" that referenced an unnamed "respected mother" and "mother of Korea." Titled "We shall defend to the death the high command of the revolution led by great comrade Kim Chong-il,"[28] this document sought to portray Ko by way of code word as Kim Chong-il's closest and most fervent supporter,[29] noting that "the esteemed mother (Ko) is the most loyal among the endlessly loyal to the revered supreme commander comrade (Kim Chong-il)."[30] The document went on to cite numerous instances of this "respected mother" accompanying her husband on inspections of the military and his on-site guidance tours and gave examples of how well she understood and looked after the safety and health of the leader. These descriptions, as well as the use of the phrase "mother of Korea," were reminiscent of how the North Korean media described Kim's mother, Kim Chong-suk, during his grooming process.[31]

Kim's use of the "respected mother" campaign was a clear indication that he was drawing from his own experience to set the path for his own successor.[32] Unlike Kim Il-sung, who could build his credentials as a leader by exaggerating and beatifying his own experience in Korea's anti-Japanese struggle, Kim Chong-il complemented his weakness of having no experience in the anti-Japanese struggle by according his birth mother Kim Chong-suk a status for worship as a "revolutionary patriot." Therefore, it is not surprising that Kim Chong-il took pains to highlight the "legitimate line of descent" from "the family of Mangyongdae and Mt. Paektu" as the foundation for his own successor.

A BROTHER-IN-LAW GOES MISSING

If it is true that Kim was using his own succession as a blueprint for ensuring his own successor, he could not be content to just name an heir and socialize this choice within the North Korean leadership. He would also need to enforce this choice within his own family. This meant "cutting the branches" to ensure that no pretenders to the throne could claim the mantle of leadership, either as another center of power during Kim's lifetime or as a threat to his chosen heir after his death.

In 2003, the Pyongyang watching community was beginning to discuss succession, but there was no clear consensus on whom Kim Chong-il would name as his heir apparent or even when this would take place. Kim Chong-nam's arrest at Narita seemed to dim his chances. Many believed Kim Chong-chol was the logical choice given that he was next in line among the male offspring. Kenji Fujimoto, Kim Chong-il's former chef, who had left his employer after 13 years to return to Japan, claimed that Kim was partial to his third son, Kim Chong-un. Despite this speculation, there was a growing consensus that the de facto number two man in the regime was Chang Song-taek, Kim's brother-in-law. Hwang Chang-yop even speculated that if Kim were to die, Chang would be the logical successor.

Hwang's assessment made sense given Chang's career trajectory. Chang quickly emerged as one of Kim's closest confidants in the 1970s and 1980s, assisting his brother-in-law in his battles within the family as he "cut the branches" (namely his uncle Kim Yong-chu and his half brother Kim Pyong-il) to clear his way as Kim Il-sung's successor. The fact that Chang was also a hard drinker afforded him special access to Kim as a central member of the "drinking team" who joined the Dear Leader at his late-night parties where plans were made and plots hatched. By the early 1990s, Kim's confidence in Chang was clearly revealed when the latter was given responsibility over 3 of the 22 departments in the Party's Central Committee—Youth Department, Organization Guidance Department, and the Three Revolutions Team Department.[33] Even though Kim maintained the directorship of the Organization Guidance Department, Chang, as the first vice director for administrative affairs, not only oversaw the party's surveillance apparatus, but had oversight responsibilities for Office 39, which was in charge of raising hard currency for the Kim family's private use.

Following Kim Il-sung's death, Chang's power base within the regime began to expand to the point that it was second only to Kim Chong-il's. Chang was in charge of party life and policy guidance over judicial, prosecutorial, and public security institutions. Chang's oldest brother Chang Song-u (age 71, vice marshal) had recently assumed the post of chief of the KWP Civil Defense Department, and his second oldest brother Chang Song-kil (age 65, lieutenant general) was the political commissar at the 820th Tank Corps.

Though it is doubtful that Hwang's statement carried much sway in Pyongyang, some Pyongyang watchers raised it as a possible motive for Chang's disappearance from public view in 2003. Later, reports began to emerge from defector channels that painted a story of jealousy and suspicion within the House of Kim.

The first indications of a problem reportedly came in early 2003 when Sin Il-nam, the chairman of the Capital Construction Committee and a Chang protégé, ignored repeated requests by Kim's newly chosen premier, Pak Pong-chu, to release materials needed for the capital modernization project. The plan to build Pyongyang into an international city based on the "Shanghai experience" had been a priority ever since Kim had returned from his visit to China in January 2001. The fact that delays in the supply chain were occurring allegedly caught Kim's attention. And the fact that the delay seemed to be coming from a sector controlled by Chang Song-taek probably raised Kim's suspicions about his closest associate.[34]

Sometime in the spring, Kim reportedly ordered an investigation into Chang Song-taek's affairs. Because Chang was a senior party member, the investigation would have been handled by the KWP Organization Guidance Department. Other internal security agencies, such as the Ministry of People's Security or the State Security Department, were prohibited from investigating the central party apparatus.[35] The investigation was probably handled by Ri Che-kang, the first vice director in charge of party affairs. By the summer, the investigation had reached some preliminary conclusions, which Ri most likely passed on to Kim Chong-il. On July 5, Chang accompanied Kim during a visit to Chagang Province. With the exception of a brief appearance at the central report meeting on the sixth anniversary of Kim Chong-il's election to party general secretary on October 7, it would be the last time he would be seen in public for three years.[36]

According to defector reporting, Chang continued his party work throughout 2003, although his access to Kim had been severely curtailed, if not altogether eliminated. It was during this period of internal exile (in February 2004) that Chang allegedly made a serious mistake by attending a wedding party for the child of one of his colleagues within the Organization Guidance Department. This gathering violated a central rule of security within the regime that prohibited the gathering of senior cadres without Kim Chong-il's express permission.

When the report of the event reached Kim, he took immediate steps. In March, Chang was relieved from his duties within the KWP Organization Guidance Department. South Korea's National Intelligence Service later reported that Chang had been charged with "sectarian acts" and "abuse of power" and placed under house arrest. The Capital Construction Committee, which sparked the investigation in the first place, was dismantled and reorganized into the Pyongyang Capital Construction General Bureau. Many of Chang's confidants who attended the wedding were also purged, including Trade Minister Ri Kwang-kun and Sports Guidance Committee Chairman Pak Myong-chol, who were expelled to the countryside. The Minister of People's Security Choe Yong-su, who had been recommended by Chang, was replaced after only a little over a year in office. First vice director of KWP Propaganda and Agitation Department Choe Chun-hwang was replaced with Ri Che-il. The director of the KWP International Department, Chi Chae-ryong, who had been close to Chang since the 1970s as chairman of the Kim Il-sung Socialist Youth League, stopped appearing at public functions in March.

For many Pyongyang watchers, such a simple misstep leading to such drastic consequences did not ring true. They pointed to additional defector testimony that placed Chang Song-taek's purge in context. By 2003, some defectors argued, a struggle for power within the Kim family was brewing between Chang and Kim's wife, Ko Yong-hui. As noted above, Ko was seeking to position her son, Kim Chong-chol, as the eventual heir. Chang and Kim Kyong-hui, however, opposed this move in favor of other heirs who would be more closely tied to them. Both Chang and his wife had ties to Kim's first son, Kim Chong-nam. Kim Kyong-hui reportedly took personal responsibility for grooming Kim Chong-nam and even overseeing his education abroad.[37] They were also rumored to be the foster parents of Kim Il-sung's last son, Kim Hyon. Because Kim Il-sung wanted to avoid undermining Kim Chong-il's position, he had kept Kim Hyon's identity a secret, placing him in the care of his daughter Kim Kyong-hui and Chang Song-taek.[38]

During this period, the dynamics within the family were shifting. Kim Kyong-hui, who had been Kim Chong-il's closest confidant since their childhood, was rumored to be ill and struggling with a severe alcohol problem. Like her husband, she also disappeared from public view in 2003 after posing for a commemorative photograph of the 11th SPA in September. At the same time, even as her own idolization campaign was raging, Ko Yong-hui was dying of breast cancer. Although she had received treatment, the cancer had reoccurred, and she was in critical condition.[39] Kim Chong-il, who was reportedly distraught over her illness, began to isolate himself. This allowed Ko's allies within the regime, such as Kim Ok, Kim Chong-il's technical secretary and mistress, and Ri Che-kang, backed by powerful elements within the military, to move against Chang Song-taek and his patronage network.

Despite his organizational power and influence, Chang was defenseless against the influence of a dying wife. Though it is only speculation, Ko most likely warned Kim Chong-il of the threat his sister and Chang Song-taek posed to her sons and to his own status as the unchallenged leader. Such warnings were probably validated when Kim found out about the wedding ceremony attended by Chang and many of his protégés. Kim Kyong-hui's illness and her lack of access to her brother prevented her from intervening on Chang's behalf.

LEADERSHIP TURNOVER AND AN EXPLOSION IN YONGCHON

Although struggles within the house of Kim centered on succession, the battles being waged within Kim's close aide network remained focused on the tradeoff between economic reform and regime stability. In an effort to deal with this tradeoff, from both sides of the equation, Kim oversaw a dramatic turnover of personnel throughout the regime in 2003.

Turnover in the Military and Security Apparatuses

Kim carried out a reshuffle of many of the key operational commanders in the summer. Between the annual promotions and the reshuffle of the corps in May, all of the corps commanders were elevated to at least colonel general, with some commanders holding the rank of full general. Most of the newly promoted generals were in their 40s and 50s. One vice marshal, Chang Song-u, moved from commander of the Third Corps to chief of the Capital Defense Command.

Though there is very little information in the public domain concerning the Korean People's Army (KPA) at the corps level, a few points can be gleaned from an historical analysis of the various commanders.

- Horizontal loyalties (such as military academy classes) appear to be restricted, as are career bonds that could come about between officers through sequential appointments to same commands.

- First-time promotions to corps commandership (especially front-line corps) appear to come from divisions within those corps.
- There are lateral transfers from front-line corps to rear-area corps and vise versa.
- It is not uncommon that commanders have commanded or have links to more than one corps.
- It is not uncommon for commanders to serve time in senior-level commands (General Staff, Artillery Command) before returning to the corps.
- On occasion, commanders have backgrounds in other services (Air Force, Navy).
- Corps commanders have very little interaction with provincial secretaries. Adherence to chains of command is mandated.
- Senior corps officers normally rank between 60 and 80 on protocol lists, but their influence is often not reflected because of ties they sometimes have to senior KPA officials or Kim Chong-il.
- When purges occur at the senior level of the high command, it can lead to reshuffles in the corps because of links with military leaders now out of favor.
- With very few exceptions, corps commanders do not travel outside North Korea.[40]

In July, Kim replaced key members of his security apparatus. VMAR Pak Ki-so, who had commanded the Pyongyang Defense Command since 1995, was replaced by Col. Gen. Ri Yong-ho. According to informed sources, Pak was replaced for age reasons (he was born in 1929). The Pyongyang Defense Command is the corps-level unit responsible for the protection of Pyongyang and the surrounding areas. It takes its tasking from the General Staff, but has close ties to Kim Chong-il. Prior to the 1980s, it was subordinated to the Guard Bureau (now Guard Command), but was part of a realignment to streamline the chain of command and de-conflict information flow. The Pyongyang Defense Command is composed of 70,000 troops and outfitted with numerous tanks, armored personnel carriers, and artillery systems. It works closely with the Third Corps in ensuring the security of the capital.

The long-time commander of the Guard Command, Ri Ul-sol retired in 2003 and was replaced by Col. Gen. Yun Chong-in. The Guard Command's origins stretch back to 1946, when the elements of the 90th Training Command were carved out to provide security for North Korea's emerging leadership. It has gone through a number of reorganizations and, since the 1990s, has been growing in importance as the heart of the regime's Praetorian Guard.

Although formally subordinated to the Ministry for People's Armed Forces, the Guard Command reports directly to Kim Chong-il in his capacity as head of the party. It is responsible for the personal security of Kim and other high-ranking officials, as well as surveillance of high-ranking political and military officials. It also shares responsibility for the defense of the capital with the Pyongyang Defense Command and the Pyongyang Antiaircraft Artillery Command. Located in Puksae-tong, Moranbong-kuyok, Pyongyang, the corps-sized Guard Command is equipped with tanks, artillery, and airplanes. One brigade is deployed at each of Kim's residences located throughout North Korea.

Finally, Gen. Won Ung-hui, the head of the dreaded Military Security Command, a counterintelligence organization responsible for internal security within the KPA, was replaced by Col. Gen. Kim Won-hong,[41] an officer who was first publicly identified in 1997, when he signed Choe Kwang's obituary. His career had largely been confined to the field commands, especially the Seventh and Ninth Corps.

Organized under the Ministry of People's Armed Forces, the Security Command enjoyed a great deal of autonomy because of Won's close relationship with Kim. Like the General Political Bureau, it has its own agencies at every level of the military down to the battalion level. Through its own field agencies, it seeks out antiregime activity, investigates political crimes, and conducts extensive political surveillance. Even the political officers of the General Political Bureau are not immune from its close scrutiny.[42] The Security Command was upgraded from a bureau in the mid-1990s, allegedly in response to its contribution to uncovering the corruption in the Sixth Corps in 1995. In 1998, the command assumed responsibility for key internal security and law enforcement activities, until then the jurisdiction of civilian authorities.

In the fall, Kim completed the reshuffle of the defense and security apparatuses. The National Defense Commission underwent a substantial reshuffle at the 11th SPA in September 2003. Yon Hyong-muk, who served as premier during the third seven-year economic plan (1987–93) and as a member of the NDC since 1998, was promoted to vice chairman. Choe Yong-su, who replaced Paek Hak-rim as Minister of People's Security in July 2003, and Paek Se-bong,[43] an SPA member, joined the NDC as members. Three elderly members (Ri Ul-sol, Paek Hak-rim, and Kim Chol-man) were removed from the commission. Within the new commission, the vice chairmen had clear-cut roles. VM Ri Yong-mu took charge of military affairs, and Yon Hyong-muk had oversight of economic affairs.[44]

Generational Turnover in the Cabinet

Whether for security reasons or as a matter of procedure, the reshuffle of the military and security apparatuses gave Kim the space to address some issues that had been long opposed by hardliners within the leadership. Wrestling with the shortcomings of military-first politics, Kim Chong-il, according to some reports, continued to entertain the arguments of pragmatists around him who contended that such a policy had proven an economic disaster, inhibiting the reduction of sanctions and availability of South Korean and Chinese assistance, which was critical to the country's survival.[45]

At the 11th SPA, a new Cabinet made up of young reform-minded ministers was appointed. The obscure Minister of Chemical Industry, Pak Pong-chu,[46] was appointed premier, replacing Hong Song-nam, who became chief secretary of the South Hamgyong Provincial Party Committee. The move caught most Pyongyang watchers off guard, not just because Pak was a rather unknown figure, but because his rapidly rising status suggested a newly invigorated Cabinet, which had real power.

Pak's cabinet was composed of economic technocrats, many of whom had knowledge of western economic thought and had been part of delegations to South Korea where they were able to observe Seoul's planning and policymaking up close. Pak Nam-ki, who headed the October 2002 delegation to Seoul, was named chief of the Supreme People's Assembly's budget committee and Kim Kwang-nin replaced Pak Nam-ki as State Planning Commission chairman. Other top Cabinet officials such as Ri Kwang-nam, minister of extractive industries, Kim Sung-hyon, minister of metal and machine-building industries, Ri Mu-yong, minister of chemical industry, and Choe Ik-kyu, minister of culture, were people who had field experience and professional knowledge gained from long careers in their respective agencies.

The appointment of Yim Kyong-man (57 years old) in April 2004 as minister of foreign trade, replacing Ri Kwang-kun, continued this trend. A graduate of the foreign literature department of Kim Il-sung University, Yim was rumored to be a student of capitalist market economics. After a career in a variety of Asian postings, he served as chief of the trade representative office in Dalian, China, between August 2001 and March 2004. Yim's appointment was seen by many within the Pyongyang watching community as an indication of North Korea's intention to engage in active economic diplomacy in the future. In a related move, North Korea's economic theory publication, *Kyongje Yongu,* advocated an "active economic diplomacy, that is, trade activities, aimed at boldly penetrating capitalist countries to ensure practical gains by proactively and efficiently taking advantage of the characteristics of capitalist markets."

The rise of these technocrats was part of a broader turnover of the elite as younger and better educated functionaries came to dominate the second and third echelons of the regime. Fifty-three percent of the delegates elected to the 11th Supreme People's Assembly were below the age of 55, up 5 percent from the previous Assembly. The percentage of university graduates in the SPA also rose, to 91 percent from 85 percent.[47] The Cabinet reshuffle also lowered the average age of top government officials across the board. In a more general context, this was reflective of the rise within the general population of a new generation of young and capable professionals equipped with the skills to thrive in the wake of the "July 1st Measures."[48]

Standing in opposition to this cadre of technocrats was the old guard and powerful elements within the military and security apparatus. These were the major proponents of the isolationist agenda. At the end of 2002, they had successfully rolled back the euphoria surrounding the July reforms, as evidenced in the New Year's joint editorial, which claimed the year as "a year of total march toward the peak of a powerful state, a year of bold offensive battles, and a year of a gigantic change under the military-first banner."[49] The resonance of this security argument was reflected in Pak Pong-chu's oath taken at the 11th SPA, which made it clear that whatever reforms were implemented would fall within the boundaries of the "the *songun* [military-first] revolutionary line of the Worker's Party of Korea." Now, the isolationists looked on with increasing suspicion and trepidation as the Cabinet pushed an agenda that touted the path to a "strong and prosperous state" as based on economic rationality and incentive-based reforms. Any reforms along these lines, the isolationists contended, would make North Korea vulnerable to the infiltration of foreign ideas and exploitation.

Kim's leadership style and the fact that he had become somewhat disengaged and distracted by Ko's illness likely encouraged this competition,[50] which lasted until April, when it came to an abrupt halt in the wake of what for all intents and purposes appeared to be a major attack on the stability of the regime. Upon his return home from China, Kim's train passed through the town of Yongchon, a city of 130,000 close to the border with China. According to initial reports, approximately nine hours after Kim's train passed, the Yongchon railroad station was devastated by a massive blast that left at least 161 people dead and 1,300 others injured.[51] These reports claimed that the source of the blast was the collision of two trains loaded with ammonium nitrate and fuel. Later reports speculated that the explosion resulted from a failed assassination attempt.[52]

Regardless of the reason for the explosion, the Yongchon incident gave the critics of reform the opportunity to reinvigorate military-first politics and roll back the gains that had been made in the name of *silli* (pragmatism). Kim Chong-il was reminded that pragmatism as an approach existed within the range of regime stability. According to South Korean reporting, the SSD concluded that the Yongchon explosion was a result of a conspiracy by anti-North Korean government forces to harm North Korean leader Kim Chong-il. A "North Korean official" was cited as saying that the security agency had evidence that "cell phones had been used in triggering the explosion and reported to the North Korean leader that the use of cell phones should be banned for the sake of the leader's safety." On May 19, North Korea instituted a nationwide ban on the private use of cell phones.

Talk of Succession amid Confusion in Leadership Politics

The summer and fall of 2004 were a swirl of confusion and mixed signals coming out of Pyongyang. The North Korean regime appeared to be
wrestling with a number of different issues, in terms of both its politics
and policies. Though signs were mixed over whether the regime would
roll back the 2002 economic reforms, North Korea once again turned to
diplomacy in a number of overtures to the international community. In a
surprising move, Pyongyang in May agreed to Seoul's long-standing offer to hold inter-Korean general-level military talks, something the two
countries had not done since the end of the Korean War. This was followed
by Prime Minister Koizumi's second trip to Pyongyang, where in return
for substantial economic aid, North Korea released five Japanese abduct-
ees. Finally, in June, the third round of the Six Party Talks took place in
Beijing.

Amid this flurry of activity on the international stage, reports began to
surface in the foreign press about a number of leadership issues, not the
least of which was succession. Since 2002 and the Ko Yong-hui articles,
rumors had persisted that Ko's first son, Kim Chong-chol, had replaced
Kim Chong-nam as the odds-on favorite to become the heir apparent.[53] In
September 2003, a mysterious figure named Paek Se-bong appeared in
the National Defense Commission lineup. Some Pyongyang watchers speculated that the name, which can be translated as "new bud (or peak) from
Paekto," a reference to the Paekto Mountain bloodline, was a cover for
Kim's heir, possibly Kim Chong-chol.[54]

But it was not until 2004 that signs began to appear in the official media
that suggested that this speculation might have some merit. In May, the
name "Kim Chong-chol" appeared in the North Korean media for the
first time, but as with his mother's name two years before, the reference
was not directly associated with the family of Kim Chong-il. Instead, it
was tied to a story of the emergency response to the train explosion at
Yongchon train station. Although not describing it as an assassination attempt, the story highlighted accounts of heroism, in particular the actions
of a public security agent Kim Chong-chol, who "went out to the units
[fighting the fire] . . . and participated in rescue battles." This act of
bravery and selflessness was contrasted earlier in the article by the actions of a "functionary" Kim Chong-nam, who did nothing more than follow orders and rush to the scene of the incident. The article stood out for
its ties to a real incident that the foreign press was speculating could have
been an assassination attempt on Kim Chong-il, and for the fact that the
names of two of the primary contenders in the succession race were un-
precedentedly mentioned and their actions seemingly juxtaposed.[55]

Taken by itself, this article could easily be dismissed as a coincidence.
But in 2004, stories involving the North Korean leadership suggested that

at the very least various agendas were at work inside Pyongyang. The most intriguing rumor of the summer was Ko Yong-hui's health. In June, reports began to surface that Ko had returned to North Korea from Paris, where she had been receiving treatment for breast cancer since April.[56] In August, rumors began to reach the outside world that Kim's fourth wife/mistress (her marital status had never been determined) had died of a heart attack.

There was no immediate confirmation of Ko's death. However, Kim Chong-il's movements during this period and reports from sources inside Pyongyang suggested that something was amiss. Kim Chong-il, who met with King Norodom Sihanouk of Cambodia on July 31, suddenly disappeared from public view for about two weeks, reemerging in mid-August to make an inspection tour of military units. In the meantime, rumors began to mount that the regime had placed Pyongyang under a "state of emergency," ceasing the issuance of foreign visas, controlling internal travel in and out of the capital, and restricting international telephone service, including the telephone lines available to foreign missions.

Sandwiched between the stories of Ko's illness and eventual death was an intriguing commentary in Nodong Sinmun and a high-profile reshuffle in the Ministry of People's Security. In an unusual editorial marking the tenth anniversary of Kim Il-sung's death, Nodong Sinmun highlighted the qualifications for the country's next leader, noting that it would boil down to "outstanding accomplishments in ideology and theory and a relevant initiative."[57] Though the commentary was couched in a discussion of the merits that led to the late leader's grooming of his son, Kim Chong-il, it marked the first time that the North Korean media had discussed (even obliquely) Kim's own succession.[58]

Two days after the editorial on July 9, KCNA announced the replacement of Minister of People's Security Choe Yong-su by Chu Sang-song. What made this unusual was that Choe had only served in his post for one year, suggesting that the move was politically motivated. Some Pyongyang watchers speculated that the move was tied to the removal of Chang Song-taek, but little evidence was presented linking the fallen minister and Kim's brother-in-law.[59] Others argued that the timing of the reshuffle was probably related to the Yongchon explosion and the ministry's shortcomings in responding to the event. Rumors surrounding the event suggested that the SSD, not the Ministry of People's Security, took the lead in investigation, something that would have given it a boost in the ongoing turf battles among the North Korean security agencies.[60]

Questions about the internal cohesion within the regime continued in the fall, with publication of a picture of Kim Chong-il's estranged half brother, Kim Pyong-il, the ambassador to Poland. Taken on the occasion of Kim Chong-il's birthday (February 16), the photo appeared on the Korean Friendship Association (KFA) website on September 10.[61] Given the fact that any information regarding the Kim family is treated as a state secret, not to mention that Kim Chong-il reportedly viewed his half brother as a threat and had banned him from the country, the photograph took on special significance. When a report was leaked through Japanese channels one week later that Kim Kyong-hui, Kim's sister, had just returned to Pyongyang from treatment in Paris for alcoholism and mental illness,[62] many Pyongyang watchers saw tentative evidence that Ko Yong-hui's death had unleashed a rush by a number of factions to fill a power vacuum within the Kim family.[63]

As the year drew to a close, speculation surrounding infighting within the Kim family had deepened to the point that some Pyongyang watchers began to hypothesize about Kim's own status as leader. They pointed to a Japanese Radiopress report that the glorifying description "Dear Leader" had been dropped by the official media,[64] as well as Russian ITAR-TASS reports that Kim's portraits were being removed throughout the capital in an effort to downplay his personality cult.[65]

Upon closer examination, however, this speculation was based on international media confusion and partial data. The rumors began when Pyongyang radio failed to mention Kim's title "great leader of our party and people" during coverage of his visit to a military unit on November 16. As the Japanese and South Korean press latched on to this omission, English language translations of the stories incorrectly reported that the title "Dear Leader," which had become widely used in the West, had been dropped. In fact, since Kim Chong-il assumed power in 1994, the North Korean media had normally referred to him by the honorific title "Great Leader" (*widaehan ryo'ngdoja*).[66] "Dear Leader" was rarely used and normally only in a historical context. As for the omission, Pyongyang radio on November 19 and 22 carried reports on Kim's visits to military units, both of which referred to him as "great leader of our party and people."[67] As for the portraits, pro–North Korean media corroborated that Kim's portrait had been removed from some North Korean venues, but argued that this was done to obscure the personality cult from foreign eyes, not to question his undisputed power inside the country. After all, a *Choson Sinbo* article argued, portraits of both leaders were "still hanging on the walls of homes and public institutions of the DPRK."[68] In a follow-up article along the same lines, the Tokyo-based Korean language newspaper went on the offensive in its refutation of Western media–inspired rumors of "an unstable [North Korean] domestic situation."

The Western countries' media are spreading words on the "unstable domestic situation" and "changed political situation" based on their arbitrary interpretation and deliberate distortion of the reality of the DPRK.

This year marks the 10th anniversary of President Kim Il-sung's passing away. The DPRK people call the by-gone days "ten years of the eternal leader." In the past, there were times when the preceding leaders' idea and accomplishments suffered setback and insult in the later days. Seen in an objective light, the military-first politics of giving priority to and attaching importance to the military unfolded by General Kim Chong-il has been the greatest element that has helped defend the ten years of President Kim Il-sung's eternal life amid confrontation with the hostile countries.[69]

The *Choson Sinbo* defense was no doubt part of a larger North Korean effort to defuse international speculation about its internal affairs, something that the regime feared could be used by the United States and its allies as part of an information warfare campaign. It dovetailed with Kim's own steady pace of military guidance inspections aimed at boosting morale and, in the words of a South Korean government report, tightening his grip on power.[70] Whether it was also used to mask dissention within the Kim family is unknown. By the beginning of 2005, the rumor mill had gone quiet.

CONCLUSION

The North Korean regime has been referred to as a "Byzantine Court on the Taedong River" where Kim Chong-il and a handful of families run a "modern-day *Chuche* Constantinople."[71] This description evokes images of kings and kingmakers and powerful wives conducting politics within the halls of power and behind bedroom doors. It is a world that is opaque to the outside world, which is left to only guess who is up and who is down by reading obscure references in the official media and connecting the dots based on interviews with former insiders whose own knowledge is often based on rumors and innuendo.

Despite the opacity and the reliance on tea leaves, 2004 had all the earmarks of an unusual year. In a country that places great importance on symbolism, it was awash in meaning. It marked the 40th anniversary of Kim Chong-il's entry into the KWP Central Committee apparatus (1964), the 30th anniversary of his designation as the heir apparent (1974), and the 10th anniversary of his assumption of power after the death of the Great Leader (1994). It also fell within a period of a generational turnover within the North Korean leadership as the third generation began to assume some responsibilities at the operational level. Finally, it fell in a period of profound change within the Kim family itself with Ko Yong-hui's illness.

The question for Pyongyang watchers was whether these turf battles and shifts within the leadership had any impact on policy. When one considers the fact that this early foray into succession politics was probably accompanied by an intensification of the competition for Kim's attention, devotion, and favors, at the very least, it was a distraction from the day-to-day operations of the regime. More important, in retrospect, 2004 was the culmination of a decade-long trend in which the fabric that had held the regime together for nearly six decades had become seriously frayed.

Markets and technology had provided the population with some modicum of independence and information of the outside world. Devine worship of the Leader had dimmed and the infallibility of *Chuche* was in serious question. Elite unity, and even the unity within the Kim family, appeared in doubt.

The situation demanded action by the king, or in this case the Great Leader. Kim could act as his father had done on several occasions and institute a purge to rebuild fear and cohesion or he could continue his strategy of power building, which relied more on calibrating and recalibrating policies while keeping leadership turnover to a minimum. Whatever path he took would have profound consequences for North Korea's future.

The next four years would suggest that Kim would maintain his own counsel. As a consequence, the engine of reform, which had been unleashed two years earlier, would sputter to a halt.

CHAPTER 4

Rollback of Reforms

Running in parallel with the apparent struggle for power within the Kim family was the regime's ongoing debate about what to do about the economy. As noted, Pak Pong-chu, the Minister for Chemical Industry and a member of the economic delegation that toured South Korea the year before, became Premier in 2003, replacing Hong Song-nam. The Cabinet, which had been elevated in status because of the July 1st Measures, became increasingly aggressive in pushing the reform agenda. But, by 2004 and 2005, the reform agenda came to a fundamental fork in the road where another set of decisions had to be made regarding international support. Once again, the regime needed to weigh the costs and benefits of its nuclear deterrent. The decisions that would be made over the next four years would cast the regime down a familiar path of retrenchment, driven by its own calculus for survival.

In the Pyongyang watching community there are two views about why North Korea began to retrench and roll back its reforms. One view holds that the actions of the Bush administration in blocking North Korea's access to the international financial system forced Pyongyang to seek defensive and protective policies, instead of confident reform measures. Another view contends that with increased confidence in its ability to survive, North Korea simply returned to the status quo. Although conclusive evidence to support one interpretation over another is lacking and Pyongyang watchers are left with trying to connect the dots, it is not a wasted effort. After all, at the heart of this debate is the question of whether Kim Chong-il's North Korea is even capable of change.

A MIXED MESSAGE

The New Year's Joint Editorial for 2005 gave the impression that North Korea was in a holding pattern. The security measures imposed after the Yongchon explosion appeared to stop with the confiscation of cell phones. A wider rollback of reforms did not appear imminent. In fact, the domestic agenda dominated the Joint Editorial, which emphasized that 2005 would be "a year of hope" when the people's hard labor would be rewarded with "prosperity and wealth." From the standpoint of language, the New Year's message was decidedly more optimistic than the somber 2004 forecast of an era of "turbulent struggle." Lest anyone get the impression that Pyongyang was on the verge of abandoning its decade-long priorities, the editorial continued to reaffirm the importance of the regime's "military-first" policy, stating that the country should "give precedence" to the military and "supply everything necessary on a priority basis" to the national defense industry.

ASSESSING THE REFORM EFFORT

The Joint Editorial left many wondering whether the regime was on the verge of another spasm of economic initiatives. It made references to "storms of giant strides" and "another leap and innovation that will surprise the world." The editorial also promised a "radical turn" in economic construction and an increase in the population's standard of living. Finally, it boasted that 2005 would be a "rewarding year" as Kim Chong-il's "plans of great reform" led to "great changes" (*pyo'nhyo'k*) for the people.[1]

The consequences of the 2002 reforms in terms of economic benefits and political costs were a mixed picture. The government had taken a number of measures that were paying dividends. In sectors directly tied to people's livelihood, such as agriculture, light industry, and commerce, the government facilitated managerial independence and vitality, while retaining the planned economic system with regard to basic industries, where it allocated most state-controlled resources. It replaced quotas with profitability as the basic measure of performance, for both the enterprise and the worker. Workers in their 30s and 40s with special skills were deployed throughout the economy as managers to revitalize the inefficient organizational culture. State-designated prices were adjusted periodically to reflect supply and demand. The government reduced its mandatory purchase quotas from 80 percent to 60 percent to facilitate farming efficiency and significantly raise farmers' wages. A new land-lease system reduced rental prices on land and expanded the size of plots individuals could farm for their own personal use and profit. Farmers' markets were reorganized into consolidated markets to expand their distribution. Nonproductive and nonoperating enterprises were closed and/or merged. To entice foreign investment, North Korea opened up Sinuiju, Kaesong, and Mt. Kumgang.

In terms of performance, the overall economic indicators suggested that the reforms had led to a modest recovery. North Korea's economic growth rate had begun to creep up and certain sectors, such as mining and agriculture, showed dramatic improvement.[2] Hyperinflation, which resulted from the price reforms designed to bring prices in state-run enterprises in line with those in farmers' markets, had begun to subside by 2005. Enterprise profitability and wages tied to productivity enhanced work motivation and economic efficiency, especially in the agricultural and light industrial sectors. Fears of famine subsided as harvests gradually improved and Chinese food aid soared.

By 2004–2005, however, economic life in North Korea began to take on a new character somewhat troubling to the regime. Though the increased reliance on the market system had yielded benefits, it also had unintended negative consequences. As the planned economy shrank and markets expanded, enterprises and individuals became more autonomous. The gap between wages and prices, caused by the hyperinflation following the 2002 reforms, had weakened the state's control over the population. The traditional means of tying people to state business enterprises and strict residential districts were diminishing as a rising sector of the population was attempting to engage in small business enterprises. With an increase in private economic activity, the gap between rich and poor was growing. An increasing number of high-ranking party and government officials and international trade employees were accumulating wealth through influence-peddling or foreign currency manipulation. This led to a widening gap in the regime between "winners" and "losers," a potentially destabilizing phenomenon. But most troubling was the fact that as the population became increasingly conscious of the consequences of the reforms, momentum was growing for a market-oriented economy, a trend that would be increasingly difficult to reverse.[3]

REEXERTING CONTROL

As early as January 2004, Kim's economic advisers had been searching for the right vehicle to combine the planned economy with the market economy, thus giving the government more control over this spontaneous marketization, which had become the country's coping mechanism. The uptick in the economic indicators in 2005 and the receding concern about famine gave the regime some breathing space to begin a partial rollback of the reforms. But to simply decree a reinstitutionalization of centralized control risked a backlash. Instead, the Kim regime tied the rollback to the larger struggle for national security.

Although the Joint Editorial had placed an emphasis on economic development, it did make reference to the continuing importance of the military-first policy. It stressed that "only the *Chuche* military-first idea" should "brim over in our revolutionary ranks" as a way of inoculating the country from "mean imperialist maneuvers" that threaten to "erode our ideology and institutions." In an obvious reference to the regime's concern about the negative consequences of the markets, the editorial went on to warn against the "penetration of reactionary ideological poison" and "rotten bourgeois way of living." In retrospect, these parts of the Joint Editorial provided the rationale for what was to come. The need to deter the external threat would justify the reassertion of control. Over the next several months, this plan would be put in place.

On February 2, North Korea convened an unprecedented meeting of party and military officials in what the official media called a "Meeting on the General March of the Military-First Revolution." Inside the April 25 Palace of Culture in Pyongyang, functionaries of party, military, and power organs, ministries, and central organs gathered for speeches on the state of the regime and the challenges it faced in the future. President of the SPA Presidium Kim Yong-nam urged the army and people to "always maintain a combat mobilization posture in coping with the acute situation where the U.S. imperialists' maneuvers of aggression are becoming more blatant."[4] This set the stage for Premier Pak Pong-chu, the generally recognized father of the reform effort, to deliver a message that seemed better suited coming from a senior military figure.[5]

After elaborating on the "greatness of our party's military-first politics," Kim Chong-il's achievement of strengthening the army, and various achievements in economic constructions under Kim Chong-il's leadership, the premier turned to the importance of "thoroughly embodying the military-first politics in all sectors" and urged the army and people to "resolutely smash the U.S. imperialists' maneuvers to isolate and crush the Republic and to create an epochal turning point in fulfilling the cause of building a powerful socialist state through the general march of the military-first revolution." Pak then talked of safeguarding North Korean-style socialism by military ideological vigilance and an "economic blockade with overall revitalization of and a great revolutionary upsurge in the socialist self-supporting economy [sahoejuu'ijaripkyo'ngje]."[6] In the oblique manner in which North Korea often made policy pronouncements, Pak had served notice to the regime's enemies, both domestic and foreign, that Pyongyang intended to stand firm behind the military-first strategy as it navigated the dangerous future that lay ahead.

On February 8, 2005, at the conclusion of this military-party policy meeting, the North Korean high command pledged its loyalty to Kim Chong-il, praising his leadership and the military-first policy. Two days later, the Ministry of Foreign Affairs announced the country's possession of nuclear weapons and an indefinite suspension of participation in the Six Party Talks. This declaration signaled a shift in North Korea's public diplomacy, which had until then been based on innuendo and obfuscation.

Many international observers were quick to ascribe North Korea's admission to purely external reasons. Following stories in the *New York Times* and *Washington Post* linking North Korea to Libya's burgeoning nuclear program, hardliners in the Pentagon and Vice President Dick Cheney's office argued for a quarantine of North Korea to bring about regime change. Without a doubt, North Korea's announcement seemed to fit the timing of a response to this threat. It certainly fit the pattern of bellicosity the regime resorted to from time to time when it felt cornered by the international community. But, in this case, the domestic driver for such an announcement was just as compelling. In order to carry out the delicate and most likely unpopular task of returning the reform genie to its bottle, the nation had to be unified behind a greater need. As one Pyongyang watcher noted at the time, "The experiment in putting the socialist Humpty Dumpty back together is being done against the backdrop of increasing militarization of society."[7]

Against the backdrop of heightened tension, North Korea convened the Third Session of the Eleventh SPA in April.[8] Contrary to the expectations of many international observers, the reports to the assembly made no mention of the nuclear issue, but instead focused on Cabinet-related issues. With Kim Chong-il in attendance (he missed the 2004 meeting of the SPA), Pak Pong-chu talked about the need to find an administrative solution to food distribution in order to meet the grain production targets. Without specifically saying so, he was in fact announcing the reintroduction of the Public Distribution System (PDS) that had reportedly been abandoned with the 2002 reforms. But careful not to retrench too far, Pak outlined a continued role for markets both as a mechanism for bringing advanced technology into the country and as a conduit for exporting North Korean goods to foreign markets. He also tried to balance ideological principles with market principles in a clumsy embrace of profits as the preferred method to measure performance: "All economic guidance functionaries . . . should organize and conduct the activities of production and management by strictly adhering to the principle of socialism and the principle of guaranteeing actual profits."[9]

By the waning months of 2005, the regime had taken a number of measures for the reintroduction and normalization of the PDS and the regulation of the markets. Justified under the banner of "preserving the principle of socialism," these measures included the implementation of age restrictions for market participation, closing of unofficial trading companies, and enactment of market price controls. Pyongyang resumed the twice-monthly sale of up to a 15-day supply of rations, but tied it to a number of qualifications including workplace attendance and performance. Probably most disconcerting for a large segment of the population, the regime banned the sale of food and produce in local markets and required farmers to deliver and sell all of their produce to the goverment.[10] Initially restricted to the Unification Street Market in Pyongyang, this ban was extended to all of North Korea by November.

One month before the institution of the PDS in October, Pak Nam-gi, the former chairman of the State Planning Commission and director of the KWP Heavy Industry Department, began to appear in the North Korean media under a new title, the director of the KWP Planning and Finance Department. Though his appointment went largely unnoticed by the Pyongyang watching community, it signaled the beginning of a change in how the North Korean economy was run. The July 1st Measures had been accompanied by the abolishment of several party departments that dealt with the economy (including the Department of Economic Policy Supervision and the Department of Agricultural Policy Supervision) in order to give the Cabinet more autonomy and responsibility to handle the economy. Pak's appointment suggested that the party had begun to take back some of its oversight responsibilities with the aim of suppressing the market and restoring a considerable portion of the planned system. Therefore by the end of 2005, competing centers of power had been established with regard to economic policy: the reform line represented by Pak Pong-chu and the conservative line (favoring heavy industrialization and communal agricultural production and distribution) represented by Pak Nam-gi.

CHANG SONG-TAEK RETURNS

In the latter half of 2005, a sense of normality seemed to be returning to North Korea's strategy for regime survival. Rather than relying on domestic reforms to pull itself out of the economic quagmire, Pyongyang had moved back to its comfort zone of internal control while using diplomacy to entice the aid necessary to hold things together. Inter-Korean relations continued apace as South Korean tourists flooded into North Korea to visit such resort areas as Mt. Kumgang. Pyongyang also promised to open Mt. Paektu to tourism. In May, South Korea shipped nearly 200,000 tons of fertilizer to North Korea and in July laid power lines for the future transmission of electricity once the North's power grid could be modernized. In the summer and fall, hopes were raised as North Korea agreed to return to the Six Party Talks reaching a tentative agreement in September for Pyongyang's gradual abandonment of the nuclear program in return for security, economic, and energy benefits.[11]

Over the next year, however, this survival strategy began to shift again as North Korea entered a new period of isolationism. Following on the heels of the BDA affair and the collapse of the Six Party Talks,[12] North Korea broke off its dialogue with South Korea. There was a test launch of a number of missiles, including the Taepodong 2, in July 2006; and on October 9, KCNA announced "the science and technology sector safely and successfully carried out an underground nuclear test." North Korea by its own definition had joined the club of nuclear weapon states.

Driven by external pressure surrounding North Korea's proliferation activity, which undermined Pyongyang's diplomacy on several fronts, as well as an increasing concern within the regime regarding the negative impact of the markets, Kim Chong-il now appeared intent on hunkering down. Instead of reaching out diplomatically and reforming domestic policies to achieve stability, as during 2002–2004, North Korea now retrenched on all fronts.[13] To the outside world, Pyongyang touted its enhanced deterrence. Internally, the regime took measures to enhance domestic security and regain central control of the economy. This naturally had consequences for leadership dynamics within the regime. To underline this fact, as if on cue, Chang Song-taek returned from the shadows.

Chang Song-taek returned to the public eye in January 2006 after a two-year absence. Described as a first vice director of a KWP Central Committee Department, KCNA listed him as one of the attendees at a dinner party hosted by National Defense Commission Chairman Kim Chong-il for China's Ambassador to Pyongyang in honor of the Lunar Chinese New Year.[14] Chang's return had been preceded by months of speculation beginning in August, when rumors surfaced that the Presidium of the Supreme People's Assembly had adopted a "decree" sanctioning a general amnesty to be granted on September 1 on the occasion of the liberation day and the 60th anniversary of the founding of the party.[15] Though Chang did not appear to be a part of this amnesty, his name again surfaced toward the end of the year when North Korean sources began reporting that he had been rehabilitated and had assumed the post of first vice director of the KWP Organizations and Capital Development Department.

Several things about Chang's rehabilitation stood out for Pyongyang watchers. First, he was not returned to the KWP Organization Guidance Department. That department now was under the firm control of Chang's rumored rivals Ri Che-kang and Ri Yong-chol. Instead, he was back where his career began, in charge of party social organizations and Pyongyang-based construction projects. The KWP Organizations and Capital Development Department had oversight of such entities as the Kim Il-sung Socialist Youth League, the General Federation of Trade Unions of Korea, and the Union of Agricultural Working People of Korea. It also had long-established ties to the powerful Pyongyang municipal party apparatus dating back to the 1970s and 1980s, when the KWP Working Organizations Work Department oversaw youth mobilization efforts to assist numerous capital construction projects.[16]

Chang's return also overlapped with the cessation of the Ko Yong-hui glorification campaign in the central media.[17] This did not appear to be a coincidence, but a conscious effort by Kim to smooth Chang's reintroduction into the leadership while avoiding friction with Ri Che-kang, who had allegedly continued to push the Ko agenda even after her death.[18] Whether a condition for Chang's return was his endorsement of the Ko matriarchal line as far as any future succession was concerned is not clear. In any case, by the beginning of 2007, Kim Chong-il reportedly banned all discussion about succession, expressing his will to continue exercising power for the "long term."[19]

Speculation ran high as to what role Chang would assume within the leadership. His reinstatement just days after Kim's trip to China to examine special economic zones led many to believe that Chang's responsibilities would be tied to the economy, more specifically, economic reconstruction. This view was bolstered in early February when Chang accompanied Kim on a guidance inspection of military and industrial sites in Kanggye City, which is located in the defense industrial heartland of Chagang Province. The fact that the patron for the province, Yon Hyong-muk, had died the previous October made this visit particularly important as an exercise in showing the face of the central leadership.

The Kanggye City inspection also prepared Chang for his next major task, which was to lead a 30-member delegation in early March through China to study the special economic zones Kim had visited three months earlier.[20] The delegation was endowed with the mission of working out policy alternatives that could tackle the economic difficulties in North Korea. As part of the trip, Chang met with Liu Qi, the fourth-ranking member of the Chinese leadership and a member of the CCP Political Bureau. The trip gave China a chance to again stress the need for North Korea to pursue economic reforms along the lines of the Chinese model.

The international media covered Chang's trip and his activities as he worked his way back into the good graces of the Kim regime. Embedded in much of this reporting was the belief that Chang was a proponent of markets and was emerging as the official responsible for implementing Kim's second phase of economic reform.[21] After all, Chang had in the past toured South Korea's economic miracle and was rumored to have ties to the Chinese leadership. As the months, passed, however, this optimism faded. Chang was linked to even more drastic measures to restrict the markets, such as the ban on private hiring and the narrowing of age and gender restrictions on who could participate in market activity.[22] According to a 2009 South Korean assessment of this period, Chang Song-taek was more than likely leading a defensive and constricted economic policy that stressed social stability.[23] His meager reform goals focused on the special economic zones, which were linked more tightly to Chinese economic activity along the border.

CONCLUSION

The reinstitution of the PDS and the regime's actions in the following months to curtail the markets led to a fundamental reassessment of the goals and objectives of the 2002 reforms by many Pyongyang watchers.

Many had taken Kim Chong-il's declaration to adapt socialist economic management to the demands of the times and press references to "New Economic Policy" to describe this program as an admission that the planned economy had failed and that the country was moving toward "market socialism." Now, it appeared that the reform measures were transitory and aimed at restoring and normalizing the planned economy while importing some elements of the market system. According to one Pyongyang watcher, "The goal was simply to narrow the gap created in the 1990s between state and private sectors, thus reducing the power and influence of the black market."[24]

In retrospect, it is likely that Kim Chong-il strengthened the Cabinet's authority while pursuing economic reform in order to overcome economic stagnation, but eventually sided with the party and its more conservative policies of a planned economy once stability had been achieved. The record seems to indicate that Kim and many of his closest associates, especially within the military, were concerned about the spread and pace of change unleashed by the reforms. Recent scholarship, however, suggests a somewhat more complex reasoning for the retrenchment. Instead of being solely tied to domestic considerations, it was tied to the regime's holistic view of its situation.

What is little understood is that the military-first economic policy is not a rigid line of economic thinking, but one born out of necessity and able to accommodate the principles of centralized economic planning and market reform.[25] As such, it is a very eclectic line that can flexibly swing between planning and the market depending on necessity. When North Korea undertook the 2002 reforms, the regime was less concerned about the security threat posed from the United States and South Korea, both of which had adopted somewhat less confrontational stances toward Pyongyang. This allowed the North Korean leadership to concentrate more on economic recovery and development.

As the international situation worsened in the aftermath of the Bush "axis of evil" speech, the contradiction between North Korea's economic policy and national security policy became untenable. Decoupled in 2002, Pyongyang tried to rationalize the two policies by undertaking a major diplomatic initiative to finally acquire the security guarantees it had long sought from the United States. The success of North Korea's economic reforms depended on support from the outside world. The improvement of relations with the United States was vital. When North Korea was not able to implement its strategy of survival and prosperity through comprehensive give-and-take with the United States, it made a decision in 2005 to begin retrenchment on both the domestic and external fronts. Economic and national security policies were recoupled through such provocative actions as North Korea's announcement of its possession of nuclear weapons and decision not to return to the Six Party Talks until certain conditions were met by U.S. actions. Within this context, the clamp down on the markets served the larger purpose of internal security against what appeared to be a more threatening international environment.

What was not clear from this timeline of events was Pyongyang's honest view of reform. Was it something only to be trotted out when necessity demanded? Or was it something the regime aspired to, but could only do under certain, controlled circumstances? It would be a question that continued to perplex Pyongyang watchers.

CHAPTER 5

New Faces Emerge as North Korea Takes a Different Tack at Reform

The New Year's Joint Editorial for 2006 suggested a level of calm had descended over the leadership after the year of wrangling with the markets and making promises about the future of the economy. The most positive language in years was used to describe the country's accomplishments. Encouraging the population to "leap higher full of far-reaching aspirations and confidence," the editorial boasted that North Korea had "achieved greater successes in the socialist construction field" in 2005 than "in the past few years combined" and made "new progress in agricultural production."[1] The editorial predicted that 2006 would mark the "opening of an era of great prosperity." Such optimism was no doubt driven by North Korea's largest harvest in ten years.[2]

In contrast to its upbeat domestic assessment, the Joint Editorial expressed concerns about what it saw as an increasingly unnerving international environment. Though the editorial continued the policy line laid down in 2002 of encouraging inter-Korean cooperation, it warned of the growing influence of "pro-U.S. and conservative forces in South Korea," a reference to the South's conservative Grand National Party (GNP), which was highly critical of the sunshine policy. As for the United States, the Joint Editorial tempered its rhetoric, but did suggest the need for a deterrent in the face of a country that would not "hesitate to inflict a nuclear disaster on our brethren" if it would further its "strategy against the DPRK." In addition, the editorial hinted at U.S. efforts to undermine the regime in its emphatic call for greater attention to ideological education as a counter to "enemies' mean ideological and cultural infiltration and psychological smear campaign."[3]

The editorial capped a year of radical policy swings by the leadership in Pyongyang. And, reading between the lines of the editorial, some Pyongyang watchers discerned that more changes were on the horizon. For some, the regime's intentions would be manifest in Kim's personnel policy. In his landmark book *North Korea's National Strategy and Power Elite*, Hyon Song-il, former North Korean diplomat and paternal nephew of General Hyon Chol-hae, laid out several axioms about the North Korean regime under Kim Chong-il. Two of the most important had to do with Kim's close aides and their ties to the policy-making process. First, Hyon noted, Kim's close aides rotated and very few were permanent residents near the center of power. Second, an examination of Kim's close aides could provide clues to reading the direction of North Korean policy.

Over the next two years, as North Korea wrestled with the predicament of rolling back market forces while casting an increasingly wary eye toward the outside world, Pyongyang watchers were presented with a number of changes in the leadership. New faces tied to the Kim family captured the attention of the international media, and reshuffles occurred across the board in the military, party, and cabinet, some seemingly tied to new policy directions. Lingering in the background of all this activity was the health of one member of the leadership, which would become increasingly the focus not only inside North Korea, but across the world.

EMERGENCE OF KIM OK AND KIM SOL-SONG

Despite attempts to clamp down on the markets and staunch information from seeping into or leaking out of North Korea, rumors about the leadership continued to fuel stories in the international media in 2006. Rumors of succession continued to proliferate, with the focus remaining primarily on Kim's second son, Kim Chong-chol. However, 2006 was different in that the stories were also being driven by the appearance and disappearance of notable figures.[4]

Chang Song-taek's reemergence was the most notable change to the North Korean leadership. He was the subject of several story lines throughout the year, some having to do with his personal life. While his star continued to rise, he suffered two major tragedies. On July 11, 2006, his older brother, General Chang Song-gil, died. General Chang had been in frail health for some time, retired from active service in the KPA.[5] At the time of his death, he was serving as an honorary curator of the Ministry of People's Armed Forces Revolutionary Museum in Pyongyang. Approximately two months later, in September, Chang Song-taek and Kim Kyong-hui's only daughter, Chang Kum-song, died in her Paris apartment, possibly of a drug/alcohol overdose.[6] In addition to these tragedies, Chang himself was reportedly involved in a serious traffic accident in October.[7] While being driven to work, his car was struck by an oncoming truck. Any speculation of foul play quickly faded when Chang appeared in the North Korean press as part of a Kim guidance inspection of Hamhung University of Chemical Industry in mid-November.[8]

One month after Kim's trip to China (January 2006), sources in China began to talk about a woman who accompanied him as his technical secretary and sat next to him at formal dinners.[9] These sources also noted that members of Kim's delegation privately described the woman as the leader's new wife. When the media provided photographs of the woman taken on the trip to Kim's former chef, Kenji Fujimoto, he identified her as "comrade Ok Hui," Kim Chong-il's secretary cum mistress.[10] Subsequent reporting revealed that this mysterious woman was Kim Ok.

Born in 1963 or 1964, Kim Ok attended the Pyongyang Kumsu Middle School and Kumsong Senior Middle School, the latter specifically catering to students who showed promise in the cultural arts. She excelled as a pianist. After graduating in 1985, she was recruited into the newly founded Wang Chae-san Light Music Orchestra. According to defector accounts, this orchestra was sponsored by Kim Chong-il and regularly performed for members of the leadership. Sometime in the 1980s, Kim recognized the petite pianist and brought her into his personal secretariat.[11]

In the North Korean party system, each member of the Politburo is assigned a personal secretary, who is responsible for taking care of the Politburo member's health and managing his or her office. As General Secretary, Kim Chong-il has several such secretaries in his office and Kim Ok was the secretary who dealt with administrative affairs.[12] According to some sources, Kim Ok also held a position as a director within the National Defense Commission. Chinese interlocutors who met her during Kim's 2006 trip to China described her as intelligent and very conversant on international issues.[13] As international media outlets began to scour their photo archives of North Korean delegations, it became apparent that Kim Ok was a major figure within the regime. She not only figured prominently in Kim Chong-il's trips to China and Russia (2001),[14] she was also part of the Cho Myong-nok delegation that met with President Clinton in 2000.[15]

Kim Ok's influence stemmed from her proximity to Kim Chong-il. Reportedly she became his mistress in the 1980s. This personal relationship bolstered her credentials among the North Korean leadership. By the mid-1990s, her status had risen to the point that even Central Committee secretaries and director-level top-ranking cadres called her "Comrade Ok-i," a title used when addressing a superior within the North Korean nomenclature.[16] Kim Ok reportedly served as an information filter and gatekeeper for Kim Chong-il, kept his schedule, frequently accompanied him on guidance inspections, and was a constant presence in his meetings with foreign delegations. According to several accounts of those who had meetings with Kim Chong-il, Kim Ok sat directly behind the General Secretary. She apparently had the latitude to speak to him without asking permission.

Within the Kim family, Kim Ok's influence and role was less clear. Her relationship with Ko Yong-hui, for example, is the source of much debate within the Pyongyang watching community. According to Kenji Fujimoto, their relationship was close, almost like sisters. Kim Ok often stood in for Ko Yong-hui at official functions, especially after the latter became ill in 2000.[17] As Ko's health continued to deteriorate, according to some sources, she pushed Kim Ok forward as her replacement.[18] Her relationship with Ko's two sons, Kim Chong-chol and Kim Chong-un, was also allegedly close.

This interpretation is disputed by a number of North Korean defectors, who contend that the Ko Yong-hui–Kim Ok relationship was contentious. They note that Ko Yong-hui was far from comfortable with Kim Ok's relationship with her husband, something she complained about to Kim Chong-il's sister, Kim Kyong-hui. They also assert that by the late 1990s, the relationship became so strained that Kim Chong-il had to send Kim Ok to Macau, where she lived under the name Chong Il-son, a pseudonym frequently used by North Korea's royal family on their diplomatic passports when they go abroad.[19] In 2010, Kim Chong-nam weighed into the discussion when he repeated a rumor that has circulated in the defector community for years, namely that Kim Ok is the mother of Kim Chong-un. This was reportedly a secret only known to a few members of the Kim family (Kim Kyong-hui and Chang Song-taek) and key individuals within the leadership (O Kuk-yol).[20]

After Ko Yong-hui's death in 2004, Kim Ok assumed the role of first lady, filling the vacuum of power and extending her network. Cadre close to her, such as Hwang Pyong-so, vice director (in charge of military affairs) of the KWP Organization and Guidance Department, began to appear more frequently as part of Kim Chong-il's guidance inspections. By 2006, she appeared to be exerting increasing control over the succession process and is believed to have played a role in Kim's decision to halt discussion of the matter in leadership circles.[21]

As information on the Kim family continued to find its way out of the regime in 2006, the international media also shined a spotlight on Kim Chong-il's oldest daughter, Kim Sol-song.[22] Arguably Kim Chong-il's favorite child, Kim Sol-song was the first grandchild named by Kim Il-sung. Born in 1974, Kim Sol-song is the daughter of Kim Chong-il's second wife, Kim Yong-suk. After graduating from Kim Il-sung University with a degree in economics, she entered the Central Committee apparatus, reportedly taking a position in the KWP Organization Guidance Department.[23] She later transferred to the KWP Propaganda and Agitation Department.[24] Since the late 1990s, she has held a position within her father's personal secretariat, presiding over Office 99, which is responsible for managing some of the Kim family's financial accounts. She has traveled abroad with her father as an aide and has even acted as his interpreter. According to some accounts, Kim Sol-song holds the rank of lieutenant colonel in the General Guard Command and has some responsibility for providing for her father's schedule and security arrangements.[25] She frequently accompanies Kim Chong-il on guidance inspections and reportedly has close ties to many of her father's closest associates, such as MAR Ri Ul-sol, Gen. Hyon Chol-hae, Gen. Ri Myong-su, VMAR Ri Yong-mu, Kim Ki-nam, and Kang Sok-chu. Her ties with her aunt and uncle (Kim Kyong-hui and Chang Song-taek) are believed to be close. High-level defectors have claimed that Kim Chong-il has remarked on occasion: "I am extremely fond of Kim Sol-song. She has brains and capabilities, and my daughter resembles me in many aspects."[26]

With the revelations about Kim Ok and Kim Sol-song, Kim Chong-il's gatekeeping mechanism came into focus. It was not only tied to his personal secretariat, it was tied to his family. It is through this mechanism that the concentric circles of the North Korean leadership connect to the leader.

BIG BANG DIPLOMACY

The international media's focus on the trials and tribulations of the Kim family reached a fever pitch at the end of June, with feature-length articles and pictures of Kim Chong-chol, Kim Chong-il's second son, during his time in Switzerland (presumably in the 1990s).[27] In July, however, the focus shifted, with North Korea's launch on July 4 of seven missiles (including one intercontinental-range Taepo Dong 2 missile that failed after 42 seconds) over the Sea of Japan. Three months later, on October 9, North Korean officials informed the Chinese embassy in Pyongyang that a nuclear test was imminent. Twenty minutes later, at 10:36 A.M. Korea time, an explosion was detected by seismic monitors deep inside the mountain at the Panggye test site near Kilju City, 385 kilometers northeast of Pyongyang.[28]

Intelligence analysts and Pyongyang watchers wrestled with North Korea's motives for returning to its well-worn brinksmanship strategy. After all, the ensuing sanctions could do little to improve the economic quagmire in which the regime found itself. Many speculated that Kim Chong-il had little choice and sanctioned the test to placate an increasingly powerful military. They pointed to what appeared to be the changing relationship between the party and the military, largely ascribed to three factors.

- First, Kim needed to rely on the military rather than the party and the cabinet to maintain internal stability at a time when the North suffered from a shortage of resources necessary for the management of the party and the state.

- Second, the international sanctions against North Korea had created an expanded sense of insecurity within the regime, thus enhancing the status of the military.

- Third, only the military could serve as the engine for implementing economic programs at a time when the state could hardly mobilize the labor force and the state budget was lacking.[29]

During the summer of 2006, many Pyongyang watchers believed that this trend had passed a threshold, leaving the North Korean military as the dominant power in making policy decisions. Military leaders had begun to appear more prominently on leadership rostrums and the high command ordered enhanced training during the annual summer exercises (focusing on large-scale maritime maneuvers and amphibious training).[30] The high command's influence was presumably manifested outside of military channels in the regime's decision to place all government departments on alert, carry out enhanced crackdowns against foreign intrusion throughout the country, and bolster border controls.

Even more telling, for many Pyongyang watchers, was North Korea's decision to cancel the May scheduled start of train services between the North and the South. This was not the first time the North had flip flopped on agreements with the South. But instead of backing out during the planning phase, this time North Korea had changed its mind after massive preparations were complete. North Korea had renovated the Kaesung train station by employing about a thousand workers and announced it was ready to give the rail line the green light, according to a South Korean government official who refused to be identified. According to the official, the North Korea military changed its mind and wanted to scrap the trial services.[31]

This assessment of the military's role in and influence on policy making is too simplistic and ignores many of the checks and balances within the system. Indeed, the decisions regarding the missile and nuclear tests took place through a series of interactions within the KWP Central Military Committee (CMC) and the National Defense Commission (NDC), with Kim Chong-il having final say on when to test. His principal advisers most likely were Chon Pyong-ho, the KWP secretary in charge of the Munitions Industry, and Chu Kyu-chang, the director of the KWP Munitions Industry Department, which has direct oversight of the Second Academy of Natural Sciences, North Korea's defense research and industrial complex. During the decision-making process, Kim likely tasked the relevant party secretaries (logistics, industry, external relations, and military affairs) for their input on consequences related to a test. Upon receiving these inputs, Kim might meet with individual members of the NDC to discuss security ramifications before passing his final decision down through party channels, via the KWP CMC to conduct the test. Under this decision-making scheme, the military's input, though vital, would be centered mainly on requirements and technical aspects of the test, not on the decision on when and if to test.

A closer examination of the leadership and policy dynamics in North Korea at the end of 2006 and in early 2007 suggests that though issues of most interest to the military (security and development of a deterrent capability) obviously factored into the decision to conduct the missile and nuclear tests, they were not the only considerations. In fact, they probably were not the overriding considerations. In the summer and fall of 2006, pressures along two axes were beginning to attract the attention and concern of the leadership in Pyongyang. One was known only to a close circle of aides around Kim Chong-il and was only apparent to the larger leadership through tea leaves and backroom gossip. The other was a more tangible threat that was becoming impossible to ignore.

The first of these pressures was the Kim Chong-il succession. The question of succession had for two years been nothing more than speculation, a parlor game that the North Korean elite engaged in from time to time. Ko Yong-hui's death in 2004 and the resulting demise of her idolization campaign had dimmed the focus on a particular individual, but the central media had continued to signal the need for a hereditary succession. In 2006, media agit-prop increased. Articles appeared that attached the phrase "generation after generation" to the code phrase "command post of the revolution," a designation for Kim Chong-il.[32] "The command post of the revolution" construct had particularly important connotations as it was tied to the concept of unity within the regime of the party, military, and the people. By attaching the phrase "generation after generation" to this construct, the media seemed to indicate a new level of importance to the notion of hereditary succession.[33]

Alone, this new code phrase could be ascribed to nothing more than a continuation of the on again, off again hereditary succession campaign, which began in 2001 with the *Nodong Sinmun* political essay titled "A Brilliant Succession."[34] But, in 2006, a steady stream of rumors began to surface regarding Kim Chong-il's health. During his trip to China in January, some sources reported that he received medical treatment in Shanghai. A South Korean politician made news in September by claiming that Kim suffered from liver and kidney problems and could not walk "more than 30 meters without assistance." Although the ROK National Intelligence Service disputed the claim, the story did fit with an unusually high spike in speculation on the North Korean leader's health. Even within South Korean intelligence circles, a consensus was crystallizing that Kim Chong-il had sanctioned the commencement of the succession process.[35] If true, the regime would want to tie any progress in military technology to an eventual succession as a way of building support for Kim's eventual heir.

As if on cue, the North Korean media found a way of tying succession and military technology together. After the July missile and October nuclear tests, editorials in *Nodong Sinmun* began to parrot another phrase attributed to Kim Chong-il: "The Day for the strong and prosperous state (*kangsong taeguk*) is dawning." An apparent reference to Deng Xiaoping's Four Great Strategies for Modernization, this slogan suggested that the regime sought its salvation through economic reforms and enhanced military power through nuclear weapons and ballistic missiles. As with the "command post of the revolution" construct, the "strong and prosperous state" construct was given a new twist. Within the North Korean lexicon, the sun and dawn were references to the leader. Some Pyongyang watchers interpreted the reference to "dawning" as having succession (most likely hereditary) connotations.[36]

A second, and more pressing, reason for the missile and nuclear tests was the economy. At the beginning of 2006, it looked as if North Korea, even with its clamp down on the markets, would be able to achieve a level of self-sufficiency in food production. Grain production was on pace to reach 3.64 million tons. North Korea needed another 1.5 million tons to feed its 22 million people, but annual contributions from China and South Korea of a half-million tons would go far in meeting the shortfall. As a consequence, Pyongyang started off the year by asking Western aid organizations and their irksome monitoring regime to leave the country.[37] But, as fate would have it, in July, North Korea was hit by a devastating monsoon. Rain pelted the country with a savagery not seen since 1995, washing away farmland and leaving hundreds of thousands of people homeless.

It became increasingly clear that Kim's hunkering down strategy would no longer suffice. Pyongyang would have to reengage with the world. But, it would do so on its own terms, not as a weak country looking for a handout, but as a "powerful" nation commanding the world's respect, if not fear. From Pyongyang's perspective, the missile and nuclear tests were not just demonstrations of military prowess, or even a validation of the technology, but bargaining chips to be used to coax the United States back to the negotiating table. Throughout the spring of 2006, North Korea signaled that it was willing to return to the Six Party Talks if the United States lifted the BDA sanctions and held bilateral meetings. Its frustration grew as its signals met with silence from Washington. The missile test came only a month after a North Korean invitation for the United States to send its nuclear envoy to Pyongyang for bilateral talks, a move that was rebuffed.[38] When the missile test failed to achieve the desired results, Pyongyang upped the ante in October with the nuclear test, agreed to return to the Six Party Talks, and declared 2007 to be the "year of economic development."

NUCLEAR WEAPONS AND ECONOMIC POLICY

Over the next several months, Kim Chong-il began to prepare the regime for yet another course correction in terms of domestic policy. The nuclear test had completely changed the regime's decision-making calculus. Kim could now make the argument that North Korea had successfully laid the framework for reengaging the world on its own terms and under a "new nuclear umbrella," and, as such, the environment was now conducive to devoting additional attention and resources to the economy.

In November, he conducted a rare series of high-profile guidance inspections focused exclusively on the economy in South Hamgyong Province. An examination of his media appearances since 1994 revealed that it was extremely rare for Kim Chong-il to conduct such a large number of economic events uninterrupted by inspections of military facilities.[39] Because Kim used his appearances in the media to highlight his priorities and concerns and signal shifts in policy, it seemed credible to many Pyongyang watchers that a renewed emphasis was being placed on the economy.

What was perplexing, however, was the disappearance of Pak Pong-chu. Long touted as the brain behind North Korea's economic reforms, Pak had become a nonentity. His appearances had dropped dramatically from the final quarter of 2005, when he appeared with Kim 17 times. During the first quarter of 2006, he only appeared 6 times among Kim's cadre. Over the last three quarters of the year, he appeared only once in Kim's entourage, on May 10, when the state media reported him as having accompanied Kim on a visit to a music university. This sudden drop in media coverage of the premier suggested that he had fallen out of favor.[40]

According to defector reporting, during this period, Pak's operational space was rapidly shrinking thanks in large measure to several political missteps. In October 2006, the premier and the minister for Coal Industry, Chu Tong-il, were severely reprimanded for advocating a reorientation of the country's energy policy as a means of breaking the impasse facing the economy. According to one source, Chu Tong-il was dismissed for suggesting that power should be diverted in these lean times from Kim Chong-il's villas to private farms and ordinary households. The Cabinet's decision to cease shipments of coal to China and divert it to domestic use was reversed by the National Defense Commission, which argued that foreign currency generated from the sale of coal was indispensable for strengthening military power.[41]

The NDC decision was in keeping with the new policy line that challenged the Cabinet's authority in the economic realm. This shift was reflected in the Joint Editorial for 2007. Although emphasizing the importance of demonstrating economic progress, the 2007 editorial called for the elevation of the "responsibilities and roles" of all "economic organ functionaries," not just the Cabinet, in order to "build a powerful socialist state."[42] This marked a significant departure from the previous three joint editorials (2004 to 2006), which focused exclusively on the Cabinet as the "executor and organizer" of the country's economy. The 2007 Joint Editorial also went on to imply that the Cabinet had come up short in its efforts to date, but was still at the "helm of socialist economic construction."[43]

In January, Pak was again sharply criticized by party functionaries at an enlarged plenary meeting of the Cabinet for his plan to introduce an "hourly wage system," a "daily wage system," and a "weekly wage system" to domestic enterprises. Pak wanted to build up a system in which salaries were paid according to achievements, in order to increase productivity.[44] His critics, however, argued that the premier was "attempting to introduce capitalist systems." As such, the proposal was reportedly voted down and Pak's political influence drastically declined.

Pak's fall appeared to signal that Kim had begun to see economic reform in a fundamentally different way. The goal of reform remained the same, the creation of a strong and prosperous state. However, the strategy and management style for achieving these results had changed. For over a year, the regime had done little more than take measures designed to rein in the markets. This not only reflected Kim's increasing concern over the growing influence of the markets, but his discomfort with the decentralization of control, which was the hallmark of Pak's July 1st Measures. As a result, Pak's moves to jump start the economy by resorting to "capitalist" incentives and measures of performance found little traction.

The regime's rhetoric surrounding the nuclear test indicated a return to a more traditional method of running the economy. *Nodong Sinmun* noted that the party's (not the Cabinet's) "line of economic construction in the military-first era" and "policy on reconstruction and modernizing the people's economy" had been "brilliantly implemented" and that a "foundation for a new leap forward" was "being provided."[45] This suggested that the more conservative party line of running the economy had come back into vogue, something that was supported by the return of Chang Song-taek, whose profile had begun to rise. Though he had briefly reappeared in the media in early 2006, Chang now took a prominent role as part of Kim's South Hamgyong tour. This was by far his most concentrated spate of activities in the official media since 2003. The fact that Chang accompanied Kim at each guidance stop reinforced the rumors coming from inside North Korea since his trip to China in March that Kim's brother-in-law, not Pak Pong-chu, was now "in charge of all aspects of the economy."[46]

Under the enhanced deterrent capability, North Korea's leadership no longer had to worry about international interference in its domestic affairs and could also now see a new pathway to foreign aid opened up by the nuclear test. This circumstance would allow for the reinstitution of centralized control over the economy. Reform would now come from above through the redistribution of resources from Pyongyang instead of relying on the vagaries of the market place and capitalist economics. As was noted in the newspaper of the pro-Pyongyang General Association of Korean Residents in Japan (Chosen Soren), "It seems that North Korea will now step up economic rehabilitation by relying on the peace and stability guaranteed by the possession of nuclear weapons."[47]

RETURN TO SIX PARTY TALKS

One month after the nuclear test, the United States agreed to meet with North Korea to discuss outstanding issues between the two countries, including, much to Pyongyang's delight, the frozen assets at Banco Delta Asia. Following a meeting in Berlin between U.S.–North Korea envoy Christopher Hill and his counterpart, Kim Kye-kwan, the North Korean Ministry of Foreign Affairs on January 19 announced that it had reached an agreement with the United States that would allow for the resumption of the Six Party Talks.[48] The bilateral talks, which Pak Pong-chu and his cabinet had been pushing for years, appeared to be bearing fruit.

The Foreign Ministry announcement, however, was not met with universal support within the regime. *Nodong Sinmun,* the mouthpiece for the party, took a decidedly mixed view of the evolving relationship with the United States. On the same day as the Foreign Ministry announcement, the paper ran a commentary that accused the United States of "viciously pursuing a policy hostile to Korea."[49] Though it is not clear what sparked the apparent disagreement between the party and Cabinet on the wisdom of bilateral talks with the United States, dissention within the party was quickly stamped out by Kim Ki-nam, the KWP Secretary for Propaganda, who on January 20 released a statement backing the Cabinet's foreign policy.[50]

Over the next two months, the Six Party Talks resumed, leading to a North Korean agreement to seal and dismantle the Yongbyon nuclear facility and provide a list of nuclear facilities in exchange for resolution of the BDA issue. North Korea also agreed to "disablement of all existing nuclear facilities" and provision of a complete declaration of all nuclear programs in exchange for energy assistance, including heavy fuel oil. Both Japan and the United States agreed to move toward normalization, with promises of additional economic aid.[51] Pak Pong-chu also met with South Korean Minister of Unification Lee Jae-joung for four days in Pyongyang and requested the resumption of rice and fertilizer aid, economic projects, and a peace treaty ending the Korean War.

NEW PREMIER, SAME AS THE OLD
PREMIER . . . NOT QUITE

Pak was "relieved of premiership" at the 5th session of the 11th Supreme People's Assembly in April.[52] He was replaced by the Minister of Land and Marine Transport Kim Yong-il. According to South Korean sources, Kim Chong-il held Pak personally responsible for the lack of progress on economic reform, rather than the economic policies themselves.[53] This was borne out in coverage of the new premier's first major policy meeting on the state budget, covered in the Cabinet's mouthpiece *Minju Choson.* At the meeting, Kim Yong-il articulated many of his predecessor's goals, stressing the need for all of the "economic guidance functionaries to strictly guarantee actual profits in industrial management and to attain their units' state budgetary payment plans without fail every month and every quarter . . . [while] routinely maintaining the principle of socialism."[54]

In follow-on speeches, Kim noted the importance of promoting agricultural and light industry development while continuing to adhere to military-first policies: "We will firmly adhere to the socialist economic construction line of the military-first era and while developing the national defense industry first, we will vigorously ignite the flames of the agricultural revolution and the light industry revolution, thus the food problem and the issue of the people's consumer goods should be smoothly resolved."[55] According to one Pyongyang watcher, "The new premier is not as outspoken and effective as his predecessor, but he still presents the same institutional policy line."[56]

As the months passed, however, it became apparent that the Cabinet under Kim Yong-il was no longer the leading agent of policy change. Instead, the party's influence, which had lay dormant since the 2002 reforms, began to reemerge in a culture where social stability trumped any lingering issues of economic reform. Pak's agricultural and corporate reform measures were cancelled. Small land farming was restricted.

MILITARY-FIRST POLICY, BUT TO A POINT

Kim Chong-il not only used the 5th session of the 11th Supreme People's Assembly to take the unusual step of dismissing a premier midway through his term. He also used it to announce a major break with past policy by underscoring his apparent commitment to the reallocation of some military resources to the civilian economy.

Since the succession period in the 1970s, the economy had been divided into three parts: the party economy (which included the finances of the Kim family), the defense economy (included in the Second Economic Committee), and the state economy (managed by the Cabinet). Over the decades, the party and defense economies expanded at the expense of the state economy. As the party's status became diminished under military-first politics, the cabinet under Pak Pong-chu was able to limit its encroachment, as was evidenced by Kim Chong-il's 2004 order to return all state enterprises that had been subsumed into the party economy. Pak, however, was not able to touch the defense economy.

Under military-first politics, the defense economy had been a constant drain on state coffers, estimated by outside sources to make up nearly one quarter of the country's gross national product (GNP).[57] In accordance with the "economic construction line of the military-first era," Kim Chong-il demanded that the light industrial and agricultural sectors of the economy be developed while "giving priority to the country's national defense."[58]

As such, production and trade units moved from the Cabinet to the Second Economic Committee and state assistance to the defense industrial sector was reinforced over the first decade of the Kim Chong-il era.

The January Joint Editorial signaled that this equation had changed. Departing from previous editorial lines that described the defense industry as "the top priority" (2006 Joint Editorial) and "the foundation of the nation's military and economic strength" that warranted "everything necessary . . . as required by the party's economic construction line" (2005 Joint Editorial), the 2007 Joint Editorial simply stated that "primary efforts" should be channeled into the development of the nation's defense industry.[59]

With Kim in attendance, Vice Premier Kwak Pom-ki made the argument before the SPA that North Korea's newfound nuclear deterrent had created a peace dividend.

Thanks to the fact that we have come to possess a powerful self-defensive nuclear deterrent . . . our Republic has now come to possess invincible military capabilities as a dignified nuclear state and is able to devote all its strength to economic construction.[60]

Kwak then went on to lay out the economic priorities for 2007, including "the main task of improving the standard of people's living . . . pushing forward the modernization of the national economy."[61]

Vice Premier Ro Tu-chol then announced the specifics of the decrease in defense spending. Ro stated that 16 percent of expenditures were devoted to defense in 2006, a number that slightly exceeded the amount projected at the April 2006 Supreme People's Assembly (15.9 percent). For 2007, he revealed, only 15.8 percent would be devoted to the defense sector. When taken in the context of SPA budget readouts over the previous four years, 15.8 percent represented the first downturn in projected defense sending.[62] But, it should be noted that though this may have been a signal that the defense economy was no longer off limits, the minor reduction was also meant to calm fears within the high command and defense industry that assure that the military still held a priority role within the regime and that deep cuts would not be forthcoming.[63]

INSTITUTIONALIZATION OF COMMAND AND CONTROL AT THE NATIONAL LEVEL

With the new policy line in place, Kim moved on to organizational changes to institutionalize command and control at the national level. Since 1998, the National Defense Commission had been, at least on paper, the command center from which Kim maintained situational awareness over the regime. It was the highest executive organ in charge of management and direction of all military affairs and defense projects. Though nominally under the Supreme People's Assembly, the 1998 constitution confirmed it as the highest state body, with ultimate executive power. North Korean media in the lead-up to the Supreme People's Assembly suggested that the NDC's responsibilities would be broadened. For example, the March 18 edition of *Minju Choson* urged the NDC "to devise, instruct, and promote a strategy for all defense-related projects and for all national projects that are related to politics, economy, and culture."

Just as important, if not more so, was the need to create a leadership body that could manage affairs in a crisis. The NDC ranks had been depleted through death and illness, and given the new policy agenda, it needed to be revitalized as an institution. In addition, rumors of succession planning and Kim Chong-il's health suggested that the regime needed to begin constructing a leadership system that could effectively operate after Kim's demise or incapacitation. The SPA took the first steps in addressing these issues by confirming the promotion of VMAR Kim Yong-chun to vice chairman of the National Defense Commission, filling a void created by Yon Hyong-muk's death in 2005. This move in many respects was a hedge against the aging leadership at the top of the military high command.[64]

If need be, Kim Yong-chun could succeed VMAR Cho Myong-nok as NDC first vice chairman. Cho had been suffering from chronic renal failure and was rarely seen in public.[65] Although the role of the first vice chairman of the NDC is not spelled out in the constitution, it is rumored to play a key role in crisis management. This would be particularly true if Kim Chong-il died or became incapacitated. The first vice chairman would likely oversee the affairs of the NDC, which would be critical in the interim until a new leadership configuration could be established.

Over the next month, a number of bureaucratic appointments were made to the NDC in an apparent effort to institutionalize its role by giving it a more extensive apparatus and bringing into it some of the informal chains of command Kim had relied on in the past.[66] Ever since its elevation in status in the 1998 constitution, the NDC had been a leading body in name only. It was a superstructure without an infrastructure. The appointment of Ri Myong-su and (rumored appointment of) Kang Sok-chu to the NDC tied the commission more closely to Kim's personal apparatus.[67] These were two of Kim's closest advisers on security and foreign policy. Ri, the former director of the General Staff's Operations Bureau, had been Kim's tie to the operational side of the KPA, and First Vice Foreign Minister Kang was one of the primary architects of North Korea's nuclear policy. Both would be serving as councilors to the NDC. In the North Korean system, councilors play a vital role in making the bureaucracy work, in that they are skilled in interpreting Kim Chong-il's intentions, developing policy strategies, and composing important documents that reflect and initiate policy within the regime. This meant that they, along with Gen. Hyon Chol-hae, who was appointed the director of the NDC Standing Bureau, would be vital to the daily running of the NDC and its interactions with the rest of the military and government establishment. Another former NDC councilor, Kim Yang-kon, took over the KWP United Front Department.[68]

The NDC appointments preceded a significant turnover within the high command. There is debate over whether this represented a generational turnover,[69] but all of the appointees owed their military careers to Kim Chong-il. These were military figures who were promoted to lieutenant general and colonel general as part of the 1992 reshuffle that marked Kim Chong-il's first series of promotions after becoming Supreme Commander in 1991. They had spent nearly 15 years as corps-level commanders and political commissars.

Gen. Kim Kyok-sik replaced VMAR Kim Yong-chun as chief of the General Staff. After spending time in Syria in the 1970s as a military attaché, Kim Kyok-sik returned to North Korea to take up a long career as an operational commander. In the 1980s, he oversaw the 815th Mechanized Corps before becoming the commander of the frontline Second Corps. He became a four-star general in 1997. In the same year, he also oversaw the military parade commemorating the 65th anniversary of the founding of the armed forces, a role he reprised ten years later on the eve of his appointment to head the General Staff.[70] According to some reports, he oversaw the missile test in 2006. At 67, he hailed from Kim Chong-il's second generation, but the subdued North Korean reporting on his activities suggested that he was not particularly close to the Leader. In terms of his political pedigree, Kim was a member of the KWP Central Committee, but had lost his seat in the SPA in 2003.[71]

Gen. Kim Myong-guk replaced Gen. Ri Myong-su as the director of the General Staff's Operations Bureau, a post Ri had held throughout most of the 1990s. Kim then served as the commander of the Fifth Corps and as commander of the 108th Mechanized Corps.[72] He was rumored to be close to Kim Chong-il, who was known to visit his house on occasion. His return to the General Staff was not publicized, but was gleaned by Pyongyang watchers based on his responsibilities tied to the military parade. During military reviews, the director of operations typically stands behind Kim Chong-il and provides the briefing of the events.

Within the General Political Bureau, Lt. Gen. Chong Tae-kun replaced Gen. Pak Chae-kyong as vice director in charge of propaganda. This post is responsible for supervising the ideological and propaganda work of the People's Army. Chong had been the political commissar of the Third Corps since 1992. As for Pak Chae-kyong, he was transferred (by way of Kim Chong-il's "special order") to the post of vice minister of the Ministry of People's Armed Forces in charge of external affairs.[73] A frequent cohort on Kim's guidance inspections, Pak often served as the Leader's special envoy on trips abroad. In 2000, for example, he acted as the courier of a gift of pine mushrooms from Kim Chong-il to various South Korean leaders as *Chusok* (Korean Thanksgiving Day) gifts.[74]

Whether the turnover in the NDC and the high command represented a generational turnover or not, it fit with Kim's increasing proclivity to tie individuals in whom he had trust more tightly to the chain of command. This not only enhanced his confidence that his orders and directives would be carried out in the spirit in which they were intended, but it fulfilled his 2006 pledge to expand the knowledge base of the cadre at the lower echelons and attach importance to expertise and ability in the appointment of cadres. What impact this would have on close aide politics remained to be seen.

RUMORS OF HIS DEATH ARE PREMATURE

Following on the heels of this flurry of changes across the North Korean leadership in the summer of 2007, reports began to appear in the Japanese and South Korean press in late June that Kim Chong-il had died. For over two months rumors had circulated in the foreign press that Kim's health had taken a turn for the worse. According to one Western diplomat who attended the military parade in Pyongyang to celebrate the 75th anniversary of the founding of the KPA:

General Secretary Kim ascended the rostrum in the middle of the parade propped up by people around him. He then clapped to the soldiers passing the square in an exaggerated manner and moved left for a few meters, leaning on the handrail. Then he raised his right hand limply toward the soldiers to cheer them, after which he descended the rostrum from the exit in the back, again leaning on the handrail. This took place in just a few minutes.[75]

This was followed by reports in May that Kim suffered a cardiac infarction after which a medical team was urgently dispatched from the Berlin Heart Institute to Pyongyang to perform an emergency cardiac bypass operation. Upon further investigation, these reports appeared to lack credibility.[76] The German doctors, who in fact visited Pyongyang, denied operating on the North Korean leader, saying that they only conducted three routine operations on ordinary citizens. The newspapers also echoed stories of Kim's health that had been making the rounds for over a year, namely that he could not walk more than 30 meters at a time and had to be accompanied by an assistant carrying a chair so that he could sit and catch his breath.

Then, on June 21, *Shukan Shincho*, a Japanese weekly tabloid magazine, reported that sources close to the Japanese Prime Minister's office had received intelligence that Kim Chong-il had died due to complications related to diabetes. This speculation was reportedly backed up by a variety of actions on the part on the North Korean regime one would expect to see in the early days following Kim's demise.

- As if reacting to these rumors, the North Korean state-run Korean Central News Agency filed several consecutive reports in early June on Kim's activities, which could be interpreted as an effort to reassure internal audiences that might have heard reports about his death and give the regime time to prepare for the succession.

- In February, the children of all diplomats and officials overseas were ordered to return home. In May, even students studying in Beijing received the same order. This was the first such incident since students overseas were ordered to return home during the reforms in East Europe in 1990.

- Kim's public appearances declined significantly compared to the same period in previous years. The number of reports in North Korean radio broadcasts on Kim's activities in the first half of 2007 totaled 31. This was less than the comparatively low 43 reports in the first half of 2005 and a significant decrease from the 67 reports of the same period in 2006.

By the end of June, the speculation ceased with the arrival of Christopher Hill in Pyongyang for meetings with his North Korean counterparts, marking the highest-ranking visit by a U.S. official since Hill's predecessor in 2002. Such a visit would not have been sanctioned if Kim's health was in question and most definitely would not have occurred if he had died. In a meeting with various political editors, a representative of South Korea's National Intelligence Service explained that although "rumors of deteriorating health" came up when Chairman Kim failed to appear in public gatherings for approximately a month after visiting a military unit on May 5, "It is common for Chairman Kim to halt public activity for long periods of 30 days or more, something that has happened as many as 17 times since the death of Kim Il-sung."[77] Kim reappeared on June 25 when he attended a performance given by the Russian State Academic People's Chorus Named after M. E. Pyatnichki.[78]

Though the stories of the summer of 2007 proved to be idle speculation based on rumor and random connecting of dots, they did highlight a new set of calculations countries would have to make when dealing with the Hermit Kingdom. The current leadership configuration would not last forever and given the opacity of the regime, dramatic changes not only in terms of leadership, but also policy lines could come with little or no notice.

COMING IN FROM THE COLD

When Christopher Hill arrived in Pyongyang for bilateral meetings designed to get the Six Party Talks back on track, he found little had changed in the North Korean position since February. Once the BDA funds were unfrozen, Hill's interlocutors promised that North Korea would abide by the agreement reached at the Six Party Talks, namely the step-by-step dismantlement of North Korea's nuclear facilities in return for fuel and other aid.[79] Two days after Hill's visit, the North Korean Foreign Ministry confirmed the $27 million of Banco Delta Asia accounts had been transferred to North Korean-controlled accounts in a Russian bank. With the BDA issue resolved, the "first phase obligations" on both sides went into effect. IAEA inspectors were allowed to visit Yongbyon, South Korea announced the resumption of aid, the first shipment of oil under the February agreement landed in the North, and Pyongyang announced the closure of the Yongbyon reactor.[80]

Throughout the summer, North Korea continued its diplomatic outreach. Pyongyang shut down the Yongbyon reactor in July and in October agreed to disable the nuclear facility and provide a complete nuclear declaration by December 31. In the meantime, another Korean summit took place in Pyongyang with Kim Chong-il meeting with the unpopular South Korean President Roh Moon-hyun. At the meetings, the two sides reaffirmed the spirit of the June 15 Joint Declaration and had discussions on various issues related to realizing the advancement of South–North relations—peace on the Korean Peninsula, common prosperity of the Korean people, and unification of Korea. On October 4, 2007, President Roh Moo-hyun and Kim Chong-il signed a peace declaration, which called for international talks to replace the armistice that ended the Korean War with a permanent peace treaty. Although there was a question of whether South Korea could follow through, Roh promised several multi-year, multi-billion-dollar economic projects.[81]

But, it must be noted that this diplomatic outreach, while necessary in terms of economic policy, was tentative and raised a number of issues for Pyongyang in terms of security policy. A careful reading of the North Korean media suggests that Kim for months was engaged in a delicate balancing act both in regard to engagement with the United States and South Korea and denuclearization. The high command sounded a cautious note regarding negotiations with the United States. In a July article detailing the history (from North Korea's point of view) of U.S.–North Korean confrontation, the chief of the Korean People's Army Panmunjom Mission touted the untrustworthiness of the United States on the nuclear issue as a way of highlighting North Korea's need to maintain a deterrent. Though the article did not say so specifically, it hinted that the possession of a nuclear deterrent might be North Korea's most prudent course.

If the United States continues to pressure us using the nuclear issue as an excuse and refuses to discontinue the large-scale war exercises it stages as an annual event and the massive arms buildup maneuvers [it carries out] in South Korea as preparations for a preemptive strike at us, our army and people cannot help but devote all our strength to further perfecting our counterattack means to the level corresponding to preparations for the United States' nuclear attacks and preemptive attacks in order to defend their dignity, sovereignty, and right to existence.[82]

The article went on to threaten that the February agreement and the Six Party Talks could be in jeopardy if the U.S.–South Korean military exercises continued. Stretching into September, party commentaries continued to harp on the exercises and reiterated the warnings regarding U.S. motives, pointing out that U.S. and IAEA inspections took place in Iraq on the eve of the U.S. invasion.[83]

The fact that this commentary was aired in official channels speaks to the balancing act that the regime was engaged in, both in regard to its external relations (especially with the United States) and its evolving policy toward nuclear weapons. On the one hand, the commentary did not openly oppose the established policy of engagement. But on the other hand, it urged caution. It is likely that Pyongyang continued to harbor reservations about the Six Party process and the willingness of the United States and its partners to fulfill their commitments, and thus a hedging strategy on North Korea's own obligations made sense.

The strategy also made sense because Kim had, either inadvertently or consciously as a means of deferring a decision, sanctioned two divergent public messages of denuclearization. Although North Korea continued to pursue denuclearization, which would allow it to achieve its long-sought goal of improved relations with the United States, such a policy risked undercutting the domestic message on the transcendent importance of the country's new status as a nuclear state. By continuing to preach the need for an active self defense, the regime was able to keep diplomacy on track while building consensus within security circles on how to proceed with regard to the country's new-found nuclear deterrent.

As the regime moved toward the October second phase agreement, the divergent paths seemed to melt away. Kim's endorsement of the Six Party Talks suggested that denuclearization was still the stated policy of the regime. His signature on the joint inter-Korean summit declaration included the clause stating that the Koreas "agreed to make joint efforts to smooth implementation of the 19 September Joint Statement and the 13 February agreement made at the Six Party Talks for the resolution of the Korean Peninsula's nuclear issue." Though the North Korean media had in the past cited Kim as endorsing the Six Party process, this was the first time he had put his name on an official public document that directly referenced the issue.

PREPARING THE REGIME FOR
OUTSIDE ENGAGEMENT

It is simple to assume that North Korea had gone through a policy deliberation process and come out the other end with an understanding that it needed to engage the outside world in order to jump start its economy. According to a veteran U.S. intelligence analyst who visited North Korea during this period as part of a delegation to the Yongbyon nuclear complex, "The lines you are not supposed to cross have been redrawn."[84] The increasing number of foreign visitors spoke of change in the air. According to one frequent visitor to Pyongyang,

On the once-empty streets of Pyongyang, more and more motorcycles were visible, suggesting official tolerance for a means of transport that gave citizens in a tightly controlled society greater mobility. . . . More telephone kiosks were evident on street corners, often with lines of people waiting to use them, and more people were using mobile phones—another sign of a slight easing of social controls on internal communications. Small shops and vendors were visible, and officially sanctioned free markets offering goods ranging from food to clothing to electrical appliances and tools. Visitors reported a clear sense of greater economic possibility emerging, with a greater receptivity both to foreign business and the profit motive.[85]

But this was North Korea and nothing is what it appeared. Behind the scenes, the government was grappling with the consequences of its engagement policy. Initially, the plan had been to open up slowly and in a controlled manner through the isolated economic zones at Sinuiju and Raseon. The agreements reached during the inter-Korean summit, however, held out the real danger of this plan getting out of control. If this strategy was going to work, the country would need to be prepared. This meant instituting control mechanisms from the center and getting rid of those regime elements that could not be trusted in such close proximity with the outside world.

Kim Chong-il once again looked to his brother-in-law, Chang Song-taek, to carry out the important task of ensuring regime stability as the regime explored avenues to the outside world. In October, according to North Korean sources, Chang was appointed director of the newly reestablished KWP Administrative Department,[86] which had oversight of the internal security apparatus, including the State Security Department, the Ministry of People's Security, the Central Prosecutor's Office, and the Central Court—essentially restoring the portfolio he once held as first vice chairman of the KWP Organization Guidance Department.[87] From an organizational point of view, Chang's appointment made sense in that Kim, in line with his evolving close aide policy, consolidated the reporting lines for domestic policy in Chang, giving him two of the most critical portfolios tied to regime stability, the economy and internal security. Not only did Chang now have a strong say in how policy was crafted, but in how it was managed. From his informal position as a senior adviser on the economy, Chang could more effectively utilize the levers of power to prevent the spread of destabilizing forces unleashed by the markets and international engagement.

At the national level, Chang moved to reestablish the party's control over the economy. On the eve of his appointment, he began a campaign to dismantle an apparatus tied to North–South cooperation that had been established in the months after his purge in 2004 by engineering the transfer of the National Economic Cooperation Committee (NECC), which oversaw economic cooperation projects with the South Korean private sector, from the Cabinet to the KWP United Front Department.[88] The timing of this move suggests the regime was preparing for the inter-Korean summit. Now the party, not the Cabinet, would oversee the aid coming from the South.

With the creation of the KWP Administrative Department, Chang Song-taek began to assert his authority over how the regime dealt with the consequences of economic reform. This raised his profile among Kim's close aides even further while diminishing the status of key rival, Ri Che-kang. Since February, the KWP Organization Guidance Department had been conducting an intensive investigation of the KWP United Front Department for a number of irregularities (corruption).[89] Led by first vice director Ri Che-kang and vice director Hong In-pom, by September the investigation had spread to the NECC.[90] But as the investigation was about to expand beyond the party, this "social cleanup" drive to eradicate corruption throughout society was turned over to the KWP Administrative Department,[91] thus consolidating Chang's responsibility for carrying out an economic policy that was not only top down, but concentrated on the promotion of social stability.

At the local level, people began to feel the weight of the state as more restrictions were placed on the market. Trade was banned outside marketplaces, and a return-to-work order was promulgated. By forcing the people back into the factories, many of which were not even operational, the regime was able to reinstitute its system of indoctrination and surveillance, which had waned since the 1990s. In December, the regime extended the ban on market trade to females below 50 years of age. This decision went far beyond any measures taken in the past and seemed designed to not just curb the markets, but kill them. After all, middle-aged women represented most of the vendors and small entrepreneurs. The government also reinstituted requisition-style securing of provisions, something that had not been seen since the early 2000s. In a particularly egregious example of this practice, special collection squads were dispatched to Hwanghae Province to secure rice for the military and the capital, Pyongyang.

Even the military was not beyond Chang's reach. On December 23, a directive was passed down to reorganize non-sanctioned trading companies attached to individual military units. Under the directive, intensive inspection was tightened on trading companies of military units and the border region, including heightened inspection in Sinuiju in March 2008.[92] Enhanced inspections were conducted along the border with China in an effort to crack down on refugee traffic. Military and border security elements came under increased scrutiny, presumably hampering what had become a lucrative source of hard currency and goods.

As 2007 came to a close and the "social stabilization" campaign gathered momentum into 2008, it seemed that a subtle, but important, shift was occurring in North Korean domestic policy. It had been clear for some time that although the North Korean media continued to tout economic development as the "main front in the construction of a powerful state," such development was not centered on bold new, internally driven policies. The question was whether such statements were even about preparing the country for a dramatic enhancement of international aid. When the South Korean people in December elected Lee Myung-bak as the country's first conservative president in a decade, Pyongyang most likely began to scale back its expectations for the promised aid from Seoul. The priority now was to ensure that the regime could survive another period of austere measures. Economic policy blended with security policy as Pyongyang took steps to strengthen its control over society and its resources.

GRASPING AT STRAWS

For years, Kim Chong-il had wrestled with how to carry out economic reform in North Korea. He had listened to the advice of the Chinese leaders. North Korea had exchanged delegations with Vietnam in an attempt to explore yet another communist model for reform.[93] Kim had seen some of the virtues of the capitalist system, such as profit and efficiency. Finally, he had found reason to hope for untold riches to pour in from South Korea as Pyongyang discovered the true potential of the Sunshine Policy. But, as he watched the hopes he had placed on Seoul fade away, no new set of policies presented themselves. The New Year's Joint Editorial for 2008 suggested that the regime had entered a holding pattern. Unlike in the previous few years, the editorial contained no new policy initiatives and even reiterated traditional communist principles of economic management. The Cabinet was no longer hailed as the leading agent for the economy, but one among many leading institutions that should "strictly adhere to the socialist principle and the collectivist principle in conducting economic management."

North Korea's concerns about the Sunshine Policy were confirmed in February when Lee Myung-bak took office. Turning his back on the decade-long experiment with engagement, the new president pledged to adopt a more skeptical posture toward the North. While he put forth the progressive "Vision 3000" policy that promised to raise the average per capita income in North Korea to $3,000, some three times the current level (which translated into a 10 percent growth rate over the next decade), it was tied to the resolution of the nuclear crisis and Pyongyang's commitment to reform.[94]

Although Pyongyang had been restrained in its criticism of Lee's policies before he took office, it wasted little time in launching rhetorical attacks after he announced his government's new policy line. In March, the Committee for the Peaceful Reunification of the Fatherland called the new government "a successor to a previous authoritarian regime that shocked other countries with its fascist rule and trampled the human rights of South Koreans." It went on to note that "the pro-U.S. conservative forces in South Korea are now clinging more impatiently to a racket of confrontation against their fellow country with the backing of outside forces."[95]

The deteriorating external situation was reflected in Pyongyang's handling of the spring session of the Supreme People's Assembly. Premier Kim Yong-il in his report to the session stated that the top priority in the "economic field" was to "ensure the increase of defense capabilities." In contrast to the descriptions of the Cabinet's priorities for the past decade, the premier did not emphasize the need to improve the standard of people's living. Instead, he emphasized the need for North Korea to secure a "strong self-defensive nuclear deterrent" and by increasing its defense capabilities, the country would ensure "the advance in the building of an economic power."[96] The budget report reinforced the commitment to the defense sector by maintaining projected military spending at 15.8 percent.[97]

In April, the North's position became increasingly confrontational as it refused to accept humanitarian aid from Seoul. Instead, it turned to China, which for its own domestic reasons was restricted in the amount of grain and agricultural products it could provide.[98] By May, the North Korean leadership began to prepare the population for a deterioration in the food situation.[99] Because of weak harvests and a drop-off in commercial imports and aid, North Korea's public distribution system, which had been reinstituted in 2005, again broke down. Refusing to admit this fact, the regime sought to rationalize impending hardships by citing external circumstances as the underlying cause for its inability to provide the population with sustained food security.[100]

As with China, Pyongyang ramped up its diplomatic efforts toward the United States as its relations with Seoul soured. In a departure from past practice, the speeches at the Supreme People's Assembly did not blame the United States for North Korea's poor economic performance. In fact, the Ministry of Foreign Affairs welcomed recent U.S.–North Korean talks in Singapore, noting that the two sides had reached a "consensus" on the nuclear declaration issue.[101] Pyongyang continued to send signals of its commitment to the Six Party Talks, urging the United States to hold to its promise to take North Korea off the terrorism list and ease up on sanctions as "the key" to progress. Despite a temporary setback as information became public in April about North Korea's nuclear ties to Syria, by the summer, the United States and North Korea were once again engaged in the step-by-step game of diplomacy. North Korea destroyed the Yongbyon reactor's cooling tower, a largely symbolic move that signaled the regime's decision to dismantle the nuclear site. The United States began the process of delisting and came through with a promise of 500,000 metric tons of rice, which arrived at the end of June just as North Korean officials turned over a 60-page declaration providing previously undisclosed details about Pyongyang's nuclear program.[102]

A cursory examination of North Korean media pronouncements over the course of the first eight months of 2008 painted the picture of a regime that was unclear about the way forward. According to North Korean officials, the regime was increasingly frustrated by the slow pace of promised aid and increasingly concerned with the changing ground rules regarding sanctions. In the July round of the Six Party Talks, the parties agreed in principle to establish a verification and monitoring mechanism as well as a more precise timetable so that fuel oil assistance and disablement could take place in parallel. However, the United States made removal of North Korea from the list of state sponsors of terrorism contingent on an initial verification protocol. By August, a stalemate had taken over the process, with North Korea refusing to budge on verification and the United States not moving on delisting. In September, Pyongyang expelled the IAEA inspectors, halted the disablement process of its nuclear facilities, and threatened to restart the Yongbyon reactor.

A VERY ATYPICAL MILITARY PARADE

By 6:00 P.M. on September 9, it was clear to many Pyongyang watchers that something was wrong. This was the 60th anniversary of the founding of the state. The regime no doubt had commemorated the event with a military parade. Though such parades normally were held in the morning (around 10:00 A.M.), they did not air until the afternoon or early evening. The last military parade held in April 2007 to celebrate the 75th anniversary of the founding of the KPA was broadcast at 6:00 P.M. On this day, 6:00 P.M. came and went with no coverage of the parade.

When the coverage did begin at 9:00 P.M., it was clear why the delay had occurred. Kim Chong-il was absent. Suspicions had been raised the day before when he failed to show up at the national meeting commemorating the anniversary. But his continued absence suggested that something was amiss. The capricious leader had never failed to attend the commemorative meetings and parades marking the 60th founding anniversaries for both the party (October 10, 2005) and military (April 25, 1992) and had attended every military parade marking major—quinquennial and decennial—founding anniversaries for the state, party, and military since 1995.

Aware that Kim's absence would be noticed, the regime apparently tried to restructure events—perhaps at the last minute—to compensate for this fact and convey a sense of continuity and unity in governance.

National Defense Commission First Vice Chairman VMAR Cho Myong-nok, 78, who had not been seen in public since 2007, was standing (feeble-looking, but upright) in his usual spot on the dais next to the titular head of state, Kim Yong-nam. To Cho's right was Vice Chairman of the NDC VMAR Kim Yong-chun. Dressed in traditional workers' garb reminiscent of the Kim family leadership, the chief of the General Staff Department opened the festivities with a statement that he had been "entrusted by Kim Chong-il with the honor of ardently welcoming all of our citizens."

The parade itself was unusual for the occasion. Film footage suggested that it did not start at 10:00 A.M., but some time in the afternoon. Some Pyongyang watchers suggested that the regime leadership did not make the decision to proceed with the parade without Kim until the last minute and needed extra time to coordinate parade adjustments and media coverage. Instead of military troops, the Worker and Peasant Red Guard (a militia reserve force) marched in the parade. Following the infantry units, units under the Pyongyang Defense Command made up of trucks carrying anti-aircraft guns, moved past the parade stand. After eight trucks passed by, the parade ended after only 30 minutes.[103]

In the following weeks, information began to seep out of North Korea that Kim had suffered a stroke in August. Some sources placed the stroke around August 22,[104] others closer to the last time he had been seen in public,[105] on August 14 when he had inspected KPA Unit 1319.[106] One report that emerged in 2009 stated that Kim was at one of his resorts when he complained of not feeling well and was immediately transported to a medical facility where,[107] according to NIS Director Kim Chong-ho, he was operated on by "an overseas medical team."[108] Japanese and South Korean sources contended that this medical team was made up of five specialists dispatched from China.[109] Though not admitting this fact, Chinese sources later noted that Kim suffered a "brain infarction resulting from a cerebral blood vessel blockage, which led to hemorrhaging and eventual breakage of the blood vessel."[110] After the operation, he underwent several weeks rest and rehabilitation at the Ponghwa Recuperation Center located in Pyongyang City's Potonggang District.[111]

CONCLUSION

Over the next several weeks, the North Korean regime consistently denied that there was anything wrong with General Secretary Kim. In a September 10 interview with a visiting delegation from the Japanese news agency *Kyodo*, Kim Yong-nam, stated "While we wanted to celebrate the 60th anniversary of the country with General Secretary Kim Chong-il, we celebrated on our own . . . There are no problems [with his health]."[112] The regime also began to release leadership messages attributed to Kim, such as congratulatory birthday messages to Russian President Dmitri

Medvedev and Syrian President Bashar al-Asad. But, most of all, the regime released numerous undated photographs.

On October 4, after a 51-day absence, Kim reappeared in the pages of the central media in a photograph that showed him enjoying a soccer match. This picture was the beginning of a propaganda campaign designed to show that he was still in charge. Foreign observers tried to grasp Kim's medical condition by focusing on the limited evidence the North Koreans provided. In the end, Pyongyang watchers were left to speculate about the impact Kim's stroke would have on the North Korean leadership. Who was actually in charge and how decisions were being made became a source of constant discussion. One thing was clear; nothing would be as it was before. Kim was mortal. He would not live forever. Odds are, he only had a few years left. Who or what would follow him was no longer a parlor game. It was real.

PART II

Passing the Torch to a Third Generation

The North Korean regime is a leader-centric system. Not since the regime's early beginnings has anything approximating a collective leadership existed in Pyongyang. For more than six decades, two men (one family) have molded the regime to fit their unique leadership styles. At the Third Party Conference in September 2010, the world was introduced to Kim Chong-un, the putative beneficiary of a future dynastic transfer of power. At 28 years old, not many Pyongyang watchers believe he will be able to take measures in his own hands to seize power after his father departs the political scene, much less consolidate that power. He will have to rely on leaders that have grown up in the Kim Chong-il (and some in the Kim Il-sung) era, many of whom owe their loyalty to Kim the elder, not Kim the junior. Kim Chong-un will also inherit a system of rule based on informal relationships and back-channel communications where chains of command are often ignored. Given these challenges, what does the future hold?

This section will examine the leadership dynamics of the most recent history of the Kim Chong-il era as it prepares for the eventual transfer of power to the next generation. It will argue that Kim's power consolidation strategy in the 1990s led to significant changes in how the regime operates, thus laying the foundation for problems that the next leader(s) will face once Kim leaves the political scene. No matter who follows Kim Chong-il, he or they will likely be weaker. Finally, the level of stability in the regime and the potential for regime collapse will be considered.

CHAPTER 6

Third Hereditary Succession

Succession in a totalitarian regime is always a sensitive, and potentially dangerous, time. It is a time when the leader needs to create another center of power in the person of his chosen heir apparent while at the same time maintaining his own authority to govern the regime. In most cases, including North Korea, there are no formal rules pertaining to the transfer of power; no amendments in the constitution or ruling party by-laws. Instead, succession depends on the leader's ability to build consensus around his choice and the successor's ability to show his legitimacy.

An examination of the succession process as it played out in 2009 and 2010 in North Korea reveals that the regime has a plan to secure a third hereditary transfer of power. Though not set down in any codified set of rules, this plan seems to be anchored in Kim Chong-il's own succession experience. The model consists of three phases:

- First, a preparatory or apprentice phase for the successor
- Second, a limited duopoly phase that begins with the announcement of the successor-designate and limited power sharing, with Kim Chong-il retaining the preponderance of power
- Third, a transition phase in which the son's power begins to eclipse that of the father

At the time of this writing, North Korea appears to be in the second phase. Kim Chong-un emerged into the public spotlight at the Third Party Conference held in September 2010. In the lead up to this event, the regime underwent what appears to have been a labored process of securing the needed consensus highlighted by a failed currency revaluation and the sinking of a South Korean military vessel.

This chapter will focus on how the succession process unfolded. It will look at the propaganda campaign, which was for all intents and purposes the only part of the process that was visible to the outside world. It will highlight how Kim has taken measures to prepare the regime for the transfer of power, both in terms of shoring up his position and building a consensus around Kim Chong-un. Finally, it will briefly consider how the succession process may unfold as it moves toward the penultimate third phase.

A BIRTHDAY TRIBUTE

As soon as the international media began reporting that Kim Chong-il had chosen his third son, Kim Chong-un, as his successor in early January 2009,[1] Pyongyang watchers began to scour the North Korean media for any sort of validation. The evidence was thin. The edition of *Nodong Sinmun* published on Kim Chong-un's birthday (January 8) included an out-of-place song titled "Let Us Raise a Toast."[2] Though the song did not mention the heir apparent by name, it was set off on the page and in unusual fashion surrounded by a special border. It used a term for "leader"—*hyangdo* or "guide"—not typically associated with Kim Chong-il, who was referred to primarily as *ryo'ngdoja* (leader) or *changgun* (general) in North Korean media.[3] The next month, the succession-related song "Footsteps" (*Pal Keol Um*) made its debut in the central media. It was performed live for Kim Chong-il and the leadership on February 23.[4]

If the theory of a three-phased succession based on Kim's own experience was correct, North Korea had entered the first phase. Kim Chong-un had been designated within internal channels as the heir apparent. But who is Kim Chong-un?

His name had been known within Pyongyang watching circles since around 2003, but personal details were lacking. In January 2009, Kim Chong-il's former chef, Kenji Fujimoto, provided the Japanese media with a photograph alleged to be that of a 10-year-old Kim Chong-un.[5] According to Fujimoto, Kim Chong-un was born in 1983 or 1984 to Kim's fourth wife, Ko Yong-hui, and was allegedly his father's favorite son.[6] He is rumored to have studied at the International School of Berne in Guemlingen, Switzerland. Upon returning to North Korea sometime after 2000, his studies continued, most likely at Kim Il-sung Military University, where he allegedly graduated in 2007.[7] There are varying reports that he speaks German, French, and English.

Kim Chong-un's career background has been just as opaque. In 2004, reports began to surface that he and his brother were accompanying their father on guidance inspections of military installations. In 2007, a flurry of reports emerged placing the third son in either the party's powerful Organization Guidance Department or the military's influential General Political Bureau.[8] Both of these bodies are charged with surveillance and monitoring of the regime's powerful party, military, and security bodies. Still other sources placed him in some nondescript role in the National Defense Commission. According to the well regarded *NK Daily,* inside Pyongyang, Kim Chong-un was at "the center of three sets of rumors concerning training in kingcraft:" the theory about him being trained at the State Security Department, the theory about him being appointed a colonel at the Ministry of People's Armed Forces, and the story about his serving as a guidance officer in the same department.

As for his character and personal traits, information was practically nonexistent. Fujimoto in his book pointed out that, unlike his older brother Kim Chong-chol, Kim Chong-un has a forthright character.[9] Some defector reporting highlighted in the South Korean press contended that the third son has a "cool-headed personality," is "intelligent," and has "strong political instincts."[10] These leadership skills, according to some South Korean intelligence officials who referenced unnamed sources, "were recognized within the regime from an early age."[11] As for his health, there were reports that Kim Chong-un may share some of the ailments of his father, such as diabetes and hypertension, and may have been in a car accident in 2008.[12]

Given his age and obvious lack of experience, the Pyongyang watching community could only speculate about why Kim Chong-il had chosen to anoint his third son as his successor. A popular theory was that Kim Chong-un's relative anonymity was his greatest attribute. Unlike his older brothers, Kim Chong-un's time abroad escaped the media's attention, something that could make it easier for the regime to bolster his claim to ideological purity and build a myth around his "achievements." If this could be done, Kim Chong-il could rationalize his decision to depart from Confucian tradition in selecting someone other than his oldest son as successor, in addition to the historical rationale that a number of Korean kings were second or lesser sons selected largely due to acumen.

BUILDING A SUPPORT BASE

For the first phase of the succession to go forth, Kim most likely had to secure the support of his family and close aides for his chosen successor. This would be necessary for two primary reasons. First, the first phase was a time for educating the heir apparent in the broader aspects of the regime. He would be expected to assume key roles in the party, and possibly the military, apparatus. He would be expected to begin cultivating relationships within various leadership networks. Finally, he would be expected to begin the process of showing his leadership qualities by participating in national-level campaigns. To do any of this, Kim Chong-un would need the mentorship of many of his father's close aides. Second, and probably more important, only with the support of close aides and the Kim family could Kim Chong-il build wider senior-elite consensus and bureaucratic support behind his son. And, in much the same way as Kim Il-sung's partisan group helped Kim Chong-il in the 1970s, the wider Kim family would be vital to conferring legitimacy to Kim Chong-un as a third hereditary successor.

How Kim Chong-il secured the initial support for his chosen successor is not really known. As noted in the last chapter, Chang Song-taek's support seemed to be critical to this process. At the beginning of 2009, the Kim family was still a house divided. Kim Chong-il's mistress, Kim Ok, had in 2008 apparently taken up Ko Yong-hui's campaign and had enlisted Ri Che-kang's support for the youngest son Kim Chong-un's succession.[13] On the other side of the family were Kim's sister, Kim Kyong-hui, and brother-in-law, Chang Song-taek, who by all indications still maintained ties to the first son, Kim Chong-nam. It was only after Chang switched his allegiance that Kim Chong-il was able to formally nominate Kim Chong-un as his successor.[14] According to South Korean reporting based on "multiple sources," Kim Chong-il's nomination was made at Chang's "recommendation."[15]

Whether Chang's motives were tied to his own aspirations, as suggested earlier, or his recognition of Kim's "special affection" for his third son, there is little doubt that he would not have given his support without already being sure that such a move met with the approval of his wife (Kim Kyong-hui) and their extended networks throughout the leadership. In other words, Chang's support ensured that the succession could go forward without tearing the family apart. In the months ahead, there would be hints that Chang's support was part of a Machiavellian masterstroke that would remove any opposition to his own power in the regime.[16]

2009 RESHUFFLE AND PREPARATIONS FOR THE POST-KIM LEADERSHIP CONFIGURATION

In the aftermath of this reported Kim–Chang agreement, the regime witnessed one of the most widespread reshuffles of leading cadre in years. There is little doubt that this rewiring of the upper echelons of the state apparatus was designed to address some of the inherent weaknesses in the regime. It brought new blood into the senior leadership, changed the dynamics within the regime in terms of command and control to better accommodate Kim Chong-il's health problems, and marked a major step in creating a new leadership environment for succession.

In February, Pyongyang carried out its most significant public military leadership shakeup in decades, simultaneously replacing both its defense minister and chief of the General Staff. Kim Yong-chun, the former chief of the General Staff and current vice chairman of the NDC, was appointed minister of the People's Armed Forces, replacing Kim Il-chol, who became first vice minister. Ri Yong-ho, the Pyongyang Defense Commander, was promoted to chief of the General Staff, replacing Kim Kyok-sik, who was appointed commander of the Fourth Corps.[17] Two weeks later, O Kuk-yol, the director of the KWP's Operations Department, was appointed vice chairman of the NDC.

This was followed in April by the 12th Supreme People's Assembly, which ratified a new leadership makeup.[18] The changes to the National Defense Commission were particularly interesting for what they said about evolving leadership dynamics and potentially about the upcoming succession. On April 10, *Nodong Sinmun* published photographs of the individual members of the National Defense Commission who had been appointed the day before. It was an unprecedented public release in a country that traditionally keeps faceless the power elite who engage in confidential national affairs.

The photos, according to some sources, gave notice that a power group had been formed at the center of the North Korean system to assist Kim in running the regime. The North's revised 1998 constitution defined the authority of the National Defense Commission as limited to the military and defense. However, with the military-oriented policy promoted by the regime, the commission's power had been expanded to become the de facto general administration.[19] The reshuffle of the National Defense Commission could be interpreted as an intention to make it the core of the national governing system; something akin to a standing Politburo.[20]

The NDC membership increased from eight to twelve. In addition to Kim being elected to a third term as chairman, Cho Myong-nok remained as the first vice chairman. The three vice chairmen—Kim Yong-chun, Ri Yong-mu, and O Kuk-yol—remained in their posts. Chong Pyong-ho, Kim Il-chol, and Paek Se-bong remained as members, and Chang Song-taek, Chu Sang-song, U Tong-chuk, Chu Kyu-chang, and Kim Chong-gak were newly elected. This enhanced membership represented the most important officials from the military, defense industry, the party's administrative organs, police, secret police, and other key fields critical to running the country.

According to several sources, this new leadership configuration was part of a strategy to consolidate the reporting channels through which Kim Chong-il rules the regime. As noted above, in the past, Kim relied on informal ties into a variety of organizations that often trumped formal chains of command. This leadership style was cumbersome and relied on frequent interactions with a number of subordinates. As his health declined in 2008, Kim's ability to continue with this method of rule became untenable.[21] The enhancement of the NDC's role allowed for the creation of dedicated channels for information/guidance flow. Examples of this

Table 6.1
National Defense Commission in 2009

Name	Age	Position	Comment
Kim Chong-il	68	Chairman	
VMAR Cho Myong-nok	81	First Vice Chairman	Director, GPB
VMAR Kim Yong-chun	73	Vice Chairman	Minister of People's Armed Forces
Gen. O Kuk-yol	78	Vice Chairman	Director, KWP Operations Department
VMAR Ri Yong-mu	86	Vice Chairman	Husband of KCI's paternal aunt
Chon Pyong-ho	83	Member	KWP Secretary for Military Industry
VMAR Kim Il-chol	76	Member	1st Vice Minister of People's Armed Forces
Chang Song-taek	63	Member (made Vice Chairman in June 2010)	Director of KWP Administration Department. KCI's brother-in-law.
Chu Kyu-chang	N/A	Member	First Vice Director of KWP Munitions Industry Department
Paek Se-bong	N/A	Member	Chairman of Second Economic Committee
Gen. Chu Sang-song	66	Member	Minister of People's Security
Gen. Kim Chong-gak	66	Member	First Vice Director of GPB

consolidation could be seen in the restructuring of the lines of authority within the military and security apparatuses.

- Within the military, command and control appeared to return to its Kim Il-sung structure, with the Minister of People's Armed Forces (MPAF) once again being the primary conduit through which the Supreme Commander-in-Chief ran the armed forces.[22] After the death of Choe Kwang in 1997, Kim Chong-il moved away from his father's methods of control, preferring to align himself personally with various reporting lines into the KPA, such as the NDC, CMC, the General Staff, and the General Political Bureau. As a consequence, the influence and stature of the MPAF declined, as was evidenced by the fact that

Kim Il-chol, who succeeded Choe Kwang as MPAF, was demoted from vice chairman to member of the NDC. His authority was also diminished by the fact that Kim Chong-il relied directly on the chief of the General Staff (Kim Yong-chun) and General Staff's Operations Bureau to pass on guidance to the KPA. The 2009 reform reduced the number of checks and balances within the military and returned command and control to a hierarchical structure, with the General Staff (headed by Col. Gen. Ri Yong-ho) reporting directly to the MPAF (VMAR Kim Yong-chun), which interacts directly with the Supreme Commander.

- The reform of the reporting lines of the security services was more complicated as several organizations dedicated to operations against South Korea were transferred from the party and the Ministry of People's Armed Forces to the NDC and placed under the newly established General Bureau of Reconnaissance.[23] The director of this new bureau was allegedly the chief of the NDC Policy Department Lt. Gen. Kim Yong-chol.[24] This bureau oversees three other bureaus: Bureau 1 (Operations—the former KWP Operations Department), Bureau 2 (Reconnaissance Bureau—the former MPAF Reconnaissance Bureau), and Bureau 5 (former KWP Office 35).[25] Presumably, the chain of command for operations runs through O Kuk-yol as vice chairman of the NDC and ultimately to Kim Chong-il. Two other organizations with a portfolio for South Korean affairs, the United Front Department (headed by Kim Yang-gon) and the External Liaison Department (headed by Kang Kwan-chu),[26] apparently remained within the party chain of command. They apparently continue to report directly to Kim Chong-il through party channels.[27]

- Reporting lines related to internal security were largely consolidated under Chang Song-taek. Both Chu Sang-song (minister of People's Security) and U Tong-chuk (deputy director of the State Security Department) are protégés of Chang and report directly to him in his capacity as director of the KWP Administration Department.[28] Chang, of course, reports directly to Kim Chong-il.[29]

Therefore, unlike the past when Kim Chong-il relied on direct channels to numerous internal and external security agencies, by 2009, much of the information and guidance was apparently handled by three NDC members: Kim Yong-chun, O Kuk-yol, and Chang Song-taek.[30] Within this leadership configuration, some sources believed that Kim Chong-il broadly divided policy responsibilities among these key NDC members, with Chang Song-taek taking the lead on domestic and internal security affairs,[31] and Kim Yong-chun and O Kuk-yol allegedly playing a large role in military and foreign policy decision making.[32]

These same sources claimed that Kim Chong-il, though still a dominant figure within the regime, was no longer a micromanager. Instead, he approved broad policy parameters within which his subordinates in the NDC conducted the day-to-day affairs of the regime. This, they claimed, accounted for the military's more prominent role in the foreign affairs of the country, as evidenced by the General Staff's frequent public messages regarding the Northern Limit Line (NLL), the Ministry of Foreign Affairs' increasingly strong language regarding denuclearization and the Six Party Talks, and threats by the regime to pull out of the 1953 Armistice Agreement. As for domestic affairs, many believed that since his return to prominence in 2006, Chang had overseen a crackdown by the security forces on cross-border activity with China, as well as the so-called counter reforms that rolled back the market innovations within the economic sector in 2002.[33]

In addition to issues of command and control, the wire diagram of power within the North Korean system appeared to be changing to accommodate the upcoming succession. Kim's stroke in August seemed to have had a jarring impact on the North Korean leadership. It raised the real possibility of a near-term succession, which could come with very little warning. This may have contributed to Kim's decision to further augment the NDC organizational structure (something that began in 2007) and expand its membership beyond the military and defense industry realms to include powerful members of the party and security apparatus. Whereas in the past Kim had treated the NDC as a collection of advisers, whom he could task individually with specific guidance, now the NDC was, according to many observers, more able to serve as a venue for crisis management in the event of Kim's death or incapacitation. In essence, it is a forum for a collective leadership in the post-Kim era.

Within the NDC, many sources pointed to Chang Song-taek as being the important member with regard to succession planning.[34] Outside of Kim himself, only Chang had the gravitas and patronage relationships to ensure that the connective tissue remained in place as a succession process went forward.[35] As noted above, several 2009 appointments had ties to the Chang network.[36] According to some sources, Kim's decision to allow Chang to build such a powerful network at the regime's center (something he had allegedly been purged twice before for doing) was driven by his desire for stability. Chang's enhanced control over the security services not only served as a bulwark against factionalism within the regime, but also laid the cornerstone for the next leadership. If this theory was true, his appointment to the NDC placed this organization at the center of North Korean politics.

It would be too simplistic, however, to describe this shift in power as a zero sum game, with any gain in power of the military/security apparatus translated as an equal loss in power and status for the party.[37] Instead, though the party still retained a lofty status within North Korea, the foundation for succession had apparently been shifted to the military/state apparatus, namely the National Defense Commission. Unlike under Kim Il-sung, when Kim Chong-il used the party apparatus, more specifically, the KWP Organization Guidance Department, to build up a patronage system and his credentials to become heir apparent, the NDC looked in 2009 to be the chosen platform to usher in the post–Kim Chong-il era.

ACCELERATING THE PACE OF SUCCESSION—SPEED CAMPAIGNS AND AN OCCASIONAL SPEED BUMP

As the SPA was wrapping up its agenda, reports began to surface about an upcoming campaign to push the economy forward. The central media, through a number of publicity activities, touted a 150-Day Battle aimed at "achieving eye-catching economic success" through the mobilization of the entire residents for 150 days from May 10 through to October 10, the day that marked the 64th founding anniversary of the Korean Workers' Party.[38] The regime had hinted that such a campaign might be coming in the New Year's Joint Editorial, which referred repeatedly to the iconic *chollima* movement of the late 1950s to underscore a major point, namely the need to enforce tighter discipline and reassert control over the economy. In a May 7 editorial, *Nodong Sinmun* defined "today's 150-Day Battle" as "a grand revolutionary march demanding an extraordinary resolve, strong will, and blazing devotion." It went on to say:

The order for battle has been issued. . . . Now is the very time to fully explode the might of our single-hearted unity, which is even more powerful than nuclear weapons . . . and carry out an all-party total mobilization campaign, nationwide all-out offensive, and all-people general do-or-die battle.[39]

There was little doubt within the Pyongyang watching community that this speed battle (or *chollima*) was tied to the succession. Rumors had already spread through defector channels that Kim Chong-un had taken a leading role in organizing the April 15 fireworks in celebration of Kim Il-sung's 97th birthday. By May, his name was being associated with the 150-Day Battle.[40] During the first phase of his succession, Kim Chong-il had made use of such economic speed campaigns.[41] Like his father, Pyongyang watchers believed, Kim Chong-un would try to use the mass mobilization effort to demonstrate to the populace his leadership and performance skills.[42]

Running in parallel with the reporting on the 150-Day Battle were a number of stories on the internal propaganda campaign to announce Kim Chong-un to the wider leadership. Sources inside North Korea reported that the KPA's General Political Bureau was conveying daily special instructions from some shadowy figure called the "Morning Star General" regarding the fundamental principles for the army's frontline units.[43] These instructions were designed to set straight the ideological mindset of the soldiers. Although reportedly North Korean military officials did not know the identity of the "Morning Star General," they were under the impression that it was one of Kim Chong-il's sons.[44]

Within internal security channels, information on the succession seemed to be more transparent. In April, the State Security Department and Ministry of People's Security had reportedly begun special lecture sessions targeting chiefs of security offices and directors of security departments in counties and districts. The title of this special lecture session was "Sagacious General Kim Chong-un, the One and Only Successor of Great Leader (ryo'ngdoja) Comrade Kim Chong-il." According to one security officer who participated in the lecture session:

As soon as the director of the provincial security bureau announced the title of the special lecture session, participants of the special lecture session stood up, applauding and shouting hurrahs. Sagacious General Kim Chong-un's revolutionary family, his academic background, and a brief history of his revolutionary activities were introduced at the special lecture session. General Kim Chong-un graduated from Kim Il-sung University and Kim Il-sung Military University and is now assisting the military-first leadership of general [Kim Chong-il]. It is an honor and a pride of our nation—which is blessed with the fortune of the leader and the fortune of the general from generation to generation—to be serving another military-first brilliant commander who is succeeding and developing the general's [Kim Chong-il's] excellent art of command on a lofty stage.[45]

But, just as talk of the succession was reaching a crescendo both inside North Korea and within the international media, things went quiet. The June 10 edition of the *Nodong Sinmun* ran a political commentary emphasizing that when Kim began resuming his regular duties following his stroke, he "had the youthfulness of one in his 20s." Political commentaries dated June 22 and 23 continued to make references to the succession issue. A commentary dated June 27 emphasized the legitimacy of a "hereditary" succession: "It is the lineage of Mt. Paektu that remains unchanged after hundreds of generations have passed." Then in July, these succession-related commentaries suddenly stopped.[46] Even veiled references to a young leader disappeared and the North Korean media avoided explicit mention of succession-related songs "Let Us Raise a Toast" and "Footsteps." Finally, on September 6, Kim Yong-nam, the President of the SPA Presidium and the second-highest-ranking official in the regime, gave a rare interview with the Japanese news agency *Kyodo* in which he stated that the regime leadership in North Korea "hasn't even had discussions about such an issue [succession]."[47]

The reason for this deceleration of the succession campaign is not clear. According to some sources, Kim Chong-il had become concerned that much like 2005 when he prevented open discussion of the succession within the regime, rampant speculation was adversely affecting the succession process. Other rumors surfaced that Kim objected to personnel moves that Kim Chong-un made soon after his designation as heir apparent. If his son was as ambitious as his father had been, this could be true. But, more than likely, it had to do with process. The decision to appoint a successor can create a dual power structure, thus weakening the power base of the current leader. If Kim Chong-il was following the model of his own succession, this duopoly of power should not occur until after the successor had been publicly named, thus moving the succession into the second phase. If it was already occurring in the regime as the propaganda campaign was accelerated and the 150-Day Battle was mobilizing the population, Kim might have become worried that this momentum could undermine his own position as key elements within the regime realigned their loyalties with an eye toward the future.[48] By slowing down the pace of the succession propaganda campaign, Kim emphasized his continued leadership.[49]

Far from disavowing the third hereditary succession, Kim Chong-un's presence remained just below the surface in a number of activities inside the regime. In June, the Kim family bloodline attracted attention as Kim Kyong-hui began to appear in the central media for the first time ever. Pyongyang watchers speculated that Kim was bringing his family close in his time of need, wanting to show a united front to the larger North Korean leadership. Even after the propaganda campaign surrounding the succession went into hiatus, Kim Kyong-hui continued to show up in her brother's guidance inspections, as well as at national events. On July 8, she was on the reporting rostrum for the 15th anniversary of Kim Il-sung's death. It was the first time that both Kim Kyong-hui and O Kuk-yol, two of Kim's closest confidants, had appeared on a rostrum hierarchy.[50]

In September, more signs emerged pointing to the succession as toned down, but continuing apace. The North Korean media on September 21 carried a rare and authoritative KWP Central Committee "press release" announcing that a 100-Day Battle was under way, having followed on the heels of the just-completed 150-Day Battle. Within leadership circles, this speed campaign no doubt had succession implications, although it was formally tied to Kim Chong-il. Over the course of the next three months, Cabinet editorials described the various aspects of the battle, including two areas that would later become associated with Kim Chong-un: achievements in Computer Numerical Control (CNC) Technology and modern housing construction in Pyongyang.[51]

A more concrete sign of the succession was not generated by the regime, but emerged through unofficial channels. On September 22, a photojournalist who goes by the pseudonym "hanming huang" acquired and posted to the Internet a photograph of a public propaganda poster in North Korea extolling Kim Chong-un. Reportedly taken in Wonsan, Kangwon Province, the header on the poster read: "The glory of our nation, which enjoys the blessing of the general [*changgun*] and the general [*taejang*] . . . Young General Comrade Kim-Chong-un, who is continuing the Mangyongdae bloodline and the Paektu bloodline." This was followed by the words from the song "Footsteps." If authentic, and there was no reason to doubt that it was,[52] this poster was the first public recognition of the third son by the regime to make it to the outside world.

Table 6.2
July 8, 2009 Central Memorial Meeting on the Occasion of the 15th Anniversary of Kim Il-sung's Death

Ranking	Person	Position
1	Kim Chong-il	Chairman of the National Defense Commission
2	Kim Yong-nam	President of the Supreme People's Assembly
3	Kim Yong-il	Cabinet Premier
4	Kim Yong-chun	Vice Chairman of the NDC, Minister of People's Armed Forces
5	Chon Pyong-ho	Member of the NDC
6	Ri Yong-mu	Vice Chairman of the NDC
7	O Kuk-yol	Vice Chairman of the NDC
8	Choe Thae-bok	Chairman of the SPA
9	Kim Il-chol	Member of the NDC
10	Ri Yong-ho	Chief of the General Staff Department
11	Kim Chong-gak	First Vice Director of the General Political Bureau
12	Kim Kuk-tae	Secretary of the KWP Central Committee
13	Kim Chung-rin	Secretary of the KWP Central Committee
14	Kim Ki-nam	Secretary of the KWP Central Committee
15	Kim Kyong-hui	Director of KWP Light Industry Department
16	Yang Yong-sop	Vice President of the SPA Presidium
17	Choe Yong-rim	Secretary General of the SPA Presidium
18	Kim Chol-man	Alternate Member of the Politburo
19	Ri Ul-sol	Member of the KWP Central Military Committee
20	Ri Ha-il	Member of the KWP Central Military Committee
21	Chang Song-u	Director of the KWP Civil Defense Department (Died on August 24, 2009)[a]
22	Kim Yong-dae	Chairman of the Socialist Democratic Party Central Committee
23	Ryu Mi-yong	Chairperson of the Korean Chondoist Chongu Party Central Committee

[a] "Obituary on Comrade Chang Song-u's Demise," *Nodong Sinmun,* 26 August 2009.

CURRENCY REVALUATION

Even though North Korea was increasingly focused on its internal affairs in the fall of 2009, Kim Chong-il was engaged in a diplomatic gambit that, if successful, would satisfy a critical piece of the succession puzzle. Despite the propaganda surrounding the rush toward an economically prosperous state by 2012, the Leader knew that mobilization campaigns did little to address the regime's economic shortfalls. What was needed was a massive infusion of aid; preferably in such a way that Kim could continue to tout the benefits of *Chuche*. Once again, this meant looking to China.

As North Korea was transitioning from the 150-Day Battle to the 100-Day Battle, Kim chose to take a meeting with State Councilor Dai Bingguo, who was visiting North Korea as a special envoy from President Hu Jintao. In response to a letter delivered by Dai, Kim proclaimed that North Korea wanted to "solve related problems [code for the nuclear issue] through bilateral and multilateral dialogue." He went on to note that North Korea "will continue to observe the goal of denuclearization and focus its efforts on the peace and stability of the Korean Peninsula." Though not promising to return to the Six Party Talks, North Korean interlocutors made it clear that exploring the process whereby North Korea could come back to the talks might be a worthwhile avenue of discussion between the two countries.

The Dai visit sparked a flurry of delegations between the two countries. Chinese authorities welcomed a North Korean military delegation and then a youth affairs delegation. On September 28, the Chinese Foreign Ministry announced that at the invitation of the KWP Central Committee and the North Korean government, CPC Political Bureau Standing Committee member and Premier Wen Jiabao would pay an official goodwill visit to Pyongyang in October.

Wen Jiabao was the first Chinese premier to visit North Korea since Li Peng in 1991. A reading of the Chinese press made his mandate clear—securing Kim Chong-il's commitment to return to the Six Party Talks.[53] After two days of a frank exchange of views, the results of the meeting were mixed. Chinese interlocutors suggested that Wen had made some progress, but failed to convince Kim to return to the talks. North Korean interlocutors were much more upbeat, focusing on the progress that was made—namely, a massive economic package. According to the North Korean press, China would assume the costs for a new bridge to be constructed over the Yalu River, which runs along the northern part of the Korean Peninsula. The two sides also reportedly reached agreements on cooperation in education and tourism, with China providing grants worth an estimated $200 million.[54]

What happened next is a matter of much debate within Pyongyang watching circles. How confident was Kim in the agreements reached with

Wen? What was the nature of the agreements in terms of amounts of aid and time lines for delivery? The lack of transparency about what transpired in the talks makes it difficult to discern the nature of the agreements struck between the two countries. This was complicated further by the disparities between the Chinese and North Korean media treatment of the visit. Therefore, whether one can connect the dots between Wen's visit and North Korea's aggressive economic decision making over the next several months is open to interpretation.

What is clearer is Kim's desire to blunt the influence of the markets through the reinstitution of a socialist planned economy.[55] At the same time, Kim probably recognized the need to cushion the adverse impact of squeezing the market economy. This could explain Pyongyang's move in August to reverse its antagonistic policy toward South Korean President Lee Myung-bak and to move to restore North–South cooperation on projects that earned substantial revenue for the North.[56] If Wen did in fact promise a substantial aid package, Kim may have believed that he had secured the safety net that would allow him to take the steps necessary to rein in the economy, close the markets, and build the economic base for the successor regime.

By the end of November, Kim's next move seemed to be in place. On November 22, he inspected the Ministry of People's Security headquarters, expressing his "great satisfaction" to public security officers for "performing the assigned combat mission in a responsible manner." This was the first time that Kim had made such a publicized visit to the ministry's headquarters.[57] Though the gist of Kim's discussions with Chu Sang-song and his staff was not made public, in retrospect, this visit was probably more than just an inspection. More than likely, it was a planning meeting centered on an upcoming event that could lead to domestic unrest. On November 29, security units were deployed throughout the country and border security forces placed on high alert.

The next day, on November 30, the Cabinet issued Decision No. 423 regarding the exchange of monetary currency (*hwap'ye kyohwan*). The decision itself was rather sparse and included two subsections outlining the rationale for the move. The Cabinet Decision No. 423–1 and 423–2 pointed to "stability and improvement of the people's living standards," as well as the need to restore "the economic management system and order" as the reasons for the revaluation.[58] The decision went on to warn that "internal directions" were issued to "ruthlessly punish" any fraudulent acts regarding the currency exchange. Sometime between 11:00 A.M. and 2:00 P.M., currency exchange offices across the country began to trade old currency for the new script.[59] The exchange rate for the new currency was 100–1, so old 1,000-won notes were exchanged for new 10-won bills. Severe restrictions were placed on the amount of currency that could be exchanged. The upper limit for each family was said to be between 100,000 and 150,000 won, which is about the monthly average per-family cost of living. If people had any money in excess of this amount, it would have to be deposited into banks, up to 300,000 won.

This was the fifth currency revaluation in North Korea's 54-year history.[60] As the days passed, it became obvious that it was in many respects unique. Most noticeable was the fact that the action was taken without preparing the public. The regime had announced its previous four redenomination decisions with authoritative government pronouncements in the central media before the relevant currency regulations took effect— a "people's committee ordinance" in 1947 (1–1 revaluation), a "cabinet decision" in 1959 (100–1 revaluation), and "Central People's Committee decrees" in 1979 (1–1 revaluation) and 1992 (1–1 revaluation). This time, however, there was no announcement through official media channels, something that led to widespread confusion as to what was happening.

The covert means by which the revaluation occurred led some Pyongyang watchers to speculate that the regime wanted to avoid a repeat of the 1992 experience, when, following the announcement of the revaluation in *Nodong Sinmun,* the public quickly bought up commodities to get rid of old currency. It also suggested that the regime viewed the revaluation not just in economic terms—as a means of dealing with inflation—but politically, as an attack on the growing middle class, which had accumulated wealth and independence through the markets. If true, it means that the regime made several assumptions regarding the outcome of the revaluation.

- The growing middle class would be brought under control and forced back under the thumb of the centrally controlled economy.
- The markets would be suppressed.
- Private wealth of traders large and small would be reduced.
- The public outcry would be muted because the population was exhausted by the 150- and 100-day campaigns.
- Senior North Korean officials would not be severely impacted by the revaluation because they held foreign currency.

It soon became clear that some of these assumptions were misplaced. The initial public response to the currency revaluation was decidedly antagonistic, especially among traders who stood to lose accumulated savings in both local and foreign currencies. This anger soon spread to the general public as prices rose dramatically. Stories began to seep out of demonstrations in the markets and citizens burning old bills as a sign of protest.

In a surprising move on January 9, *Nodong Sinmun* cited Kim in an article as saying,

Although the *Suryong* (Kim Il-sung) told us that we have to let the people eat rice with meat soup, wear silk clothes and live in a tiled roof house, we have not accomplished his will. . . . We have already reached the status of a strong country in the military field, let alone politics and ideology, but there are still quite a number of things lacking in people's lives. I am trying to implement the will [of Kim Il-sung] by solving these problems.[61]

This admission seemed to suggest that the regime had been caught off guard by the vociferous public reaction to the currency revaluation. By publicly referencing his own concerns, Kim presumably hoped to soothe public sentiment by advertising his desire to improve people's lives. This starkly contrasted with Kim's previous strategy for dealing with the dilapidated economy, essentially telling the people to just endure economic difficulties in order to become a strong country in the ideological, military, and political arenas. The article sought to insulate the Leader from criticism on this matter, highlighting Kim's tireless efforts to find the solution to people's daily problems through on-site inspections at economic entities in Wonsan, Daean, and Heungnam. It added, "Living in a train on a rigorous schedule is now a habit for the General. Until he has solved the people's living problems he cannot sleep deeply at home. Every road the General takes is paved with his sincere words, 'Let's carry out the *Suryong*'s will by solving the people's problems with one unified heart.'"[62]

The government, while apparently taken aback by the public's reaction, continued into January with its campaign against the markets. Though loosening the initial rules governing the currency conversion, it soon banned the use of foreign currency and instituted a propaganda campaign and a 40-Day Battle to enforce market closures. The New Year's Joint Editorial boldly stated the regime's intention to "bring about a radical turn in the people's standard of living by accelerating the development of light industry and agriculture once again this year that marks the 65th anniversary of the founding of the Workers' Party of Korea." By emphasizing the identity of the party as the provider of basic welfare for the North Korean people, the editorial signaled that in the future it would be the regime, not the markets, that would bring broad-based economic benefits to the people.

Despite the regime's attempts to couch the currency reforms in a positive economic light, the public's anger continued to grow. The ban on the use of foreign currency, however, proved to be particularly troubling because it impacted many within the elite who were involved in hard currency endeavors. As North Korean authorities clamped down on those in possession of foreign currency through ramped up investigations, foreign merchants (especially Chinese) who settled their business transactions in U.S. dollars and renminbi began to hold off transactions. This not only slowed the flow of goods into North Korea, but impacted the bottom line of North Korean traders and merchants (both in the official and black markets), many of whom had ties to the leadership. As outrage within this segment of society began to grow, Pyongyang took notice.

In response to a report by Chae Yong-hae, the North Hwanghae Provincial Party secretary, which outlined the confusion caused by the currency measures and the negative impact it was having on the population, Kim Chong-il convened a conference of provincial party secretaries in mid-January to study the situation.[63] At about the same time, in an effort to calm concerns and deflect blame for the crisis, Kim relieved Pak Nam-gi, director of the KWP Planning and Finance Department, the so-called control tower of the planned economy and the reported implementer of the currency reforms, of his duties.[64] Over the next month, Pyongyang began to move away from the more draconian elements of the campaign against the markets. Reportedly, some goods (such as electronics) began to be traded in some general markets in major cities. In addition, foreign currency shops reopened and the ban on the possession and use of foreign currencies was relaxed. The idea of reviving the controlled economy that was envisaged by the authorities by implementing the currency redenomination and conversion had come to a standstill.

By February, the regime was in retreat.[65] On February 5, Premier Kim Yong-il reportedly acknowledged within leadership circles that the currency reform had gone disastrously wrong. He is rumored to have read out an hour-long statement before village chiefs and other party officials at the People's Palace of Culture in Pyongyang.[66] Deflecting the blame away from Kim Chong-il and placing it squarely on the bodies executing the reform, the premier was quoted as saying, "I sincerely apologize for having caused great pain to the people by recklessly enforcing the latest currency reform without making sufficient preparations or considering the circumstances."[67] Kim also pledged to rectify the mistakes, saying he would do his best to stabilize the people's financial circumstances, an apparent reference to the skyrocketing inflation unleashed by the revaluation of the won.[68] Despite the concessions to the market forces inside the country, Kim stressed the need to stick to state-set prices, adding that the government would strictly crack down on the hoarding of goods.[69]

Although the premier's apology seemed to quell the public's anger, by February Kim Chong-il and his close aides were focused on the impact that the currency revaluation had on the stability of the regime.[70] On February 1, the Ministry of People's Security issued a decree outlining punishments for those caught contacting the outside world. One week later, North Korea's two major public security organizations, the Ministry of People's Security and the State Security Department, issued a joint statement on dealing with attempts to overthrow the system.[71] These moves came in the wake of numerous reports by the international media of public anger and demonstrations, reportedly based on information coming from inside North Korea.[72] Important targets for this decree were those who communicated with the outside via Chinese cellular phones; those who viewed South Korean videos or listened to South Korean radio; and those attempting to travel or live abroad. The decree announced that such people would be punished under the charge of "crime of treachery against the nation," which carries a possible death sentence. Following the issuance of this decree, most of the North's sources of information, which had been flowing out to South Korean NGOs, were cut off.[73] On March 5, the *Daily NK* reported that the security organs were making preparations for the issuance of new citizenship certificates, a familiar regime strategy in times of economic or social peril. Ostensibly aimed at weeding out potential spies, the recertification campaign affords the internal security apparatus with an opportunity to mobilize its forces throughout the country in order to validate its information on the population, including the current location of every citizen.[74]

In an indication of the seriousness with which the regime viewed the situation, on March 6 Kim Chong-il attended a mass rally in Hamhung, South Hamgyong Province, to celebrate the dedication of the February 8 Vinalon Complex, which resumed operation for the first time in 16 years. For security reasons, Kim rarely showed up at outdoor rallies, other than political or military events, such as ceremonial parades. This was the first time he had ever attended a mass rally. It was also the first time he had ever attended a popular rally outside of Pyongyang. The security implications of this move were tied to the city itself. Hamgyong Province is in a region where a great number of people had died of starvation in the 1990s. Located in the southern part of the province, Hamhung was infamous for its anti-government tendencies, and its residents had often proved resistant to government control. The fact that Kim Chong-il, who was rumored to be obsessed about his personal security, felt the need to venture out to the rally in Hamhung was no doubt a signal that the regime was eager to reassert its control over a situation it felt was getting out of hand.[75]

SINKING OF THE *CHEONAN*

As the regime wrestled with its growing domestic problems, externally Pyongyang was sending signals that it was ready to engage. On January 11, North Korea issued a rare and highly authoritative Foreign Ministry pronouncement—almost certainly vetted by Kim Chong-il himself—proposing talks for a "peace agreement" to replace the 1953 Armistice Agreement as the way forward on the nuclear issue. In addition to referencing denuclearization, the pronouncement made clear that the removal of sanctions had become a regime priority. The New Year's Joint Editorial had emphasized the benefits that could accrue from the easing of sanctions, namely improving the "people's living standards" through light industry and foreign trade. The Foreign Ministry's pronouncement emphasized this point, hinting that sanction relief would be something the regime would take very seriously in its deliberations about the resumption of the Six Party Talks.

Another indication that Pyongyang was eager to reestablish relations, especially with the United States, was its handling of the Robert Park affair. Park was a Korean American missionary who had been detained on December 25 for illegally crossing into North Korea. The North Korean media downplayed the issue, noting simply that an "American" was "under investigation."[76] The arrest was apparently not reported to the North Korean public, a departure from past handling of similar cases, in which arrests of trespassers were used to accuse the United States of trying to spy on and undermine the regime.[77] As in the case of Euna Lee and Laura Ling from several months earlier, North Korea most likely saw the Robert Park case as a chance to force the United States to again reach out, albeit through back channels, to Pyongyang, thus affording North Korea another chance to portray itself as "lenient" or "humanitarian" in the hope of promoting its diplomatic line toward Washington.

By mid-February, however, Pyongyang began to back away from its efforts at diplomatic outreach. On February 25, a Korean People's Army General Staff spokesman issued a "press statement" criticizing the UN Combined Forces Command's announcement of the annual Key Resolve and Foal Eagle (KRFE) US–South Korea combined military exercises, which would be held in March. The pronouncement mentioned that the regime could respond to the exercises by "mobilizing all the offensive and defensive means, including nuclear deterrent."[78] This was the first time since 2002 that Pyongyang had referred to a "nuclear deterrent" in response to an announcement of planned exercises, something that it probably calculated would be provocative.[79]

While many Pyongyang watchers puzzled over the fact that the North had never responded to an announcement of exercises at this level of authoritativeness, they reasoned that it was an effort by Pyongyang to reinforce its call for opening talks on a peace agreement.[80] After all, Kim Yong-nam—the President of the SPA Presidium and nominally the number two leader within the regime—just a week before had stated in an address at a national meeting marking Kim Chong-il's birthday that North Korea would "put an end to the hostile relations between the DPRK and the United States," a line in keeping with the positive line drawn in the New Year's Joint Editorial.[81]

Some Pyongyang watchers, however, believed that the hardline rhetoric coming out of Pyongyang was indicative of its growing impatience with diplomacy. According to these experts, Kim was being pulled in various directions by his close aides, namely those within the Ministry of Foreign Affairs, who advocated patience, and elements within the military, who believed that prolonged diplomacy made North Korea look weak in the eyes of its enemies. Though the truth may never be known, it is likely that the military's arguments were becoming conflated in Kim Chong-il's mind with growing anxiety among the elite surrounding the currency revaluation. In the months after the event, Kim Chong-un, the presumed heir apparent, had become attached to the revaluation. It was apparently an open secret that a 500-won per-person payment, which emerged in December, was in fact "consideration money from the New General" aimed at improving Chong-un's image. That said, several key families tied to the high command had suffered severe losses as the regime clamped down on cross-border trade with China. Their hard currency ventures were undermined by the temporary ban on the use or even possession of foreign currency.[82] A 500-won "consideration" payment would fall far short of making amends. If this were the case, Kim might have felt compelled to take steps to win over these hardline elements so as not to derail the succession.

Of course, these deliberations, if they were in fact occurring, were not known to the outside world, thus making the events of March 26 that much more shocking. At around 9:30 P.M., an explosion occurred underneath the hull of the ROK patrol ship *Cheonan* (PCC-772). The ship split in half and sank within minutes approximately one nautical mile off the southwest coast of Baengnyeong Island in the West (Yellow) Sea. Of the 104 crew members, 46 were lost. The cause of this explosion was not immediately determined, but a subsequent international investigation declared that a North Korean mini-sub had sunk the ship with a torpedo, a charge that Pyongyang vociferously denied.

On April 25, Kim made his first ever public inspection tour of KPA Unit 586, the Reconnaissance General Bureau (RGB). Accompanied by the commander of the unit, Col. Gen. Kim Yong-chol, Kim Chong-il's presence focused attention on a part of the military that normally remained in the shadows. The fact that his inspection occurred on Army Day suggested to some Pyongyang watchers that North Korea was attempting to take credit (at least internally) for the *Cheonan* sinking by bestowing honor on the unit. Though speculative, a narrative began to form of the sequence of events that led to the sinking of the *Cheonan*.

With his regime facing public anger from the currency revaluation and a military growing impatient with diplomacy and outraged from a November skirmish with the South Korean Navy in which a North Korean vessel was sunk, Kim Chong-il was looking for a way out. According to a senior defector, Kim would have been receiving advice from his close aide network, but because of his declining health, he probably did not follow his previous practice of vetting his decision through the relevant chains of command.[83] Therefore, when he made the decision to allow the military to carry out the mission, he most likely did not check with the Ministry of Foreign Affairs to get an assessment of possible fallout within the region and implications such a provocation would have on North Korea's larger diplomatic equities.

Once Kim had decided on the course of action, he probably passed orders down through the National Defense Commission via Vice Chairman O Kuk-yol. O, in turn, would issue guidance to the General Staff Department (Operations Bureau) and the Reconnaissance General Bureau for planning. The KPA Navy might have been brought into the process in a supporting role. Given the location for the provocation, Kim Kyok-sik, the commander of the Fourth Corps (former chief of the General Staff), which oversees the West Sea (Yellow Sea) Coast, was also probably involved in the planning. Subsequent reporting indicated that first vice director of the State Security Department, U Tong-chuk, was responsible for ensuring operational security surrounding the mission.[84]

Kim turned to the Reconnaissance General Bureau (RGB), which had been elevated in status in 2009 and placed under the National Defense Commission, to carry out the mission. After a purge of Pyongyang's external intelligence apparatus, the long-time covert operations unit was now in charge of southern affairs. It also had close ties with the Kim family going back decades. Its head, Kim Yong-chol, was purported to be a former bodyguard for Kim Chong-il. He was also allegedly one of Kim Chong-un's military mentors. By having the RGB conduct the attack, its success could be ascribed to the new successor.

The joint investigation into the *Cheonan* incident suggested that on the night of the incident, a mother ship transported the mini-submarine (most likely Yano class) to the coastal waters around Baengnyeong Island.[85] The submarine separated from the ship and set up a patrol in waters also patrolled by the South Korean Navy. When the *Cheonan* appeared, the submarine fired a heavy torpedo and then returned to its base, having transformed the security landscape on the Korean Peninsula.

A MUNDANE SPA MEETING

On April 8, the South Korean media picked up activity from a North Korean advance team in Beijing. Ten high-ranking officials, headed by First Vice Foreign Minister Kim Kye-kwan had apparently arrived to handle the logistics for another Kim Chong-il trip.[86] Speculation among the diplomatic community was that Pyongyang was signaling the need for consultations with Beijing in light of North Korea's deteriorating domestic situation. Opinion was growing that with North Korea's economic turmoil, Kim Chong-il's shaky health, and the fallout from the *Cheonan* affair cascading on the country, Pyongyang would need to shore up its relationship with its lone remaining ally. Reports that North Korea was seriously considering a Chinese proposal calling for the holding of a preparatory session to kick-start the Six Party Talks remained unconfirmed.

Amid the nearly daily speculation of Kim's impending trip, the leadership convened the second session of the 12th Supreme People's Assembly in Pyongyang on April 9. However, the meeting almost went unnoticed as Kim Chong-il for the fifth time since 1998 chose not to attend. There also had been speculation that Kim Chong-un would make an appearance or that there would be a reshuffle of the top leadership, but neither occurred. KCNA reported that the parliament amended the Constitution, but did not give any details.

The two themes to emerge from the meeting were that North Korea was a powerful, nuclear state and that the regime's central planning approach toward the economy was paying dividends. Despite Pyongyang's recent concessions to the markets, the propaganda surrounding the SPA sought to highlight the regime's return to orthodoxy. The Cabinet report noted that defense spending would hold steady at 15.8 percent for the fourth straight year, something in keeping with the frugal approach to spending across the board. Although left unsaid, the reports of the economic planners sought to suggest that through responsible spending and proper balancing of priorities, North Korea could move forward without having to rely on the unpredictable strategies advocated by pro-market elements within the leadership.

For Pyongyang watchers, the SPA meeting seemed to impart one bit of news. The propaganda themes surrounding the event were built around the importance of the 65th anniversary of the founding of the ruling Korean Workers' Party (October 10). The speeches characterized 2010 as a "deeply meaningful year . . . worth a special mention in history" and stated that it would be significant in the "construction of a powerful state."[87] For some, this suggested the likelihood that the party for the first time since Kim had taken power would convene a major meeting in the coming months. If true, the implications for the succession would be significant.

The meeting of the SPA was followed by the annual military promotions. One day before the 98th anniversary of Kim Il-sung's birth (April 15), Kim Chong-il, acting in his capacity as supreme commander, handed down Order No. 0045 promoting 100 military officers, including 4 generals: First Vice Director of the SSD U Tong-chuk, Air Force Commander Ri Pyong-chol, Navy Commander ADM Chong Myong-do, and Artillery Commander Chung Ho-gyun.[88] This was the largest set of promotions since 1997, when 129 officers were promoted. At that time, Kim Chong-il was in the process of consolidating his position as supreme leader. Similarly, this set of promotions was seen by Pyongyang watchers as part of the succession process designed to cement loyalty within the armed forces for Kim Chong-un. In his announcement, Kim seemed to suggest the need for heightened vigilance when he for the first time tied promotions to the "internal and external" defense of the country.

As April drew to a close, the North Korean leadership continued to evolve with the deaths of two of Kim Chong-il's close aides: Ri Yong-chol and Kim Chung-rin. Kim Chung-rin for many years had been a key player in North Korean operations against the South. As a former KWP Secretary for ROK Affairs and director of the KWP United Front Department, he was involved in policy making, including the terrorist acts against South Korean targets in the 1960s and 1980s. At the time of his death, his influence had diminished in his capacity as KWP Secretary for Working and Public Organizations. By contrast, Ri Yong-chol remained at the center of party activities until his death. As a first vice director of the KWP Organization Guidance Department, Ri played a key role in the selection, promotion, appointment, and dismissal of senior military officers.

Pyongyang watchers eagerly awaited the appointments to the posts left vacant by these deaths in the hope that they would provide insights into Kim Chong-il's thinking about the succession process. How he filled the vacancy in the Organization Guidance Department could provide a clear indication of the pace at which the succession was moving. If Kim Chong-un replaced Ri Yong-chol, it would mark a major step in the transfer of responsibility for personnel appointments. This could suggest that the succession process was moving faster than most Pyongyang watchers believed. How Kim handled the vacancy in the KWP Secretariat would likely not yield much on the succession per se, but could provide more organizational insights into how the regime might function in the future. If he chose to replace Kim Chung-rin with a close aide, it could suggest that the Secretariat would remain at the center of the Kim regime and not go the way of the Politburo, which had withered because of neglect. Finally, given the moribund state of the party, any new appointments would no doubt signal whether or not Kim was interested in generational turnover to create a support network around his son.

ANOTHER TRIP TO CHINA

Leadership watchers, however, would have to wait for these answers, for around 5:20 A.M. on May 2, Kim Chong-il's special 17-car train arrived at the Dandong border crossing in northeastern China. Local sources in the area reported a major presence of Chinese police and border guards camped out in the vicinity of the Dandong Station and around the North Korea-China Friendship Bridge. At 7:00 A.M., the train headed for Dalian instead of Shenyang, which is the route Kim's train normally took to Beijing. After spending a day wandering around Dalian and presumably having discussions on Chinese development of Rajin Port,[89] Kim's train departed for Beijing. Later reporting would identify several key figures accompanying him, including Chang Song-taek, Kim Ok, Kang Sok-chu (first vice minister of foreign affairs), Kim Yong-il (director of the KWP International Department), and Kim Yang-gon (director of the KWP United Front Department).[90]

Kim's motives for this trip to China were unclear. Presumably he would clarify Pyongyang's position on the *Cheonan* incident and appeal for Chinese help to confront the situation. Regional commentators speculated that discussions might also turn to the resumption of the Six Party Talks and economic aid. Very little information emerged in the days and weeks after Kim's trip. Kim's activities en route to Beijing seemed to reflect his interest in developing North Korea's port cities as a way to boost trade with China and Russia. Coverage of his meetings with Hu Jintao and Wen Jiabao focused on economic issues, although an obligatory brief discussion was held on creating favorable terms to revive the Six Party Talks. Hu reportedly put forward five proposals to strengthen Sino–North Korean ties:

- To maintain high-level contacts. The leaders of the two countries should keep in touch by exchanging visits, as well as sending special envoys and messages.
- To reinforce strategic coordination. The two sides should exchange views in a timely manner on major domestic and diplomatic issues, the international and regional situation, as well as on governance experience.
- To deepen economic and trade cooperation.[91] The relevant departments of the two governments should discuss and explore ways of expanding economic and trade cooperation.
- To increase personnel exchanges. The two sides should expand exchanges in the cultural, sports, and educational fields, and the contacts between the youth in particular to inherit the traditional friendship from generation to generation.
- To strengthen coordination in international and regional affairs to better serve regional peace and stability.[92]

During a meeting with Kim at Diaoyutai State Guesthouse, Prime Minister Wen Jiabao directly broached the issue of applying the Chinese reform and openness model to North Korea, saying, "China will support North Korea's economic development and improvement in its public welfare in the future, and we hope to share with North Korea China's experience with reform, openness and construction." Wen also emphasized economic ties between the two nations, saying, "There is great potential for Chinese–North Korean economic cooperation, and I hope that through joint effort and cooperation, both parties work actively at collaborative projects and enrich the livelihoods of the people of both countries by speeding up construction of infrastructure in the border region to find new areas and methods for collaboration."[93]

It is unclear how much traction Wen's offer had with Kim. It is rumored that Kim was not so much interested in the Chinese model as Chinese aid. He reportedly brought up the issue of Chinese aid first in his meeting with Hu, who referred the issue to the premier. In what appears to be the division of responsibility between Hu and Wen (regarding delivering good and bad news to Kim Chong-il), the premier delivered the news that China would respect international sanctions imposed on Pyongyang and refused to provide additional economic assistance.[94] Reportedly dismayed that his request went unheeded, Kim cut short his trip, skipping a scheduled performance by the North Korean Pibada Opera Company of *A Dream of Red Mansions*.[95]

There were no obvious indications that Kim discussed the upcoming North Korean succession with the Chinese leadership.[96] That did not, however, stop Pyongyang watchers from speculating about subtle signals about North Korean leadership dynamics on display during the summit. Of particular interest were images from the trip that ran on Chinese television, showing Chang Song-taek seated closer to Kim than his position warranted. Images of the banquet aired by China's state-run CCTV showed Kim and Hu sitting at the seats of honor at a round table, flanked by officials from both sides according to their ranks. Chang was seated in third place, right after Kim Yong-chun, the minister of the People's Armed Forces, and before First Vice Foreign Minister Kang Sok-chu, and KWP secretaries Choe Thae-bok and Kim Ki-nam.[97]

Rumored to be close to several Chinese leaders, Chang Song-taek was often pointed to by Pyongyang watchers as being a critical piece to the succession puzzle for Beijing. According to some sources, China's North Korea policy was based to a large extent on its view of the post–Kim Chong-il leadership configuration.[98] Though reportedly not enamored with the idea of the third hereditary succession, Chinese leaders were particularly interested in the collective leadership that would surround Kim's chosen successor. Given Chang's prominent role during the talks in Beijing, it is most likely that Pyongyang understood his value.[99] And within a month, Chang Song-taek's position within the regime and his role as regent began to solidify.

A TRAFFIC ACCIDENT AND ANOTHER SPA MEETING

A major sign that a shift in Chang's favor had occurred within Kim's close aide network came on June 2 with the announcement of the death of Ri Che-kang, the apparent victim of a traffic accident.[100] Details of the accident were sparse. It reportedly occurred shortly after midnight, suggesting Ri might have been driving himself home from a close aide party. The North Korean media's handling of Ri's obituary lent credence to the story that it was an accident. Of course, this may have been done to deflect speculation both inside North Korea and in the foreign press that Ri's death was due to foul play or in any way linked to the succession.[101] After all, in the space of two months, the party's Organization Guidance Department, an entity many felt had kept Chang Song-taek in check, had been weakened with the deaths of two of its three first vice directors.

Ri Che-kang's death was the second leadership event to happen in a matter of weeks. In May, the KCNA announced NDC Decision No. 06, relieving Kim Il-chol (first vice minister of the People's Armed Forces and member of the senior defense body) of all of his posts.[102] The one-paragraph announcement noted that Kim, who was 80, was retired because of his advanced age, an explanation that was undermined by the fact that two other NDC members, Cho Myong-nok (82) and Chon Pyong-ho (84), were older than Kim. Speculation inside Pyongyang was that he had fallen out of favor. Allegedly a rival of Cho Myong-nok and Kim Yong-chun, and not particularly close to Chang Song-taek, Kim Il-chol's star had been descending for years and he had begun to voice his displeasure following his replacement as minister in 2009 by Kim Yong-chun. Given the increasingly sensitive leadership environment as the succession progressed, Kim Chong-il probably did not want to risk dissention within the ranks of the nation's highest defense body. He also had to ensure that if his health failed before the succession could be completed, the NDC could not only be able to effectively rule the country in his absence, but would oversee the eventual transfer of power to his son. Though Kim Il-chol's retirement helped streamline command and control between the NDC and the armed forces, it was Chang Song-taek's promotion at an extraordinary meeting of the SPA (the third session of the 12th SPA) that signaled Kim Chong-il's driving focus on the upcoming hereditary succession.

In a hastily convened meeting of the rubber-stamp parliament on June 7, Chang Song-taek was promoted to vice chairman of the NDC, joining Cho Myong-nok (first vice chairman), Ri Yong-mu, O Kuk-yol, and Kim Yong-chun.[103] His appointment firmly tied the internal security apparatus to the NDC, thus consolidating within one institution the regime's levers of control. If, as was suspected, Chang had emerged as the regent for the heir apparent, his position was now unassailable. With Cho Myong-nok and Ri Yong-mu in declining health, Chang was now at the nexus of a triumvirate jelling around Kim Chong-il that was centered in the NDC. O Kuk-yol, as head of external intelligence and North Korea's powerful special forces, was responsible for crisis management and would step forward if the regime began to falter. Kim Yong-chun was Kim Chong-il's conduit to the armed forces, a position that was being increasingly challenged by Ri Yong-ho, the chief of the General Staff. Chang Song-taek's role as regent, however, presumably enhanced his power beyond that of his fellow vice chairmen.

In other personnel moves, the SPA also replaced the senior Cabinet leadership. Choe Yong-rim, a former aide to Kim Il-sung and long-time servant of the Kim family,[104] replaced Kim Yong-il as premier. This move seemed to be in keeping with Kim Chong-il's strategy of filling the regime's key posts with family and close aides to pave the way for the succession. In addition, Choe's appointment distanced the regime from the recently failed currency revaluation, which was ascribed to his predecessor.[105] Other appointments included the replacement of six vice premiers as well as Cabinet ministers involved in light industry, sports, food, and daily necessities.[106]

Although not given the media attention of the previous meeting in April, the Third Session of the 12th SPA was nonetheless more important.

This was made clear by the fact that unlike the April meeting, Kim Chong-il attended the meeting on June 7. Though it was unclear why the personnel reshuffle could not have been included in the earlier meeting,[107] Chang's elevation to vice chairman of the NDC seemed to complete a collective leadership, which could manage the day-to-day affairs of the regime if Kim became incapacitated. In addition, the Cabinet was now in the hands of a group of cadres, who could be relied on to follow a conservative path, relying on tried methods of central planning.

Kim must have been aware that the mechanism he had created, though useful for crisis management, was ill-suited for carrying out a transfer of power to his son that would both be institutionalized and confer legitimacy. It was possible that if Kim were to die or become incapacitated in the near future, a power struggle would break out in the NDC between power brokers. Lacking his own patronage system and without any formalized rules for succession, Kim Chong-un would be hostage to this struggle. At best, he would be a figurehead for a collection of puppeteers behind the throne. At worst, he would become an inconvenience that powerful figures such as Chang Song-taek or O Kuk-yol might marginalize or worse.

A POLITBURO ANNOUNCEMENT

As defectors and sources inside North Korea began to opine on Kim's deteriorating health and the growing responsibilities of the NDC vice chairmen, the Chosun Central News Agency (KCNA) suddenly announced on June 23 that "the Politburo of the Central Committee would summon a delegates conference at the beginning of September to elect the leading apparatus of the Workers' Party."[108] The announcement went on to say that the conference was necessary to "reflect the demands for the revolutionary development of the party, which is facing critical changes in bringing about the strong and prosperous state and *Chuche* achievements."

North Korea had only convened party conferences twice before, in 1958 (to handle the "August Incident")[109] and 1966 (to create the Secretariat and the position of General Secretary). According to the Party charter, the Central Committee is supposed to convene a Party Congress once every five years. In between congresses, a conference can be summoned to discuss urgent party issues and key policy matters. The two venues share many of the same powers in terms of personnel matters, such as appointing and expelling members from senior party bodies. However, the Party Conference differentiates itself from the Party Congress by not having to report a summary of activities to the Central Committee and the Central Auditing Committee. The Party Conference also does not have the authority to revise the Party Charter or rules.

But why the sudden focus on the party, which had become moribund since the Sixth Party Congress in 1980? Several theories were raised in Pyongyang watching circles. The first centered on the succession. Ever since Kim Chong-il had assumed the mantle of General Secretary in 1997 without convening a meeting of a leading party body, some within the North Korean leadership questioned his legitimacy as Kim Il-sung's successor. By restoring the party to its dominant position within the regime, an institutional framework would exist for the legitimate transfer of power. Kim's method of rule, the so-called hub and spoke, where he was the center of several formal and informal chains of command, would be nearly impossible to transfer to his son, especially given Kim Chong-un's age and political inexperience.[110] By surrounding his son with powerful and loyal members from his close aide network within the formal party apparatus, Kim Chong-il could enhance Chong-un's chances of surviving a near term transition. If this were done through a formal party gathering, legitimacy would automatically be conferred on the heir apparent and presumably could not easily be undone after Kim's death.

Another reason for resurrecting the party was related to the regime's plans for developing a strong and prosperous economy by 2012. Whether Kim believed this target was possible or not, it is clear that only the party had an apparatus that could reach down to the district and village level. If central planning was going to reach throughout the country, something that only the market forces had so far been able to achieve, the party would have to be the vehicle for delivery. A return to the way in which the economy had been run under Kim Il-sung, with the party assuming its rightful supervisory function, would be necessary.

As the summer came to a close, the promise of the party's resurgence led to one obvious question: Would Kim Chong-un make his first public appearance, thus sending the succession into its second phase? Since the summer of 2009, Kim Chong-un had allegedly been receiving reports to give him a broader situational awareness of the regime as part of an effort to establish a "monolithic leadership system by the party's center." He first began to receive reports from the KPA General Political Bureau, the State Security Department, and the Ministry of People's Security. These were sources of information controlled by Cho Myong-nok and Chang Song-taek. He began receiving reports from the Cabinet related to economic and foreign affairs in 2010. This led some to believe that at the upcoming Party Conference, he would receive one or more senior positions. Although there was some speculation that he might be appointed to the Politburo,[111] many Pyongyang watchers felt he would enter the KWP Secretariat as his father had done in the early 1970s when he became organizational secretary. In any case, the expectation from the Party Conference held that the regime would manifest itself as a limited duopoly with Kim Chong-il as the primary decision maker and Kim Chong-un as his chief aide.

FOLLOWING IN KIM IL-SUNG'S FOOTSTEPS
THROUGH CHINA

Talk of succession continued into August even though other topics dominated the headlines on North Korea, such as the unfolding drama surrounding former President Jimmy Carter's trip to Pyongyang to secure the release of an American teacher who was detained in January (2010) for illegally entering the country. Within 24 hours of Carter's arrival on August 25, the international media began to pick up reports that Kim Chong-il's train had once again entered China.

For his sixth trip to China since coming to power, Kim took a different route to ensure maximum secrecy. Instead of Dandong, his train crossed the border at the Manpo Railway Bridge that spans the Apnok (Yalu) River, bound for Jian in China's Jilin Province. It continued north past Jian and arrived in the city of Jilin 400 km away, where Chinese officials, including the director of the Chinese Communist Party's International Liaison Department Wang Jiarui, welcomed him. Kim then took a limousine to visit Yuwen Middle School, by the side of the Songhua River to the south of the city, which Kim Il-sung attended from 1927 to 1930. Finally, Kim arrived in Changchun, the capital of Jilin Province, where he met Hu Jintao.

Details of Kim's trip were kept private. From what little was revealed in the Chinese press, the meetings primarily focused on economic issues. Hu reiterated the need to facilitate economic exchanges, while Kim, in apparently a much more deferential mood than during his previous trip, expressed appreciation for China's economic achievements since opening and reform. Given the location of the summit, the talks most likely touched on Chinese investment along the Tumen River valley. Changchun and Jilin both utilize North Korea's Rajin Harbor as a link to maritime trade routes. This gave North Korea some leverage with China over the latter's plans to develop a "Pilot Zone" in the Tumen River valley specifically centered on the North Korean cities of Rajin and Chongjin. As such, Pyongyang watchers speculated that Kim was eager to establish specifics about Chinese investment and, if possible, speed up the economic cooperation process, using as a negotiating card the development of Rajin and Sonbong Harbor in North Korea, which were key factors in the success of the Pilot Zone's development.

Of course, given the recent announcement of the Third Party Conference, many rumors centered on whether Kim was seeking China's blessing for the succession. Widespread reports speculated that Kim Chong-un was accompanying his father,[112] but he did not appear in any of the media coverage and his name was not associated with any of the official events.[113] Chinese officials went out of their way to point out that Kim Chong-un "was not on the official list of Kim's entourage." That said, at a banquet in his honor hosted by the Chinese President, Kim reportedly said,

With the international situation remaining complicated, it is our important historical mission to hand over to the *rising generation* the baton of the traditional
friendship passed over by the revolutionary forerunners of the two countries as a
precious asset so as to carry it forward *through generations*.[114]

For Pyongyang watchers the references to "generations" were code
for the succession. Through this reference, Kim was signaling in an official setting his intention to proceed with another hereditary transfer of
power in the socialist country. If viewed in this light, this trip, which included a pilgrimage to sites considered holy in North Korea, was special
and went far beyond the Sino–North Korean relationship. As Kim Il-
sung had done decades before, Kim Chong-il was revealing to his son the
hallowed ground from which the fight for Korean independence was
waged.

LEAD UP TO THE THIRD PARTY CONFERENCE

While Kim was in China, the North Korean media reported on low-level
meetings of party delegations in the run-up to the Third Party Conference. According to KCNA, "The meetings were unanimous in saying that
the KWP Conference . . . will be a significant conference which will be a
landmark of an epochal turn in strengthening the party and a great jubi-
lee of great significance in ushering in a new surge in the revolution and
construction."

By early September, delegate elections to the conference were completed and preparations seemed to be finished. Propaganda surrounding
the conference was ubiquitous, far exceeding the campaigns associated
with the two previous (1958 and 1966) party conferences. Yet, as the days
of the month ticked off, many began to speculate on why the Third Party
Conference was delayed.[115] The reasons put forward seemed to run along
three lines.

- Kim's continuing health problems. This speculation contended that the 68-
  year-old Kim's health deteriorated after his trip to China.[116]
- Floods and other weather problems. In August, North Korea was hit by floods
  that wreaked severe damage in some border areas near China and caused an
  unspecified number of deaths. Then, on September 2, the Korean Peninsula
  was hit by Typhoon Kompasu. In the North, the storm destroyed 8,380 homes
  and 230 public buildings and severely damaged farmland, roads, railways,
  and power lines. Both events prevented provincial delegates from making
  their way to Pyongyang for the conference, thus making it impossible to reach
  a quorum. In addition, the regime was reluctant to hold the conference while
  the country was in such distress.[117]
- Power struggles and a lack of consensus over party appointments. Speculation along these lines was divided between Kim Chong-il's inability to form

a consensus around Kim Chong-un as the designated heir apparent, power struggles between key power brokers Chang Song-taek and O Kuk-yol,[118] and disagreements within the North Korean leadership over appointments to the Politburo.[119]

Without mentioning the reason for the delay, Chosun Central Broadcast, North Korea's state-run radio station, finally announced on September 21 that the Party Conference would take place on September 28. Asserting that preparations had gone off without a hitch, the conference organizing committee proclaimed that the election of delegates had been completed. And in a show of unanimity and foreshadowing of the proceedings to come, the committee noted that the delegate conferences from around the country had demonstrated their "boundless faith in the party . . . and spoke with one mind to select as a Chosun Workers' Party delegate the leader of our party and our military, great leader Comrade Kim Chong-il."[120]

Two days later, the regime carried out a high-profile reshuffle of the Ministry of Foreign Affairs. Timed to coincide with the upcoming Party Conference, the shift in diplomatic personnel highlighted the key themes in North Korean foreign policy, namely relations with the United States and the Six Party Talks. Two authoritative legislative "decrees" carried by state media announced that First Vice Foreign Minister Kang Sok-chu was promoted to cabinet vice premier, Vice Foreign Minister Kim Kye-kwan to first vice minister, and Foreign Ministry Councilor Ri Yong-ho to vice minister.

According to several Pyongyang watchers, the promotions were an effort to calm the international environment as North Korea proceeded through its succession process by signaling to domestic and foreign audiences the importance of foreign cooperation and diplomacy. For Pyongyang, tensions with Washington could dramatically impact stability within the leadership, something it did not want to have to contend with as it went through the delicate matter of reorienting the power dynamics within the party. By promoting three diplomats directly tied to U.S.–North Korean relations,[121] Pyongyang sought to dampen the constant drumbeat coming out of Washington about lack of movement by North Korea on denuclearization and the Six Party Talks.

Regardless of how interesting these appointments were for the Pyongyang watching community, they paled in comparison to the military appointments made public on September 27. In its first dispatch on the opening day of the Party Conference, 1:00 A.M. local time, KCNA announced that the Supreme Commander of the Korean People's Army Kim Chong-il issued Order No. 0051 on promoting the military ranks of commanding officers of the KPA. The order promoted Kim Kyong-hui, Kim Chong-un, Choe Ryong-hae, Hyon Yong-chol, Choe Pu-il, and Kim Kyong-ok to four-star generals.[122] For the first time, Kim Chong-un's name had appeared in the North Korean media.

The timing of the promotions and how they were handled not only made it clear that the upcoming Party Conference would be tied to the succession, but also seemed to highlight the rings of power within the regime.

- The first ring was the Kim family. The first two names listed among the promotions were Kim Kyong-hui (Kim Chong-il's sister) and Kim Chong-un (Kim Chong-il's son). The third name, Choe Ryong-hae, was the son of a former defense minister and a long-time aide to the Kim family with close ties to both Kim Chong-il and Chang Song-taek.[123]
- The second ring was the military. The fact that the military promotions preceded by one day the appointments of the Party Conference seemed to indicate the continued prominence of the military-first policy and the importance of the KPA to the stability and continuation of the regime.
- The third ring was the party. The Party Conference itself was an indication of the importance of the party's role. It was critical for the succession and the party's revitalization was necessary for the regime's survival beyond Kim Chong-il's death.

In terms of the succession, Kim Chong-il's strategy apparently was to surround his son with patronage networks along three axes so as not to make him vulnerable to any one regent or a collective leadership. Given enough time and skill at power politics, Kim Chong-un could build his own patronage system and ensure his own survival.

THE THIRD PARTY CONFERENCE

On September 28, the opening day of the Party Conference, Pyongyang was alive with activity. Under a bright blue sky, public spectacles could be found all over the city. Outdoor performances were staged at the Pyongyang Train Station and the Pyongyang Grand Theater, each drawing hundreds of spectators. Women dressed in fine clothes lined all the main thoroughfares and a forest of flags, banners, and placards gave the city a festive atmosphere.

Shortly before noon, Kim Chong-il entered the undisclosed assembly hall to the cheers and a standing ovation of the delegates. Walking toward the center of the rostrum, Kim took his seat, which faced the filled auditorium. Behind him was a large, marble statue of Kim Il-sung. In the front row of delegates, one seat in from the right aisle, was Kim Chong-un, who was dressed in a dark Mao suit and hairstyle reminiscent of photographs of his grandfather taken in the 1940s. Seated to the heir apparent's left was Hyon Chol-hae. Seated to his right were Kim Won-hong (commander of the Military Security Command), Kim Yong-chol (chief of the Reconnaissance General Bureau), and his aunt, Kim Kyong-hui.

Following an opening speech by Kim Yong-nam, the conference was declared open and the delegates stood to sing the "Song of Kim Il-sung." Kim Yong-nam then again took to the podium to deliver a speech regarding the election of Kim Chong-il as KWP General Secretary. Kim was followed by VMAR Ri Yong-ho, chief of the General Staff, who delivered a speech in his capacity as a representative of the party organization of the people's army. Several other speakers gave speeches, all expressing their support for the proposal to elect Kim Chong-il as KWP General Secretary and praising the Leader's past achievements. One hour after Kim Yong-nam's opening speech, the Party Conference unanimously supported the proposal.[124]

The Party Conference moved to the second item on the agenda, revising the Party Charter.[125] According to the KCNA, the resolution said that present reality called for revising the party rules so that "the KWP might be strengthened in every way and its leadership role further increased." Although the revised charter maintained in its preface a reference to the revolutionary principles of Marxism-Leninism,[126] it dropped the phrase "building a communist society" from the description of the party's ultimate goal. Instead, the goal was now to embody the revolutionary cause of *Chuche* (self-reliance) in the entire society. The Party Conference also took steps to smooth the hereditary transfer of power by increasing the flexibility surrounding the holding of party congresses. The new charter deleted the provision that a Party Congress had to be held every five years and replaced it with a provision stipulating that the Central Committee only needed to give a six-month notice for an upcoming Congress. This change would allow the party to deal more quickly with the unfolding demands of the succession without calling the process into question.

Probably more important, the Party Conference attempted to knit together military-first politics and the "Party Center" to create a sustainable leadership that would support the succession. The KWP Central Military Committee was newly defined as "organizing and leading all military operations." Furthermore, the new charter stipulated that the chairman of the commission would be concurrently held by the party's general secretary. This upgrade suggested that the party's military body would become a critical institution from which the heir apparent might consolidate his power, for the move would allow him to control both the party and the military when he eventually became general secretary. Finally, a reference to military-first politics was inserted into the charter, which now read that "the party will establish military-first politics as a basic political system of socialism."[127] For many Pyongyang watchers, this latter revision validated the transformation in the hierarchy of power from party-government-military that had existed under Kim Il-sung to the current party-military-government.

Having completed the revisions to the Party Charter, the conference moved to its last item of business, appointments to central leadership bodies. Key party positions, many of which had been vacant since the Sixth Party Congress, were filled in order to strengthen the party's leadership capacity and restore the party's status as a collective deliberating and decision-making institution. In particular, appointments were made to the Central Committee (increased from 151 to 229), Politburo (increased from 10 to 37), Secretariat (increased from 7 to 11), Central Military Committee (increased from 12 to 19), Central Committee departments,[128] Central Auditing Commission,[129] and Control Commission.[130]

POLITBURO

The Politburo Presidium was reconstituted, having been reduced over the years to just Kim Chong-il. Joining Kim were Kim Yong-nam (President of the SPA Presidium), Choe Yong-rim (Premier), VMAR Cho Myong-nok (director of the KPA General Political Bureau), and VMAR Ri Yong-ho (chief of the General Staff). The presence of two military officers on the party's highest decision-making body was a clear indicator of Kim Chong-il's strategy to tie the concept of the Party Center to military-first politics. Ri Yong-ho's appointment was particularly interesting because he was believed by many Pyongyang watchers to be serving as a military escort for the heir apparent, much as O Chin-u had done for Kim Chong-il.[131]

The appointments to the Politburo did not constitute a generational shift as many had expected. The average age of the 37 members was 74, with 12 being in their 80s. The youngest member was 53. Most of the appointments were drawn from Kim's inner circle of close aides and family. Kim Kyong-hui was made a full member, and Chang Song-taek became an alternate member, further backing speculation that they would serve as patrons to their nephew. Several of Chang Song-taek's protégés were also made members and alternate members, such as the minister of People's Security Chu Sang Song; the first vice director of the SSD U Tong-chuk; and Choe Ryong-hae, the new KWP secretary for military affairs. Pak Chong-sun, first vice director of the KWP Organization Guidance Department and reportedly one of the facilitators of the Kim Chong-un succession, was also made an alternate member.

Most of the Politburo membership was composed of party secretaries, senior Cabinet officials, and members of the military and security establishment. Ten members of the National Defense Commission were appointed to the Politburo,[132] as were three vice premiers. Key figures tied to the economy (Hong Sok-hyong and Tae Chong-su) and foreign affairs (Kang Sok-chu, Kim Yong-il, and Kim Yang-kon) were also brought into this senior party body in order to inform future deliberations.

Table 6.3
Politburo Membership

Name	Age	Positions	Comments[a]
Presidium			
Kim Chong-il	68	General Secretary	
Kim Yong-nam	82	President of the SPA Presidium	After graduating from a university, he worked as a teacher at the Central Party School, vice department director of the KWP Central Committee, vice minister of Foreign Affairs, and first vice department director, department director and secretary of the KWP Central Committee, vice premier of the Administration Council and concurrently minister of Foreign Affairs. He has worked as president of the Presidium of the Supreme People's Assembly since September of Chuche 87 (1998).
Choe Yong-rim	80	Premier	After graduating from university with a degree in economics, he worked as an instructor, section chief, vice department director, first vice department director and department director of the KWP Central Committee and chief secretary of the Secretaries Office of the Kumsusan Assembly Hall. He then held posts of vice premier of the Administration Council, director of the Central Public Prosecutors Office and secretary general of the SPA Presidium. He worked as chief secretary of the KWP Pyongyang City Committee until he was appointed as premier of the Cabinet in June Chuche 99 (2010).

(continued)

Table 6.3 *(Continued)*

Name	Age	Positions	Comments[a]
Cho Myong-nok	82	First Vice NDC Chairman, Director KPA General Political Bureau	He joined the KPA in December of Chuche 39 (1950). After graduating from the Aviation School, he worked as battalion commander, regimental commander, divisional commander, chief of staff and commander of the KPA Air Force, and director of the General Political Bureau. He was appointed first vice chairman of the NDC in February of Chuche 98 (2009).
Ri Yong-ho	68	Chief of the General Staff	He joined the KPA in August Chuche 48 (1959). After graduation from Kim Il-sung Military University, he worked as chief of staff of a division, director of the operations department of an army corps, head of a training center, vice director of the operations department of the General Staff, its deputy chief, head of a KPA training center, and commander of the Pyongyang Defense Command. He was appointed chief of the General Staff in February of Chuche 98 (2009).
Full Members			
Kim Yong-chun	74	Vice Chairman of the NDC, Minister of People's Armed Forces	After graduation from Kim Il-sung Military University, he held the posts of deputy director of the operations department of an army corps, chief of staff and director of the Reconnaissance Bureau of the General Staff, deputy chief of the General Staff and director of the Operations Bureau, head of a training

(continued)

150

Table 6.3   (*Continued*)

Name	Age	Positions	Comments[a]
			center, director of the General Bureau for Munitions Mobilization, commander of the Sixth Army Corps, chief of the General Staff, and vice chairman of the NDC. He was appointed minister of the People's Armed Forces in February of Chuche 98 (2009).
Chon Pyong-ho	74	Member of NDC	He joined the Worker-Peasant Red Guards in October Chuche 34 (1945). After graduating from university with a degree in engineering, he worked as deputy chief engineer of Factory No. 26, department director of the State Planning Commission, chief engineer of the Kanggye Tractor Plant, vice department director and department director of a CC department, vice chairman, first vice chairman, chief party secretary, and chairman of the Second Economy Commission, secretary and department director of the KWP Munitions Department. He worked as director of the Political Bureau of the Cabinet and chief secretary of its party committee since September of Chuche 99 (2010).
Kim Kuk-tae	86	Chairman, KWP Control Commission	After graduating from the Higher Party School, he worked as instructor, section chief, vice department director and director of a KWP department, vice director of the General Political Bureau

(*continued*)

Table 6.3 *(Continued)*

Name	Age	Positions	Comments[a]
Kim Kuk-tae *(continued)*			of the Korean People's Army, director of the Political Bureau of the Ministry of Public Security, director of Kim Il-sung Higher Party School, and director of the KWP Cadres Department. He was appointed chairman of the Central Committee's Control Commission in September Chuche 99 (2010).
Kim Ki-nam	81	KWP Secretary	See below.
Choe Tae-pok	80	KWP Secretary	See below.
Yang Hyong-sop	85	Vice President of the SPA	After graduating from Kim Il-sung University, he held the posts of instructor, section chief of the KWP Central Committee, director of the Central Party School, minister of Higher Education, KWP Secretary, president of the Academy of Social Sciences, chairman of the SPA Standing Committee. He was appointed vice president of the Presidium of the SPA in September of Chuche 87 (1998).
Kang Sok-chu	71	Vice Premier	After graduating from university, he worked as instructor of the Ministry of Foreign Affairs, instructor and section chief of the KWP Central Committee, vice minister and first vice minister of Foreign Affairs. He was appointed vice premier of the Cabinet in September of Chuche 99 (2010.)
Pyon Yong-rip	81	Secretary General of SPA Presidium	After graduating from Kim Il-sung University with a degree in physics, he worked

(continued)

Table 6.3   (*Continued*)

Name	Age	Positions	Comments[a]
			as a department head at the university, director of a department of the Ministry of Higher Education, first vice department director of the Education Commission, vice president of the State Academy of Sciences, minister of Education and president of the State Academy of Sciences. He was appointed secretary general of the Presidium of the SPA in July of Chuche 98 (2009).
Ri Yong-mu	85	Vice Chairman of the NDC	He joined the Central Guard Battalion in June Chuche 36 (1947). After graduation from Second Central Political School, he worked as an instructor of the KPA General Political Bureau, director of the political department and commander of an army division, section chief and deputy director of the organizational department of the GPB and its first vice director and director, chairman of the State Control Commission, director of the Political Bureau of the Ministry of Public Security, chairman and concurrently director of the Political Bureau of the Transport Commission. He was appointed vice chairman of the National Defense Commission in September of Chuche 87 (1998).
Chu Sang Song	77	Member of the NDC, Minister of People's Security	He joined the KPA in June of Chuche 40 (1951). After graduating from Kim Il-sung Military University he worked

(*continued*)

Table 6.3 *(Continued)*

Name	Age	Positions	Comments[a]
Chu Sang Song *(continued)*			as senior operations staff officer of an army corps, brigade commander, divisional commander, chief of staff of regional headquarters, commander of the Fourth Corps, and inspector of the General Staff. He was appointed minister of People's Security in July of Chuche 93 (2004). In March 2011, he stepped down from the MPS post "for health reasons."[b]
Hong Sok-hyong	74	KWP Secretary	See below.
Kim Kyong-hui		Director, KWP Light Industry Department	Her profile was the only one not included in the list of Politburo portfolios published by the North Korean media.
Alternate Members			
Kim Yong-gon	68	KWP Secretary	See below.
Kim Yong-il	63	KWP Secretary	See below.
Pak To-chun	66	KWP Secretary	See below.
Choe Ryong-hae	60	KWP Secretary	See below.
Chang Song-taek	64	Vice Chairman of NDC, Director of KWP Administrative Department	After graduating from Kim Il-sung University, he worked as instructor of the KWP Pyongyang City Committee and instructor, deputy section chief, section chief, vice department director, first vice department director, and department director of the KWP Organization Guidance Department. He was first vice director of the KWP Capital Construction Department and director of the KWP Administrative Department. He was

(continued)

Table 6.3 (*Continued*)

Name	Age	Positions	Comments[a]
			appointed vice chairman of the NDC in June Chuche 99 (2010).
Chu Kyu-chang	82	Member of the NDC, Director of the KWP Military Industry Department (aka Machine Industry Department)	After graduating from university with a degree in mechanical engineering, he worked as vice president, first vice president, and president of the Academy of National Defence Science, vice department director of the KWP Military Industry Department, chairman of the Second Economy Commission, president of the Second Academy of Natural Science and first vice department director of the KWP Military Industry Department. He was appointed director of the KWP Military Industry Department in September Chuche 99 (2010).
Ri Tae-nam	72	Vice Premier	He graduated from Pyongyang University of Mechanical Engineering with a degree in engineering. He worked as head of a workshop of the Coal Mining Machine Plant, instructor, deputy section chief, and section chief of the KWP Central Committee, chief secretary of the Party Committee of the Kangson Steel Complex, chairman of the Nampho City Administrative and Economic Committee, chief secretary of the Party Committee of the Hwanghae Iron and Steel Complex, and chief secretary of the KWP provincial committee. He was appointed vice premier of the Cabinet in June Chuche 99 (2010).

(*continued*)

Table 6.3   *(Continued)*

Name	Age	Positions	Comments[a]
Kim Rak-hui	77	Vice Premier	After graduating from the University of National Economics, she worked as management board chairwoman of a cooperative farm, chairwoman of a county cooperative farm management committee, chairwoman of a provincial rural economy committee, vice department director of the KWP Central Committee, and chief secretary of the KWP South Hwanghae Provincial Committee. She was appointed vice premier of the Cabinet in June Chuche 99 (2010).
Thae Chong-su	74	KWP Secretary, Director of KWP General Department	See below.
Kim Pyong-hae	69	KWP Secretary	See below.
U Tong-chuk	68	First Vice Director of the SSD	After graduating from Kim Il-sung University with a degree in philosophy, he worked as instructor and deputy section chief of the KWP Central Committee and department director and vice minister of State Security. He was appointed first vice director of State Security in September Chuche 98 (2009).
Kim Chong-gak	69	Member of the NDC, First Vice Director of the General Political Bureau	Joined the People's Army in August Chuche 48 (1959). After graduating from Kim Il-sung Military University, he served as a battalion commander, deputy commander of an army corps, chief of staff and head of a training center and

(continued)

Table 6.3   (*Continued*)

Name	Age	Positions	Comments[a]
			vice minister of the People's Armed Forces. He was appointed first vice director of the KPA General Political Bureau in March Chuche 96 (2007).
Pak Chong-sun	82	First Vice Director of the KWP Organization Guidance Department	Joined the People's Army in July Chuche 39 (1950). After graduating from the Central Party School, he worked as vice department director of a county party committee, instructor of a provincial party committee, chief instructor of the KWP Central Committee, second secretary of the KWP South Hamg-yong Provincial Commit-tee, section chief and vice department director of the KWP Central Committee, organizational secretary of the KWP Pyongyang City Committee, and vice depart-ment director and director of a KWP Department. He was appointed first vice director of the KWP Organi-zation Guidance Department in September Chuche 99 (2010).
Kim Chang-sop	64	Director of SSD Political Bureau	Joined the People's Army in July Chuche 52 (1963). After graduating from Kim Il-sung Higher Party School, he worked as instructor, chief in-structor, and deputy section chief of the KWP Central Com-mittee and vice director of State Security and vice director of its Political Bureau. He was appointed director of the SSD

(*continued*)

Table 6.3 (*Continued*)

Name	Age	Positions	Comments[a]
Kim Chang-sop (*continued*)			Political Bureau in August Chuche 98 (2009).
Mun Kyong-dok	53	KWP Secretary, Chief Secretary of the KWP Pyongyang City Committee	See below.

[a] Most of the comments are taken from the KCNA profiles of the Politburo membership published on 29 September 2010.

[b] "Minister of People's Security Dismissed 'Due to Illness,'" KCNA, 16 March 2011.

SECRETARIAT

The traditional center of Kim Chong-il's power and influence, the Secretariat, had over the years dwindled to seven members, having suffered the deaths of five secretaries since the 21st Plenum of the Sixth Party Congress in 1993. Four holdovers from the previous Secretariat (Kim Chong-il, Kim Ki-nam, Choe Tae-pok, and Hong Sok-hyong) were joined by seven new appointees—four from the provinces and three professional bureaucrats who had for years served in the Central Committee apparatus.

Within this reinvigorated Secretariat, Kim Ki-nam retained the portfolio for propaganda and Choe Tae-pok continued to oversee international affairs. Kim Yong-il, the director of the KWP International Department, was promoted to support Choe Tae-pok, focusing primarily on China. Kim Yong-gon, the director of the KWP United Front Department, would handle affairs toward the South. The newly minted four-star general Choe Ryong-hae assumed responsibility for military affairs, and Pak To-chun replaced Chon Pyong-ho as secretary for the defense industrial complex. Hyong Sok-hyong, Pak Nam-gi's successor as head of finance, and Tae Chong-su split the portfolio for the economy. Finally, Mun Kyong-tok, the youngest member of the Secretariat and a close associate of both Chang Song-taek and Choe Yong-rim, would oversee the day-to-day operations of the capital city.

CENTRAL MILITARY COMMITTEE

The last public listing of the KWP Central Military Committee was at the 21st Plenum of the Sixth Party Congress in 1993.[133] Of the 17 members, only 6 remained at the time of the Third Party Conference. Such first-generation revolutionaries as O Chin-u and Choe Kwang had passed

Table 6.4
Secretariat Membership

Name	Age	Positions	Comments[a]
Kim Chong-il	68	General Secretary	
Kim Ki-nam	81	KWP Secretary for Propaganda	After graduating from university with a degree in economics, he worked as a teacher and a dean of a faculty of Kim Il-sung University, vice director of a KWP department, editor-in-chief of *Nodong Sinmun,* first vice director of a KWP department, director of the KWP Propaganda Department, and KWP Secretary for Propaganda. He was appointed KWP Secretary for Propaganda and director of the KWP Information and Publicity Department in May, Chuche 99 (2010).
Choe Tae-pok	80	KWP Secretary for International Affairs	After graduating from university, he worked as a teacher, a dean of a faculty, president of Kim Chaek University of Technology, chairman of the Education Commission and minister of Higher Education. He was appointed KWP Secretary for International Affairs in December of Chuche 75 (1986).
Choe Ryong-hae		KWP Secretary for Military Affairs	After graduating from Kim Il-sung University with a degree in economics, he worked as vice department director, department director, and vice chairman of the League of Socialist Working Youth of Korea, first secretary of the Kim Il-sung Socialist Youth League, vice director of a KWP department, and chief secretary of the North Hwanghae Provincial Party Committee. He was appointed KWP Secretary for Military Affairs in September Chuche 99 (2010).

(continued)

Table 6.4 *(Continued)*

Name	Age	Positions	Comments[a]
Mun Kyong-dok	53	KWP Secretary for Pyongyang Affairs	After graduating from Kim Il-sung University with a degree in political economics, he worked as instructor of the KWP Pyongyang City Committe, vice chairman of the Central Committee's League of Socialist Working Youth of Korea, director of the Guidance Bureau No. 2, vice director of a KWP department, and chief secretary of the KWP Pyongyang City Committee. He was appointed KWP secretary and chief secretary of the KWP Pyongyang City Committee in September Chuche 99 (2010).
Pak To-chun		KWP Secretary for Defense Industry	After graduating from Kim Il-sung Higher Party School, he worked as secretary of a party committee for a mine, instructor, deputy section chief, and section chief of the KWP Central Committee, secretary and department director of a provincial party committee, and chief secretary of the Jagang Provincial Party Committee. He was appointed KWP Secretary for Defense Industry in September Chuche 99 (2010).
Kim Yong-il		KWP Secretary for International Affairs	After graduating from the University of International Relations, he worked as instructor of the KWP Central Committee, director and vice minister of Foreign Affairs, and KWP department director. He was appointed KWP Secretary for International Affairs and director of KWP International Affairs Department in September Chuche 99 (2010).
Kim Yang-kon		KWP Secretary for South Korean Affairs	After graduating from Kim Il-sung University with a degree in French literature, he became an instructor

(continued)

Table 6.4 (*Continued*)

Name	Age	Positions	Comments[a]
			in the KYSWL Central Commitee and instructor, section chief, vice director of the KWP International Department, and director of the KWP United Front Department. He was appointed KWP Secretary for South Korean Affairs and director of the KWP United Front Department in September Chuche 99 (2010).
Kim Pyong-hae		KWP Secretary for Personnel	After graduating from a university of education, he worked as instructor, section chief, and vice department director of a provincial party committee, instructor
			of the KWP Central Committee, department director and organizational secretary of a provincial party committee and chief secretary of the North Phyongan Provincial Party Committee. He was appointed KWP Secretary for Personnel in September Chuche 99 (2010).
Thae Chong-su	74	KWP Secretary for General Affairs	After graduating from university with a degree in engineering, he worked as school inspector of the Ministry of Common Education, instructor and section chief of the KWP Central Committee, secretary of a party provincial committee, manager of a machine-building factory, minister of Shipbuilding Industry, chief secretary of the party committee of the Taean Heavy Machine Complex, vice premier of the Cabinet, chief secretary of the South Hamgyong Provincial Party Committee, and KWP department director. He was appointed KWP Secretary for General Affairs and director of

(*continued*)

Table 6.4 (*Continued*)

Name	Age	Positions	Comments[a]
Thae Chong-su (*continued*)			the KWP General Affairs Department in September Chuche 99 (2010).
Hong Sok-hyong		KWP Secretary for Finance	After graduating from university with a degree in engineering, he worked as vice chief engineer for technical affairs of the Songjin Steel Works, first vice minister of Metal Industry, chief engineer of the Kim Chaek Iron and Steel Complex, second secretary and chief secretary of the party committee of the North Hamgyong Provincial Party Committee, chairman of the State Planning Commission, chief secretary of a provincial party committee, and director a KWP department. He was appointed director of the KWP Finance and Planning Depart-ment and KWP Secretary for Finance in September of Chuche 99 (2010). In 2011, at an "enlarged meeting of the Politburo," Hong Sok-hyong was relieved of this post "in connection with his transfer to another post."

[a] Most of the comments are taken from the KCNA profiles of the Politburo membership published on 29 September 2010.

away; others had been quietly retired or been removed from direct implementation of the party's military policies.

The Third Party Conference dramatically overhauled the Central Military Committee, boosting its membership to 19. The most significant move was the appointment of Kim Chong-un and Ri Yong-ho as vice chairmen. Other than membership in the Central Committee, this was the heir apparent's only official title, lending credence to the speculation that the succession was being firmly nested within the party apparatus, but tied to military-first politics.

The other appointments to the Central Military Committee seemed designed to both formalize the regime's control networks within the armed forces, and give Kim Chong-un access to a variety of patronage systems that could assist him in consolidating his power. In terms of operational lines of control, the new membership included the minister of People's

Table 6.5
Central Military Committee Membership

Name	Position	Comment
MAR Kim Chong-il	Chairman	Chairman of the NDC, Supreme Commander of the Armed Forces. Based on the recently revised Party Charter, the General Secretary also held the position of Chairman of the CMC.
Gen. Kim Chong-un	Vice Chairman	Member of the Central Committee. Rumored to have positions in the SSD and NDC.
VMAR Ri Yong-ho	Vice Chairman	Chief of the General Staff. Military escort for the heir apparent
VMAR Kim Yong-chun	Member	Minister of People's Armed Forces, Vice Chairman of the NDC
Gen. Kim Chong-gak	Member	First Vice Director of the KPA General Political Bureau, Member of the NDC[a]
Gen. Kim Myong-guk	Member	Director of the General Staff's Operational Bureau
Gen. Kim Kyong-ok	Member	First Vice Director of the KWP Organization Guidance Department[b]
Gen. Kim Won-hong	Member	Commander of the Military Security Command
ADM Chong Myong-do	Member	Commander of the KPA Navy
Gen. Ri Pyong-chol	Member	Commander of the KPA Air Force
Gen. Choe Pu-il	Member	Deputy Chief of the General Staff[c]
Lt. Gen. Kim Yong-chol	Member	Director of the Reconnaissance General Bureau[d]
Gen. Yun Chong-rin	Member	Commander, Guard Command
Chu Kyu-chang	Member	Member of the NDC, Director of the KWP Munitions Industry Department
Col. Gen. Choe Sang-ryo	Member	Commander of an Artillery Division
Col. Gen. Choe Kyong-song	Member	Chief of the Training Unit Guidance Bureau
Gen. U Tong-chuk	Member	Member of the NDC, First Vice Director of the SSD

(continued)

Table 6.5 *(Continued)*

Name	Position	Comment
Gen. Choe Ryong-hae	Member	KWP Secretary for Military Affairs
Chang Song-taek	Member	Vice Chairman of the NDC, KWP Director of Administrative Affairs

[a] Indications began to surface in January 2011 that Kim Chong-gak had succeeded Cho Myong-nok as director of the General Political Bureau. The position had been vacant since Cho's death in November.

[b] Gen. Kim Myong-guk presumably has responsibility for military affairs within the Organization Guidance Department.

[c] A former member of the North Korean national basketball team, Gen. Choe reportedly is close to both Kim Chong-il and Kim Chong-un.

[d] A hardliner with ties to the Kim family, Kim Yong-chol was the alleged mastermind behind the sinking of the *Cheonan*.

Armed Forces (VMAR Kim Yong-chun), chief of the General Staff's Operations Bureau (Gen. Kim Myong-guk), the commanders of the Air Force and Navy (Gen. Ri Pyong-chol and ADM Chong Myong-do), the heads of important special forces units (Lt. Gen. Kim Yong-chol and Col. Gen. Choe Kyong-song), and key members of the General Staff (Gen. Choe Pu-il and Col. Gen. Choe Sang-ryo). Other members held military and security portfolios within the party apparatus, including Gen. Choe Ryong-hae (KWP Secretary for Military Affairs), Chu Kyu-chang (director of the KWP Munitions Industry Department),[134] Chang Song-taek (director of the KWP Administrative Department), and Gen. Kim Kyong-ok (first vice director of the KWP Organization Guidance Department). The four remaining members (Gen. Kim Chong-gak, Gen. Kim Won-hong, Gen. Yun Chong-rin, and Gen. U Tong-chuk) held important internal security-related portfolios.

CONCLUSION

The Third Party Conference was a watershed in modern-day North Korean politics. It formalized a shift in leadership dynamics that had been taking place in the shadows for nearly two years. From this point on, elite politics was no longer centered on just one person. Another formal center of power was born. In more practical terms, the conference was noteworthy for a variety of reasons.

First, it established the formal ranking of power as the regime moved into the second phase of the succession. North Korean reporting over the course of several events following the conference suggested that Kim Chong-un was ranked fifth within the leadership,[135] behind only his father,

Table 6.6
Third Party Conference Leadership List

Rank	Name	Party Position	Other Positions
1	Kim Chong-il	General Secretary	Chairman of the NDC
2	Kim Yong-nam	Politburo Presidium Member	SPA Presidium President
3	Choe Yong-rim	Politburo Presidium Member	Premier
4	Ri Yong-ho	Politburo Presidium Member	Vice Chairman of the KWP Central Military Committee, Chief of the KPA General Staff
5	Kim Chong-un[a]	Politburo Presidium Member	Vice Chairman of the KWP Central Military Committee
6	Ri Ul-sol	CC Member	
7	Kim Chol-man	CC Member	
8	Kim Yong-chun	Politburo Member	NDC Vice Chairman, Minister of People's Armed Forces
9	Chon Pyong-ho	Politburo Member	NDC Member, Director of Cabinet Political Bureau
10	Kim Kuk-tae	Politburo Member	Chairman of CC Control Commission
11	Kim Ki-nam	Politburo Member	KWP Secretary for Propaganda
12	Choe Tae-bok	Politburo Member	KWP Secretary for International Affairs
13	Yang Hyong-sop	Politburo Member	SPA Presidium Vice President
14	Kang Sok-chu	Politburo Member	Vice Premier
15	Pyon Yong-nip	Politburo Member	SPA Secretary General
16	Ri Yong-mu	Politburo Member	NDC Vice Chairman
17	Chu Sang-song	Politburo Member	NDC Member, Minister of People's Security
18	Hong Sok-hyong	Politburo Member	KWP Secretary for Finance
19	Kim Kyong-hui	Politburo Member	Director of KWP Light Industry Department

(*continued*)

Table 6.6 *(Continued)*

Rank	Name	Party Position	Other Positions
20	Kim Yang-gon	Politburo Alternate Member	KWP Secretary, Director of KWP United Front Department
21	Kim Yong-il	Politburo Alternate Member	KWP Secretary, Director of KWP International Department
22	Pak To-chun	Politburo Alternate Member	KWP Secretary
23	Choe Ryong-hae	Politburo Alternate Member	KWP Secretary
24	Chang Song-taek	Politburo Alternate Member	NDC Vice Chairman, Director KWP Administrative Department
25	Chu Kyu-chang	Politburo Alternate Member	NDC Member, Director of KWP Munitions Department
26	Ri Tae-nam	Politburo Alternate Member	Vice Premier
27	Kim Rak-hui	Politburo Alternate Member	Vice Premier
28	Thae Chong-su	Politburo Alternate Member	KWP Secretary, Director of KWP General Department
29	Kim Pyong-hae	Politburo Alternate Member	KWP Secretary, Director of KWP Personnel Department
30	U Tong-chuk	Politburo Alternate Member	NDC Member, First Vice Director of SSD
31	Kim Chong-gak	Politburo Alternate Member	NDC Member, First Vice Director of KPA General Political Bureau
32	Pak Chong-sun[b]	Politburo Alternate Member	First Vice Director of KWP Organization Guidance Department

(continued)

Table 6.6   (*Continued*)

Rank	Name	Party Position	Other Positions
33	Kim Chang-sop	Politburo Alternate Member	Director of SSD Political Bureau
34	Mun Kyong-dok	Politburo Alternate Member	KWP Secretary, Pyong-yang Municipal Party Secretary

[a] By March 2011, Kim Chong-un had moved past Ri Yong-ho and Choe Yong-rim into third in the rankings of the North Korean leadership.

[b] Pak Chong-sun died in March 2011.

Supreme People's Assembly Presidium President Kim Yong-nam, Cabinet Premier Choe Yong-rim, and Chief of the General Staff Ri Yong-ho.[136]

Second, it reoriented the leadership structure in preparation for the upcoming succession by distributing power from Kim Chong-il's one-man control structure to a collective guidance system based on core groups and loyalists with alternate ties to the Kim family. Instead of the hub-and-spoke architecture of the Kim Chong-il era, where he was the sole lynch pin, key lines of control now ran through several members of the Kim family, including Kim Kyong-hui, Chang Song-taek, and even the heir apparent, Kim Chong-un. How this web of relationships evolves over the coming months and years will largely determine who eventually comes out on top as the real source of power in Pyongyang.

Third, it transferred the focus of military-first (*songun*) politics from the National Defense Commission to the party. Ten members of the NDC were now members of the Politburo and four occupied positions on the Party's Central Military Committee. By making Kim Chong-un a vice chairman of the CMC and pulling from the NDC those members with close ties to the heir apparent and giving them additional posts within the party, the Third Party Congress signaled the return of the party as the seat of military decision making.

In the months following the conference, the succession continued apace. Politburo members Cho Myong-nok and Pak Chong-sun died, leaving Pyongyang watchers to wrestle with the implications. On November 23, the campaign to build the legitimacy around Kim Chong-un seemingly began in earnest with the shelling of Yeonpyeong Island, a South Korean island situated along the disputed Northern Limit Line. This provocation increased the tensions on the peninsula and, according to some sources, brought accolades to the heir apparent, who less than an month later was being referred to by *Nodong Sinmun* as "respected general" (*chongyo'nghanu'n taejang*) instead of "young general" (*ch'o'ngnyo'n taejang*).

At the time of this writing in February 2011, the drama of the Party Conference and the shelling of Yeonpyeong have been replaced by more mundane succession-related events, such as the regime's apparent recognition of Kim Chong-un's birth date (January 8), moving him closer to the cult status of his father and grandfather. Pyongyang watchers continue to read the tea leaves of who is standing next to whom and puzzle over the fact that Kim Chong-un is now wearing an otter fur cap like his father. But expectations of future internal turmoil and foreign provocations persist. Provided there is no dramatic change in Kim Chong-il's health, Kim Chong-un will continue to engage in a campaign to both build his legitimacy as a leader and remove all sources of opposition in the lead up to the final, third, phase of the succession, which will likely begin in 2012, the 100th anniversary of Kim Il-sung's birth.

CHAPTER 7

Challenges for the Future

As the succession moves closer to its concluding third phase, Pyongyang watchers will expect to see the gradual shift in day-to-day control of the regime from Kim Chong-il to Kim Chong-un. The heir apparent will begin to gain a greater situational awareness of regime operations. He will begin to receive powerful posts, such as Supreme Commander. He will be elevated to the exalted councils of power, such as the Politburo Presidium. In time, he will begin to carve out his own role as a leader both on the domestic and foreign policy fronts. He will begin to conduct publicized inspections around the country on his own. He will travel without his father to China to begin the process of developing a relationship with the Chinese leadership. All the while, Kim Chong-il, if the process goes according to plan, will begin to fade into the background. Upon his death, the regime will undergo a three-year mourning period capped off by a gathering of party delegates at either a Party Congress or some other party venue to confer the title of General Secretary on Kim Chong-un.

This is one scenario of North Korea's future. It is not the only scenario. In 2011, it is unclear whether it is even the most likely scenario. There is a range of scenarios beyond a peaceful dynastic transfer of power, including, although unlikely in the near term, regime collapse. Much will depend on Kim Chong-il's health, the political skills of the young heir, and the ambitions and agendas of the inner circle of elites surrounding the Kim family. In the longer term, beyond the succession, stability will depend on the regime's ability to control society and manage a crumbling economy.

Merle Fainsod, one of the fathers of Kremlinology and a gifted practitioner of leadership analysis once wrote,

A totalitarian system on the march often gives the impression of remorseless and overpowering strength. Its weaknesses become fully apparent only after its downfall.[1]

The North Korean regime has survived the vicissitudes of 65 years of revolution, war, internal turmoil, famine, and international sanctions. It has also confounded numerous Pyongyang watchers, who have for two decades predicted its collapse.

But what does the future hold? Is the regime, as many believe, growing weaker as each succeeding Kim is a paler shade of the one who came before him? Is Kim Chong-un or whatever leadership configuration eventually emerges from this succession process destined to be weaker than Kim Chong-il, to say nothing of Kim Il-sung? Or is the regime capable of change in a manner that will ensure its long-term survival? Any prediction of the future is a hazardous enterprise, but as Fainsod also noted, the shape of the future is contained in the past, both in the limits it enjoins and the potentialities it unfolds. This final chapter will consider the prospects and challenges facing North Korea in the post–Kim Chong-il era. It will examine the boundaries within which the regime will have to operate and what this might mean for the leadership and policy-making dynamics.

THE LEADER-CENTRIC SYSTEM

Kim Chong-il sees North Korea, its leadership and policies, through the context of the unitary guidance system. This is the method of control that he helped establish in the late 1960s and 1970s and it is the system through which he has ruled the country for nearly two decades. By virtue of being the sole interpreter of the regime's ideology, Kim has created a ruling system that is completely dependent on the Leader. While Kim Il-sung was alive, this system, which maximizes the role of the leader to the exclusion of all else, was able to retain the form of a traditional communist system. The party was the leading body through which decisions were made and policies were executed.

As Kim Il-sung stepped into the shadows in the early 1990s as the succession process moved into its third phase, the chains of command within the regime structure began to transform to embrace Kim Chong-il's leadership style. The National Defense Commission, of which Kim became chairman in 1993, began to grow in importance, supplanting the party's Politburo as the predominant leadership body by 1998. The party became one of three branches of leadership, existing alongside the military and Cabinet. In this way, the ability of the Leader to micromanage the system became maximized. All paths of authority led back to a single point, Kim Chong-il's personal secretariat. The Leader's perceptions and belief system continued to drive every aspect of the regime.

At the Third Party Conference, it appears as if Kim has tried to restructure the regime in such a way that his successor, Kim Chong-un, will be able to rule unencumbered to the greatest extent possible. The three branches of leadership have been largely consolidated back into one with the party once again taking the unassailable lead. The party's leadership bodies have been stripped of their dead wood and filled with close supporters of the Kim family. And in an effort to head off any debate about the legitimacy of another hereditary succession, the Party Charter has been revised to reflect the party's central role in overseeing the transfer of power to a new generation.

Despite the considerable efforts to ensure a smooth succession, much still needs to be done. Although the party has been reinvigorated and filled with supporters, Kim Chong-un's control over the instruments of raw power will take time. He has been made a four star general and vice chairman of the KWP Central Military Committee. The CMC appears to have replaced the NDC as the principal organization for ensuring the Leader's unified command and control system over the military and security forces. It is only in this body where all of the key nodes of the country's national security apparatus reside. But, before Kim Chong-un can exert his control in this arena and assume the position of Supreme Commander, he will have to develop his own dedicated reporting system, something that Kim Chong-il will prevent from happening too quickly lest it undermine his own position.

In terms of stability, the Third Party Conference has most likely placed the succession on a more sure footing. It has given the heir apparent a fighting chance to succeed in the event of Kim Chong-il's medium-term (two to five years) demise by reducing the likelihood of two of the previously likely crisis scenarios: marginalization of the designated successor by a collective leadership and rise of a military strongman. By dispersing power along several axes radiating from the Kim family, it will be more difficult for a "side branch" of the family to eliminate Kim Chong-un. The longer Kim Chong-il lives, the greater Kim Chong-un's power will grow at the expense of likely regents such as Chang Song-taek and Kim Kyong-hui. In the near term (one to two years), however, the Conference has only given Kim Chong-un legitimacy, but no insulation from a regent/military strongman or a collective leadership bent on ousting him or turning him into a figurehead. As mentioned above, the North Korean regime is based on a leader-centric paradigm where skill in the use of power is at a premium—no place for a young inexperienced heir who may be perceived as a pretender to the throne.

Though elite dynamics may be the main source of instability in the near future, the regime's long term survival depends on its ability to deal with the various pressures building up on the regime, both from the inside and from afar. It is with this hurdle that Kim Chong-un and the post–Kim Chong-il leadership will face its greatest challenge.

At present, the regime is still able to control the country, but its ability to function in terms of meeting the social and economic needs of the population is sluggish and highly inefficient. As the regime grows weaker in terms of the economy, the leadership's priorities have shifted from trying to deal with the problem to ensuring the stability of the regime. Reform has given way to enhanced internal security measures and a reinstitution of centralized planning. This accounts for the recent amendment to the rules changing the party's imminent objective from "complete victory of socialism in the northern half of the Republic" to "construction of a powerful socialist state;" a change that reflects the reality that economic revival cannot be achieved in a short time, definitely not by 2012, and therefore must take a subordinate position in the list of priorities to regime stability. As one North Korean defector noted, "in North Korea, the notion of building a 'powerful socialist state' does not mean our style of socialism leads to a powerful state, but that having a powerful state is precisely our style of socialism."

This being the case, a post–Kim Chong-il leadership will find it very difficult to resurrect economic reform for the foreseeable future. Any leader, be it Kim Chong-un or a member of a collective leadership, will be reluctant in the months and possibly years after Kim Chong-il's demise to stake out a position on any domestic policy that exists outside established norms for fear of making themselves politically vulnerable. As long as North Korea remains a pariah state, surrounded by "enemies," the threat Pyongyang feels from South Korea and the United States will translate into a feeling of internal insecurity, making it impossible to entertain reform on the domestic front. To do so would also set that leader at odds with the ruling *Chuche* philosophy, which would be ideological heresy. As for Kim Chong-un, *Chuche* is at the heart of the unitary control system, thus making it even more problematic for him to back away from his father's policies. To depart from the ideology of his father and grandfather, Kim would need power and revolutionary credentials. The latter he will never have and the former will take years to accrue.

For the next few years, the regime could probably muddle through such an economic malaise. Absent reform in the long term, the state's inability to function will become a drag on its ability to exert control.[2] Indoctrination within the regime has already begun to wane. As stagnation sets in, the regime's ability to limit the markets will weaken, thus exacerbating existing trends of corruption as elite-affiliated smuggling networks try to exploit the situation. As control further weakens, the influx of information from the outside world (e.g., DVDs and MP3s) will begin to proliferate throughout the population, gnawing away at the legitimacy of the regime. At this point, the regime could face something it has never faced before: widespread public discontent. The recent backlash to the currency revaluation revealed the regime's vulnerability to public outrage.

System preservation also has a foreign policy component that will create challenges for both North Korea and the region. As the succession proceeds through its second phase, Kim Chong-un needs to show his abilities as a leader in order to gain the legitimacy needed to assume power. To build this legitimacy within a military-first system, his strategies are limited. Diplomatic pathways are cumbersome and often lead to setbacks as near-term strategies clash with larger security considerations. This leaves provocations, which can endear the young heir to large segments of the high command.

Some diplomats and scholars have pointed to North Korea's nuclear program as one area where progress may be made in a post–Kim Chong-il era. For Pyongyang, resolution of this issue holds the promise of massive aid and ties to the outside world that could ease its economic burden. This assumption, however, ignores the role the program plays in internal North Korean politics and its sense of security. Possession of nuclear weapons not only compensates for a deteriorating conventional force and provides a deterrent, it also gives North Korea a certain amount of prestige as one of the few states to possess such weapons. Although Pyongyang continues to embrace denuclearization of the Korean Peninsula as a strategic goal, internally it has engaged in a propaganda campaign to link developments in this arena to the heir apparent. Diplomatically, the regime continues to discuss the return to the Six Party Talks only on the basis that North Korea is accepted as a nuclear state, something it sees as giving it leverage in any future negotiations. Therefore, the likelihood that North Korea would embrace a Libya-style settlement of its nuclear program in the near or medium future is remote.

Another area where Pyongyang watchers look for solace on the North Korea question is China. Despite international criticism of North Korea, Beijing has significantly strengthened its bilateral ties with Pyongyang since 2009. Fearing instability on its border, China has staked out a unilateral position of support during North Korea's succession process and a policy of muted criticism with regard to Pyongyang's provocations against the Republic of Korea in the West Sea. China's leaders have subscribed to the notion that such a strategy will result in greater political influence and make the next generation of North Korean leaders more willing to implement economic reforms that China believes would strengthen internal stability and regime legitimacy as well as decrease violent behavior externally. But Pyongyang's accommodation of Beijing will only go so far. Although North Korea is likely to lean toward China in the near future as it goes through the succession, it will ultimately grow wary of overreliance on China for food, energy, and political backing. But this realignment of strategic alliances will not come quickly.

Only after North Korea has solidified its position as a nuclear state might the leadership in Pyongyang feel emboldened to broaden its international engagement beyond China in order to escape isolation, avoid dependence on Beijing, and open up new avenues for aid. But even then, there is little reason to believe that Pyongyang will eschew occasional provocations to raise tension on the Korean Peninsula in order to build cohesion within the leadership as it struggles with a deteriorating domestic situation. As long as military-first politics underwrites the regime's survival strategy, sustained engagement with the outside world in any meaningful way is probably beyond Pyongyang's capacity.

CONCLUSION

North Korea has proven to be one of the most difficult and perplexing problems for the international community. For decades, the secretive regime in Pyongyang has baffled policy makers and confounded diplomats. The regime runs by its own rules and is seldom swayed by initiatives from the outside world, be they from its enemies or allies.

At the center of this opaque regime is a leader whose life is one of legend. It can be argued that no other leader in the world exerts as much influence over his country as Kim Chong-il does over North Korea. He succeeded his father, Kim Il-sung in 1994, but in reality his control over the day-to-day affairs of the regime stretches back at least to the early 1980s, if not further. Today, all power flows to him and from him. No other centers of power are visible to the outside world. His chosen successor is only 28 and reportedly will have to rely on a collective leadership whose loyalty is far from certain.

In 2008, the world woke up to a new threat on the horizon when news began to make its way out of the Hermit Kingdom that Kim had suffered a stroke. The prospect of Kim Chong-il's death or removal from power raises serious questions about what comes next. In order to avoid a potential nightmare moment sometime in the future, North Korea needs to be brought out of isolation. This can come from a more sophisticated analysis of the leadership, which goes beyond a recitation of biographies and extends to an examination of the leadership, the culture that shapes it, and the decision-making environment that surrounds Kim Chong-il/ Kim Chong-un and their closest associates. Though this is not easy, it is not impossible. In recent years, more sources of information have become available to Pyongyang watchers. Defector networks, once closed to the outside world, have become more accessible, especially to western scholars. The author has led an effort to reach out to the Pyongyang watching community on this issue, which has led to the sharing of methodologies and techniques for garnering and vetting information. Much of these lessons learned are contained in this book, which has only begun to scratch the surface. Given the importance of the topic, both for the Korean Peninsula and for the region, much more scholarship and collaboration across national boundaries is needed.

APPENDIX A

Close Aide Politics

The greatest strength, and potentially the greatest weakness, of the Kim Chong-il regime is what is often referred to as "closed-door politics" or "politics centered on close aides." For Kim Chong-il, close aide politics is a convenient "top-down" policy-making mechanism in which he can freely exchange opinions with trusted members of the leadership at the senior and lower echelons across all policy sectors. It is a system based on trust and loyalty where Kim is at the center and all power radiates from that center.

Kim Chong-il's style of rule did not happen over night. Its origins did not even begin in 1994 when he assumed the mantle of leadership from his father. In fact, it was closely intertwined with the succession process beginning in the late 1960s and early 1970s and evolving up through his stroke in 2008. This style of rule is pervasive, touching on all aspects of Kim's rule, from the policy-making process to his situational awareness on the regime to how he makes decisions.

As the hallmark of the Kim Chong-il era, close aide politics serves as the greatest point of departure from what came before. In the Kim Il-sung era, most policy making at the national level was realized through official decision-making institutions, which met more or less on a regular basis. At the top of this infrastructure was the party's Political Bureau (Politburo), where senior level debates were held and Kim's thinking was fleshed out.[1] Kim Il-sung was also accompanied by cadres of relevant departments on his on-the-spot inspections and visits to foreign countries, so that it was not difficult to determine what policies were being pursued by North Korea by examining the cadres in attendance, which were made public through media organizations. Leadership rankings were tied to membership in official bodies.

For Kim Chong-il to build his own center of power during the succession and after, he had to work within this formal apparatus while at the same time building an unofficial network that owed its loyalty directly to him. As Kim Chong-il inherited more of his father's power and authority, the leadership system changed in important ways. Institutionally, Kim shifted the center of gravity within the party from the Political Bureau to the Secretariat, his base of power. Decision making on all policies and personnel appointments was transferred to the party Secretariat Office and specialized departments, while the Political Bureau was reduced to a rubber stamp for ratification.[2]

As Kim's establishment of the unitary guidance system became ingrained, another element of the decision making took hold as the public policy-making process disappeared and was replaced by "report politics" and "crony politics" (i.e., close aide politics). Major policies increasingly were worked out through private channels, such as close aide gatherings (often drinking parties) at one of Kim's residences.[3] Kim's remarks at these meetings, as well as during his guidance inspections, were recorded and polished in writing before being conveyed to pertinent departments or made public to the media.[4]

The makeup of Kim's close aides has evolved over the last 30 years. From early on, Kim's close personal relations with the revolution's first generation and key family members were critical to securing his authority within the leadership. These two groups formed Kim's first set of close aides, those that had personal relations with him prior to his designation as successor. These figures were revered and held up as examples for emulation. Some, such as O Chin-u, served a vital function by touting the heir apparent's legitimacy within institutions where Kim Chong-il did not have a natural base of support.

As Kim's power and influence grew, he was able to expand his close aide network beyond family and the first generation. Members of the second generation (Kim's own generation) who were the surviving children of the revolution's first generation became the inner core of the Kim Chong-il regime. These were people who got to know Kim in the 1960s in the process of working with him in the Central Committee apparatus (KWP's Organization and Guidance Department and Propaganda and Agitation Department). With Kim's appointment to organization and propaganda secretary, they naturally became his immediate subordinates and were guaranteed the position of his close aide.

Another group of close aides entered Kim's network after he became the successor-designate in the early 1970s. They helped him consolidate his power, fend off sources of opposition within the Kim family, and establish a unitary guidance system in the party, army, and government. After Kim's succession was guaranteed in the late 1980s, he formalized the selection process of close aides, subjecting them to strict checkup and verification procedures through the official personnel appointment system. This allowed him to bring his supporters en masse into the regime, thus rapidly reorganizing the leadership structure from a formalized set of institutions into an unofficial network of close aide groups.

A final group of close aides began to appear soon after Kim assumed the positions of Supreme Commander and chairman of the National Defense Commission. The early 1990s saw a reorganization of his close aides from party-centered to military-centered ranks. The frequency of key military leadership figures making an appearance in close aide events dramatically increased.

CLOSE AIDE MANAGEMENT

Laid over this web of close aide networks is a leadership style and set of processes that Kim uses to run the regime on a day-to-day basis. Often described as hub and spoke, Kim's leadership style operates on two levels. Within the formal bureaucracy, he holds the key positions within the regime that give him both authority and situational awareness. His positions of general secretary of the Korean Worker's Party and Supreme Commander of the Armed Forces give him control over the two most powerful elements of the regime. They also invest in him the legitimacy he needs to rule without obvious challenge. While unnamed, it is generally assumed that he also occupies the posts of director of the KWP Organization Guidance Department and director of the State Security Department,[5] two institutions that peer into every corner of the regime and form the basis on this modern-day police state. These positions allow him to quickly identify and destroy any potential threat to his legitimate offices.

But even these formal trappings of power are not enough. Through close aide politics, Kim has created an informal system that circumnavigates direct chains of command in order to give him alternate reservoirs of information. This allows him to access information that may otherwise be denied through formal channels. It also allows him to keep tabs on the senior leadership. He does this by forming alliances with trusted individuals within key ministries and commands. This keeps other senior leaders off balance and prevents them from using their bureaucracy as a breeding ground for antiregime cabals and plots.

At the center of this hub-and-spoke system is Kim's personal secretariat, which is located in the KWP Number 1 building at Chung District of Pyongyang.[6] The source of much speculation by North Korean watchers, Kim Chong-il's personal secretariat is where the formal and informal systems of power come together. Wielding influence by virtue

Table A.1
Kim Chong-il's Close Aides[a]

Affiliation	Period before Successor Designation[b]	Period after Successor Designation	Period after Coming to Power
Party	Kim Kuk-tae, KWP Secretary for Cadre Affairs	Kwon Min-chun, Vice Director of International Department	Kang Tong-yun, Vice OGD Director
	Kim Si-hak, Director of the Kim Il-sung Higher Party School	Kim Yong-sun, KWP Secretary for South Korean Affairs	Hang Pyong-so, Vice Military Affairs Department Director
	Kim Chi-gu, First Vice Director of the Organization Guidance Department (OGD)	Mun Song-sul	Kim Yong-gon, United Front Department
	Ri Kwan-pil, First Vice OGD Director	Pak Song-pong	
	Ri Che-kang, First Vice OGD Director	Pang Sung-un	
	Ri Chan-son, First Vice Director of KWP Department	Chang Song-taek	
	Ri Hwa-yong, Vice OGD Director	Chon Pyong-ho	
	So Yun-sok, First Vice OGD Director	Choe Ryong-hae	
	Yon Hyong-muk, Vice Chairman of National Defense Commission (NDC)	Hyon Chun-kuk	
	Yom Ki-sun, First Vice OGD Director	Ri Yong-chol, First Vice OGD Director	
	Choe Ik-kyu, Vice Director of Propaganda and Agitation Department (PAD), Minister of Culture		

(*continued*)

Affiliation	Period before Successor Designation[b]	Period after Successor Designation	Period after Coming to Power
	Hyon Chol-kyu, First Vice OGD Director		
Military	Ri Yong-mu	Kang Sang-chun	Kim Il-chol, MPAF
	O Kuk-yol, Chief of General Staff Department (GAD), Director of KWP Operations Department	Kwon Song-rin	Ri Myong-su, Vice GAD Chief
	O Chin-u, Minister of People's Armed Forces (MPAF)	Kim Kwang-chin	Kim Myong-guk, GAD Ops
		Kim Chang-son	Hyon Chol-hae, Vice GPB Director
		Kim Ha-kyu, Commander Artillery Command	Pak Chae-kyong, Vice GPB Director
		Won Ung-hui, MSC	Kim Yong-chun, GAD, MPAF
		Yun Chi-ho	Kim Kyok-sik, GAD
		Chang Song-u, commander Third Corps	Kim Ki-son, Director of the MPAF Personnel Department
		Cho Myong-rok, GPB	Kim Tae-sik, Director Reconnassiance Bureau
			Kim Won-hong, MSC
			Kim Chong-kap, Vice MPAF Minister

(*continued*)

Table A.1 *(Continued)*

Affiliation	Period before Successor Designation[b]	Period after Successor Designation	Period after Coming to Power
Military *(continued)*			Choe Pu-il, Deputy GAD Chief
			Kim Chong-gak, Vice GPB Director
Government	Ri Hwa-son	Kang Sok-chu	Chu Sang-song, MPS
	Sin In-ha	Kwon Hui-kyong	Chi Yong-chu, Director MPS Political Department
	Ho Tam	Kil Chae-kyong	
		Kim Chung-il	
		Ri Su-yong	
		Ri Chong-mok	
		Ri Won-pom	

[a] Most of Kim's close aides have come from the party, the military, and the areas of South Korean affairs and foreign affairs. Other sectors, such as the economy, administration, and science and technology, do not appear to be represented within his inner circle. There have been no known cases where technical expert elites from economy and science and technology areas were appointed to positions in Kim Chong-il personal secretariat, Organization and Guidance Department, and Propaganda and Agitation Department, which are considered his representative close aide groups. Hyon Song-il, *North Korea's National Strategy and Power Elite* (Seoul: Sunin Publishing, 2006).

[b] Positions attached to the various close aides reflect the position when the individual became a close aide, not necessarily the current position.

of its "gatekeeping" function,[7] this office is often compared to the royal order system that operated during the Chosun Dynasty (1392–1910), Kim Chong-il's personal secretariat has no official sanction and rarely is mentioned in the North Korean press. It receives, classifies, and facilitates documents addressed to the chairman (Kim Chong-il) and then issues instructions.[8] It also administers Kim's schedule, itineraries, protocol, and logistics supply and liaisons with the Guards Command to ensure his security. Because the Kim Chong-il secretariat is not an official organization, its senior cadre work externally as members of the KWP Organization Guidance Department.[9]

Table A.2
Kim Chong-il's Personal Apparatus

Name	Position
Private Office	
Kim Kang-chol	Personal Secretary
Lt. Col. Kim Sol-song	Personal Secretary (Kim Chong-il's daughter) (oversees bodyguard duties)
Chon Hui-chong	Protocol Secretary
N/A	Bodyguard for Kim Chong-il[a]
Col. Ri Ho-chun	Aide-de-camp
Personal Secretariat	
Kang Sang-chun	Director
Kim Chung-il	Vice Director, Chief, Main Office of Secretaries (oversees foreign affairs issues)
N/A	Chief Secretary (used to be Kim Chang-son)
Kim Mun-kyong	Section Chief. Granddaughter of Kim Chaek. Daughter of Kim Kuk-tae.
Kim Yon-ok	Unidentified position
Choe Pyong-yul	Chief, Office of Adjutants (bodyguard function)
Pak Yong-chin	Assistant for Intelligence
Kim Hyong-chol	Assistant for Intelligence
Ri Pyong-chun	Head, Documents Office
Pak Kyong-su	Record Keeper
Ho Myong-ok	Chief, Consolidation Division (part of Documents Office)
Ri Chae-kang	Secretary to Kim Chong-il, Head, Cadres of 5th Section (Female Entertainers)
Kim Tong-un	Chief, Office 38 (handles Kim Chong-il's funds)
Chon Il-chun	Chief, Office 39 (oversees slush fund)
Kim Sol-song (daughter)	Office 99
Paek Kun-son	First Secretary for Military Affairs
N/A	Director, Kumsusan Memorial Palace; Chief, Office of Military Officers

(*continued*)

Table A.2 *(Continued)*

Name	Position
An Yong-chol	Military Liaison Officer
Nam Yong-chol	Military Liaison Officer
Yom Ki-sun	Long-time associate of Kim Chong-il and probable adviser
Ri Su-yong (aka Ri Chol)	Deputy Public Prosecutor; roving European ambassador; vice chairman, Korean Christian Federation. Handles Kim Chong-il's personal Swiss accounts.
Pak Yong-mu (aka "Ricardo Pwag")	Procurer for Kim and his family
Hwang Ho-nam	Japanese interpreter
"Third Floor" Members not directly part of Personal Secretariat	
Kil Chae-kyong	Former ambassador to Sweden, Deputy Director of KWP CC International Department. Controls East European net for Kim Chong-il.
N/A	Chief Mangyong Trading Company. Based in Vienna, Austria. Assists in handling European funding/procurement for Kim Chong-il. Oversees Kim Chong-il overseas slush fund. Used to be Kwon Yong-nok.
Myong Kil-hyon	Director KWP CC. In charge of overseas purchases for Kim Chong-il.
Choe Yong-ho	Procurement of goods for Kim Chong-il.
Pak Song-pong	Procurement of military material.

[a] Lt. Gen. Kim Yong-chol, the current chief of the Reconnaissance General Bureau, used to be Kim's personal bodyguard. Kang Sang-chun, the director of Kim's personal secretariat, also held this position in the 1980s.

The composition of Kim's personal secretariat has changed dramatically over the years. Kil Chae-kyong, Ri Myong-che, and Ri Song-pok, who were vice directors, died of illness, and others, such as Kwon Yong-rok and Kim Chang-son, were reportedly demoted for corruption or other transgressions and replaced by cadre from the General Guard Command (i.e., Kim's bodyguards). The director of the personal secretariat, Kang Sang-chun, is a university classmate of Kim's, while the vice director, Kim Chung-il, is a confidant of the Kim family.

The son of Kang Ton, a member of Kim Il-sung's partisan group, Kang Sang-chun was born in 1944 in Jilin Province, China. After graduating from Kim Il-sung University with a degree in political economy, he joined the Bodyguard General Bureau and then moved to the KWP Secretariat in the 1980s where he became the director of the Central Committee Executive Office Building Management Section, a job that essentially served Kim Chong-il's daily needs. He moved into Kim's personal secretariat in the mid-1990s and became director in 2002.[10] In 2006, he was arrested in Macau for allegedly circulating fake U.S. dollars but was later released.[11]

Kim Chung-il is the only son of Kim Yong-nam, the president of the SPA. Born in 1938 in South Hamgyong Province, he graduated from the Pyongyang University of Foreign Studies and entered the diplomatic corps in the late 1970s. After rising to first vice foreign minister, he was laterally transferred into the KWP Propaganda and Agitation Department in 1988. He joined Kim Chong-il's personal secretariat in the early 1990s.[12] In addition to possessing fluent foreign-language skills, he reportedly enjoys Kim's "special confidence."

Closely associated with Kim Chong-il's personal secretariat (and even overlapping at times) is an entity known as the "Third Floor."[13] This element of Kim Chong-il's personal staff assists him in conducting numerous "special" operations, both inside and outside the country. The members of the "Third Floor" cadre normally have long political lives. Paek In-su (former head of Office No. 39) worked for the apparatus for 28 years, while Kwon Yong-nok and Ri Chol served for more than 20 years. While it would be difficult to replace them as they are in charge of secret affairs, their long hold on their positions is also not unrelated to Kim Chong-il's personality. These behind-the-scene members of the leadership are critical to the maintenance of the regime. For a detailed description of Kim Chong-il's personal secretariat, see: Ken E. Gause, The North Korean Leadership: Systemic Dynamics and Fault Lines. The author also authored an unpublished paper on the topic, which is reflected in and elaborated on in North Korea Leadership Watch, an excellent blog authored by Michael Madden.

These "special" operations mark a significant departure from the role of the personal secretariat as it existed under Kim Il-sung. For example, the concept of a slush fund, which is managed by Kim Chong-il's staff, did not exist. Instead, Kim Il-sung's needs were paid for by "presidential bonds," which were created by laying in 3 percent of the budget. They were akin to the resources reserved in preparation for war.[14] These secret funds are Kim Chong-il's personal money for him to buy whatever he thinks is necessary, including daily necessities from foreign countries or presents for his subordinates. In terms of system dynamics, the operation of this nefarious activity by a key component of the regime undermines Kim's legitimacy.

Decision Making at the Center of the Hub and Spoke

While close aide politics shows how Kim is able to manage the regime, it does not fully reveal the unique character of Kim's rule. This can only be seen in an examination of his decision-making process. It is a three-step process of receipt of policy reports, ratification, and implementation.[1]

The process most likely begins in close aide gatherings or during the inspection process. It is during these times that Kim sets the broad parameters for policy, be it domestic or foreign policy. Once the broad outlines are set, policy making is usually initiated by a direct request from Kim in the form of an instruction.[2] Sometimes this instruction goes to a particular department or even a particular individual.[3] On other occasions, it is farmed out to several relevant departments. In both circumstances, the KWP Organization Guidance Department makes a note of Kim's request so it can be tracked through the policy development process.

After sufficient consultation by the relevant departments, a councilor or group of councilors write a policy draft that addresses Kim's instruction.[4] It is then sent to Kim's personal secretariat either as a "document report" (*mungo'n pogo*) or "fax report" (*mosa pogo*). Reports submitted in document form include less urgent items time-wise, but still important policy-wise, such as thick "proposals," "direction of activities," and "situation materials."[5] Kim's personal secretariat prioritizes the reports and submits them for his comment and/or approval.[6]

Reports sent by fax are more urgent. These are often working-level reports or requests for clarification, which are less involved than document reports but necessary to keep the policy-making process on track. As such, they are time sensitive. These reports are faxed directly to Kim's personal secretariat and then someone is responsible for standing by until word is received as to whether the report is approved or rejected. Although Kim has fax machines at his office, his various residences, and his private train, his response may take hours, if not days.[7]

Beginning in the early 1990s, the amount of reports arriving on his desk became so numerous that it forced a change in the next step of the decision-making cycle, the ratification process. For document reports (not the urgent fax reports), Kim designated specific days on which he would conduct the review process.[8] After reviewing a document, Kim can do one of three things.

- Sign and date the document. Referred to as a "handwritten instruction," by signing and dating the document, Kim signifies that the contents of report documents should be regarded as his intentions and instructions to be implemented the way they are and that he would personally take responsibility for their results as well.

- Date, but not sign, the document. Referred to as a "handwritten document," merely dating the document signifies that Kim agrees with the contents of the report but will not be responsible for the results even though, like a "handwritten instruction," it is considered sanctioned policy.[9]

- Document returned unsigned or dated. This signifies the Kim either does not agree with or understand the document report. It also probably means that the counselor and his chain of command did not accurately judge Kim's intentions, something that probably carries with it criticism and punishment.[10]

Once a document is ratified by Kim, it becomes policy. Upon receipt of the policy guidance from Kim's personal secretariat, the originating institution of the document report is now responsible for its implementation. This begins with the head of the department or ministry either meeting with the relevant cadre responsible for implementation or convening an all-hands meeting to discuss the new policy. The report document, as received from Kim's office, is read in full and discussed. The person charged with overseeing the implementation of the policy then registers it with the institution's records office and draws up a "policy implementation plan." This plan lays out the method of implementation, the relevant department/ministries responsible for implementation, and the timeline for implementation. The policy now can be monitored by the institution's organization department, which submits progress reports to the KWP Organization Guidance Department. If the policy fails to be implemented by the date specified in the policy implementation plan, the originating institution and the cadre involved in drawing up the plan can become targets of criticism and punishment on grounds of lacking "the absolute and unconditional spirit of policy implementation" and loyalty.[11]

Notes

PREFACE

1. These points as cited in *Recognizing North Korea as a Strategic Threat: An Intelligence Challenge for the United States.* Staff Report of the House Permanent Select Committee on Intelligence Subcommittee on Intelligence Policy (28 September 2006).

2. "DPRK Media Systematically Obscure Leadership Information," FBIS Analysis, 25 April 2005.

3. Ibid.

4. The author would like to stress, however, that whenever dealing with defector accounts or regional media accounts based on defector reporting, an abundance of caution is required. This study has tried to mitigate the bias and complications inherent in these sources by finding additional sources to back up defector-based assertions. Where necessary, the author provides caveats and levels of confidence in the information.

PART I

1. "Let's Venerate the Great Leader and Complete his Feats to the End," *Nodong Sinmun,* 9 July 1994. The first official mention of Kim Il-sung's death came via Pyongyang radio at 1200 local time on 9 July. The report was attributed to the regime's ruling institutions—tahe KWP Central Committee, the KWP Central Military Committee, the National Defense Commission, the Central People's Committee, and the Administration Council.

2. "KCNA Carries Medical Diagnoses on Cause of Kim's Death," Korean Central Television, 9 July 1994.

3. The following description of North Korean coverage of Kim Il-sung's funeral and the population's reaction to his death are based on publicly available film footage from North Korean television and CNN, as well as the author's discussion with several defectors who were in Pyongyang at the time, including Hwang Chang-yop.

4. "North Koreans Begin a 2-Day Funeral for Kim," *New York Times*, 19 July 1994. See also "Crying by numbers at Kim's State Funeral," *The Independent*, 20 July 1994.

5. This paralleled a theme running through the North Korean media, which was designed to show that Kim Chong-il was an embodiment of his father's legacy. *Nodong Sinmun* in an editorial on July 11 stated that "the leader (*suryong*) had not gone" because the "dear leader (*chidoja*) Kim Chong-il embraces with exactness the leader's breath, the leader's heartbeat." "Transform Sadness to Courage and More Strength," *Nodong Sinmun*, 11 July 1994.

6. "Military Officers Express Will to Uphold Kim Chong-il," Pyongyang Korean Central Broadcasting Station, 14 July 1994.

7. *Yonhap*, 27 July 1994.

8. "Pyongyang Radio Reports Death of Kim Il-sung," Pyongyang Korean Central Broadcasting Station, 9–15 July 1994.

9. Two of the more noteworthy speakers were Vice Minister of Defense Kim Kwang-chin and diplomat and future President of the SPA Kim Yong-nam. Ho Chong-man, vice chairman of the Chosen Soren Central Committee also spoke.

10. Jei Guk-jeon, "North Korean Leadership: Kim Jong Il's Balancing Act in the Ruling Circle," *Third World Quarterly*, Vol. 21, No. 5 (2000).

CHAPTER 1

1. "Supreme Leader of the Party, State, and Army," Democratic People's Republic of Korea, No. 474 (October 1995), as cited in Adrian Buzo, *The Guerilla Dynasty: Politics and Leadership in North Korea* (Boulder, CO: Westview Press, 1999).

2. Jei Guk-jeon, "North Korean Leadership."

3. Photos of Kang Song-ae began to reappear in the North Korean media in December 1994.

4. O Kuk-yol was representative of a younger generation of officers within the KPA who were pushing for modernization of the conventional forces. These views held little sway within the Ministry of People's Armed Forces, which was headed by O Chin-u, Kim Chong-il's guardian within the military. A product of irregular guerrilla warfare, O Chin-u was reluctant to embrace the modernization being pushed by the Soviet-trained elements within the General Staff. He was also suspicious of O Kuk-yol's ambitions and growing power. According to defector reports, in 1988, O Chin-u pushed for Kim Il-sung to get rid of his young rival, replacing him with another member of the partisan first generation, Choe Kwang (then 72). These reports go further to note that Kim Chong-il intervened on his friend's behalf and saved him from banishment, or worse, convincing his father to reassign O Kuk-yol as head of the Central Committee's Civil Defense Department. There are several theories, but very little evidence, about O Kuk-yol's dismissal. Kang Myong-to relates the story that while O Chin-u was convalescing in the hospital following an automobile accident, he learned that O Kuk-yol was conducting a reshuffle of the high command. Furious, O Chin-u approached Kim Chong-il, who refused to do anything. O then went to Kim Il-sung, who intervened. Another

story suggests that O Kuk-yol authorized a major redeployment of troops onto civil construction projects, something that O Chin-u believed undermined military preparedness. Still others suggest the root of the problem was a personality clash between the senior members of the high command.

5. *Nodong Sinmun* is the major conduit for propaganda, agitation, and controlled information dissemination within the party and, by extension, throughout the populace. The editor in chief of the newspaper reports directly to the party's Propaganda and Agitation Department. He is said to have as much political clout as a vice minister in the Cabinet.

6. Kim Chong-il, "Socialism Is a Science," *Nodong Sinmun*, 14 November 1994.

7. Although Kim Chong-il chose not to take the title of *suryong*, he did sanction a change in how he was referred to in the media. Beginning in the December 27 issue, *Nodong Sinmun* ceased to call Kim Chong-Il "the Dear Leader [*ch'inaehanun chidoja*]," and began to refer to him as "the Great Leader [*widaehan yongdoja*]." On some occasions, he was even referred to as the "greatest leader" (*choego yongdoja*). The North Korean media did continue to use the term *suryong* to indicate the "leader," which one would presume was a reference to Kim Chong-il.

8. O Chin-u was the most powerful military figure in the latter half of the Kim Il-sung period. He was both the Minister of People's Armed Forces and Director of the General Political Bureau. He served as a mentor to and supporter of Kim Chong-il during his rise to power. It is worth noting that during the 2010 Third Party Conference, O's son, O Il-chong was made director of the KWP Military Department.

9. Kim Kwang-chin was rumored to be a second cousin of Kim Il-sung. A graduate of Soviet Artillery School, he commanded an artillery battalion that advanced into South Korea during the Korean War.

10. According to some Pyongyang watchers, Choe Kwang's appointment was in keeping with promotional practices within the high command since the late 1970s. Speculation was that Kim Kwang-chin would oversee the day-to-day operations of the ministry. Kim Chong-il, they speculated, was using Choe's appointment to obscure his real plan to dominate the military. Behind the scenes, he would use the Kim Kwang-chin–Kim Yong-chun line to exert command authority over the military and the Cho Myong-nok–Ri Ha-il line to ensure that the party maintained control within the armed forces.

11. In April 1995, an alleged coup d'état attempt by the Sixth Army Corps of the People's Army in Chongjin, South Hamgyong Province, was exposed. According to media reporting, scores of officers at the general and field-grade level were purged. The fact that Kim Yong-chun, who was the commander of the Sixth Corps, was not purged suggested that he was involved in suppressing the crisis.

12. Ri Ha-il was director of the KWP Military Department.

13. Ri Ul-sol was the commander of the General Guard Command. During this period, many Pyongyang watchers considered Ri Ul-sol a rival to Choe Kwang. See Haruki Wada, *North Korea: Present State of a Guerrilla Country* (Seoul: Tolbegae, 2002).

14. Cho Myong-nok was one of the leading military figures of the second generation. A graduate of the Mangyongdae Revolutionary Academy, he had been a strong supporter of the Kim Chong-il succession. He had commanded the Air Force for 17 years.

15. Kim Myong-guk was often observed shadowing Kim Chong-il throughout the parade, providing a running commentary on the proceedings. Chang Song-u,

older brother to Kim's brother-in-law Chang Song-taek, served as the parade commander. Won Ung-hui assumed a higher profile than his predecessors, most likely in return for the role he played in suppressing the April coup. For his service, his office was elevated from a bureau to a command.

16. This was not the first time North Korea had experimented with economic reform. In the early 1980s, the regime placed a focus on light industry and passed the Law of the Management of Joint Venture, a more liberal foreign trade policy designed to encourage international investment. Later, in the early 1990s, the reform-minded vice premier and chairman of the State External Economic Commission Kim Tal-hyon was promoted to the Politburo as an alternate member, leading to speculation that substantive reform might be forthcoming. Hope along these lines faded in 1993 with Kim Tal-hyon's disappearance from the political scene.

17. On October 21, 1994, the United States (represented by Assistant Secretary of State Robert Gallucci) and North Korea (represented by First Vice Foreign Minister Kang Sok-chu) signed an agreement—the Agreed Framework—calling on Pyongyang to freeze operation and construction of nuclear reactors suspected of being part of a covert nuclear weapons program in exchange for two proliferation-resistant nuclear power reactors. The agreement also called on the United States to supply North Korea with fuel oil pending construction of the reactors. An international consortium called the Korean Peninsula Energy Development Organization (KEDO) was formed to implement the agreement.

18. *Asian Yearbook of International Law, Vol. 5* (The Hague: Kluwer Law International, 1997).

19. Ibid.

20. Ibid.

21. UN Department of Humanitarian Affairs, United Nations Consolidated UN Interagency Appeal for Flood-related Emergency Humanitarian Assistance to the Democratic People's Republic of Korea (DPRK), April 1996, as cited in Jae-Cheon Lim, *Kim Jong-il's Leadership of North Korea* (London: Routledge, 2009).

22. Ibid.

23. The World Food Program estimated North Korea's total grain harvest for the year at 4.3 million tons. But with 50 percent of corn crops having been consumed in August and September, there were only 2.84 million tons left for use. Because North Korea needed at least 3.8 million tons for use as food and 5.4 million tons for use in other purposes in the next year, this meant the country was short 2.36 million tons in all.

24. *Economic Indicators of North Korea* (Seoul: Han'guk kaebal yon'guwon, 1996), as cited in Jae-Cheon Lim, *Kim Jong-il's Leadership of North Korea*.

25. The Japanese press reported in 1996 that North Korea had decided to delay the end of the mourning period for Kim Il-sung because the proper atmosphere had not been created yet for Kim Chong-il's ascension to power. See *Yomiuri Shimbun*, 26 June 1996.

26. According to one Pyongyang watcher, North Korea appeared to be under a collective leadership system comprising old first-generation revolutionaries, younger elite generals, and leading technocrats in addition to Kim Chong-il. See an interview with Ho Nam-sung, head of the North Korea Division of the Institute on National Security Affairs and adviser to the Ministry of National Defense and the Agency for National Security Planning in *Vantage Point*, April 1996.

27. Ken E. Gause, "The North Korean Leadership: System Dynamics and Fault Lines," in Kongdan Oh Hassig et al., *North Korean Policy Elites* (Alexandria, VA: Institute for Defense Analyses, 2004).

28. Kim Chong-il, "Kim Il Song chonghap taehak ch'angnip 50-tol kinyom yonsolmun" [A speech of the 50th anniversary of Kim Il-sung University], *Wolgan Choson*, April 1997, as cited in Jae-Cheon Lim, *Kim Jong-il's Leadership of North Korea*. Jae-Cheon Lim notes that the speech was brought out of the country by Hwang Chang-yop when he defected in 1997.

29. *Pukhan Kunsa Ch'eje, P'yo'ngga-wa Cho'nmang* [Evaluation of and Prospects for North Korea's Military System] (Seoul: KIDA, July 2006).

30. Kim Chong-il, "It Is Revolutionaries' Sublime Moral Duty to Respect Senior Revolutionaries," *Nodong Sinmun*, 24 December 1996.

31. Ibid.

32. *Nodong Sinmun*, 1 January 1997.

33. "Serious Aftereffects of Aging of North Korean Officials," *Chungang Ilbo*, 9 May 1996.

34. "Premier Kang Song-san Dismissed for Embezzlement," *Sankei Shimbun* 9 March 1997. He was allegedly dismissed in April 1996 after it was discovered that he was accumulating a secret wealth worth $2 million.

35. Three military officers, Ri Ul-sol, Cho Myong-nok, and Kim Yong-chun, were listed as 6th, 7th, and 8th, respectively, in the official roster of dignitaries announced before the funeral service for Choe. When his predecessor, O Chin-u, died two years earlier, these three officers had ranked between 73rd and 86th in the official roster.

36. Kim Kwang-chin's funeral service committee consisted of Ri Ul-sol, Cho Myong-nok, Kim Yong-chun, Paek Hak-rim, Kim Ik-hyon, Ri Tu-ik, Choe In-tok, Kim Yong-yon, and Ri Chong-san. Only Cho Myong-nok and Kim Yong-chun did not hail from the first generation.

37. Under the "Supreme Commander Order No. 0088" issued on April 14, 1997, a large-scale reshuffle involving the promotion of 123 generals was conducted with the aim of bolstering loyalty from the military and raising military morale.

38. But this did not mean that the military controlled Kim. On the contrary, through the KWP Organization Guidance Department and the Operations Bureau of the General Staff, Kim kept a tight surveillance over general grade officers.

39. *Nodong Sinmun*, 8 July 1997. See also "Let Us Build Our Country, Our Fatherland, to Be Richer and Stronger Under the Great Party's Leadership," KCBN, 1 January 1994.

40. *Nodong Sinmun*, 8 July 1996.

41. "Kim Elected as KWP General Secretary," Korean Central Broadcasting Network, 8 October 1997. See also *Nodong Sinmun*, 9 October 1997.

42. The message was conveyed to the people by a special report read by announcer on the Pyongyang Korean Central Broadcasting Network. The report, which was issued by the KWP Central Committee and KWP Central Military Committee, thanked Kim Chong-il for "enabling the DPRK people to uphold Kim Il-sung as their eternal leader." It went on to say that the party delegates' decision to elect Kim Chong-il as KWP general secretary showed the people's desire to uphold Kim Chong-il at the vanguard of party and revolution. It concluded with "The party's Central Committee and Central Military Committee solemnly declare

that Comrade Kim Chong-il has been elected in high esteem as the recognized general secretary of our party."

43. See Appendix A for an overview of the concept of "Close Aide Politics."

44. Hyon Song-il, *Pukhan-u'i Kukkajo'llyak-kwa P'awo' Ellit'u'* [North Korea's National Strategy and Power Elite] (Seoul: Sunin Publishing, 2006).

45. According to one source, Kim Chong-il took particular responsibility for issues related to South Korea. Party bodies, such as the External Liaison Department, Operations Department, and Office 35, all directly reported to Kim Chong-il. On important issues, KWP United Front Department vice directors could interact directly with Kim Chong-il without going through the secretary in charge of South Korean affairs. Local party organs could also directly submit proposals and report pending issues to Kim without going through the higher-level party, when necessary. Hyon Song-il, *North Korea's National Strategy and Power Elite*.

46. For a more thorough explanation of Kim's use of close aides, see Appendix A ("Close Aide Politics").

47. Choe Chu-hwal, *Pukhan Chosa Yongu* [A Study of North Korea] (Seoul: NIS's Unification Policy Institute, 2000).

48. Ri Pong-won was allegedly executed for treason, whereas So Kwan-hui was executed for espionage. Though Ri's story remains a mystery, later defector reports suggested that So was executed not for ties with agents during the Korean War, as was alleged by North Korean authorities, but for a failed agriculture policy. See Ken E. Gause, *Police State: North Korea's System of Control, Surveillance, and Punishment*, (Washington, DC: U.S. Committee for Human Rights in North Korea, 2011).

49. *Choson Ilbo*, 27 January 1998. Later reports coming out through South Korean channels alleged that the security forces had targeted the KYSL for plotting the assassination of Kim Chong-il. According to these reports, several key individuals within the KYSL had taken money from South Korean intelligence to get rid of Kim in the hope that Chang Song-taek would assume control. Chang Song-taek had close ties to the KYSL, having served as the director of the KWP Youth Department in the late 1980s and director of the KWP Youth and Three Revolution Teams in the early 1990s. The fact that Chang was not purged undermines the South Korean reports that he may have had foreknowledge of the plot. A more likely explanation of the KYSL purge was for corruption related to the organization's attempts to earn foreign currency, something that probably left it vulnerable to a South Korean intelligence operation. See *Chungang Ilbo*, 10 March 1998.

50. *Choson Ilbo*, 27 January 1998. It is not clear whether Chang was disciplined in this matter. His name did disappear from the North Korean media until September 1998.

51. *Tonga Ilbo*, 7 March 1998.

52. *Chungang Ilbo*, 7 March 1998.

53. The "Sunshine Policy" was based on the assumption that North Korean leaders would eventually embrace the Chinese reform model that would ultimately narrow the gap between the two Korean economies and facilitate a relatively painless integration and unification.

54. The Sunshine Policy was initially meant both to improve the North's economy and to induce change in the North's repressive government, though the latter goal was later (at least officially) de-emphasized.

55. Pyongyang radio, 29 April 1998, as reported by FBIS, 30 April 1998.

56. KCNA, 20 August 1997. The letter also stood in contrast to a report delivered by an alternate Politburo member on April 21 to a central symposium marking the 50th anniversary of the joint conference of representatives from political parties and public organizations in North and South Korea in which he described North–South relations as having been "aggravated to the worst state" with "grave barriers" to reunification. Pyongyang radio, 21 April 1998, as reported by FBIS, 30 April 1998.

57. "Growing Influence of DPRK Military Props Up Regime," *Hangyore*, 1 July 1998. Kim Chong-il in 1998 conducted a total of 43 official onsite inspections as of late June. Thirty-three visits to military units and other military-related activities accounted for most of these, indicating the importance placed on the military.

58. A Party Congress had not convened since the Sixth Party Congress in 1980 despite party rules that mandated that a Congress be held every five years. The plenum of the Central Committee had not been held since the 21st plenum in December 1993. And, in the summer of 1998, preparations were underway for the 10th Supreme People's Assembly. But for the first time in the history of North Korea's Communist Party, a Central Committee plenum was not going to be held before the first session of a SPA. Pyongyang watchers also suspected that there had been no Secretariat and Politburo meetings since the death of Kim Il-sung. Jinwook Choi, "The Changing Party-State System and Outlook for Reform in North Korea," *International Journal of Korean Unification Studies*, Vol. 18, No. 1 (2009).

59. The abolition of the presidency did not mean the removal of the three vice presidents (Ri Chong-ok, Pak Song-chol, and Kim Yong-chu) from the leadership. Instead, they were appointed as honorary vice chairmen of the SPA Standing Committee, positions that signaled their withdrawal from front-line political affairs. *Chungang Ilbo*, 7 September 1998.

60. Kim Yong-nam described the chairmanship of the commission as being "the highest rank of the state" responsible for commanding politics, defense, and the economy and as being a "sacred position" signifying the dignity of the state.

61. Kim Il-chol's appointment as minister of People's Armed Forces surprised Pyongyang watchers. As head of the KPA Navy, Kim was not viewed as a viable candidate for the post. However, he was the first flag officer to pledge his loyalty to Kim Chong-il following Kim Il-sung's death. *Korea Times*, 9 September 1998.

62. Its membership also reflected the generational turnover, with 24 of the 31 ministers coming from the second generation.

63. All of the ministries in the new cabinet were elevated in status from *pu* to *song* in the North Korean lexicon.

CHAPTER 2

1. This was a departure from the New Year's speeches given by Kim Il-sung, which provided hints of Pyongyang's policy directions—particularly toward Seoul and Washington. The 1999 editorial only rehashed boilerplate themes and slogans in the areas of ideology, politics, defense, economy, and reunification, while further exalting Kim Chong-il as the leader of the state, party, and military.

2. Kim Il-sung up through 1994 delivered the New Year's Statement on Chosun Central Television. Kim Chong-il discontinued this practice, favoring the joint

editorial to convey the "state of the union." According to some defectors, Kim Chong-il is "inarticulate and fast talking." It is also rumored that he stutters.

3. "DPRK Reportedly Reshuffles Political Structure," *Chungang Ilbo*, 14 January 1999. The year before, the powerful SSD first vice director, Kim Yong-ryong, had been purged on charges of corruption. See Ken E. Gause, *Police State: North Korea's System of Control, Surveillance, and Punishment* (Washington, DC: U.S. Committee for Human Rights in North Korea, 2011).

4. Ibid.

5. Hwang Chang-yop, "Kim Chong-il's Military Regime and Reform and Openness," unpublished article.

6. The Security Command is one of the DPRK's three major intelligence and surveillance organizations, with the two others being the State Security Department and People's Security Ministry. For more on North Korea's internal security apparatus, see Gause, *Police State: North Korea's System of Control, Surveillance, and Punishment*.

7. "'Security Command Engineers Purges in DPRK'—Hwang Chang-yop," *Chungang Ilbo*, 11 February 1999.

8. *Chungang Ilbo*, 8 April 1999.

9. When Kim Il-sung died, the KWP Politburo members held the 1–13 spots; Politburo candidate members held the 14–23 spots; and the KWP secretaries held the 24–29 spots.

10. The only noteworthy absence from the SPA session was Han Song-yong, KWP Secretary for the Economy.

11. "Order No. 00114 by the Supreme Commander of the Korean People's Army," Korean Central Broadcasting Network, 13 April 1999.

12. *Choson Ilbo*, 7 June 1999.

13. "Yo Ch'un-sok Appointed DPRK Armed Forces Vice Minister," *Tong-A Ilbo*, 10 September 1999.

14. Ri Chong-ok, Pak Song-chol, and Kim Yong-chu, former vice presidents of the state and currently honorary vice chairmen of the standing committee of the SPA, did not show up at the memorial service.

15. "North Korean Army Getting Corrupt by Irregularities and Graft," *Pukhan*, 1 May 1999.

16. Ibid.

17. "Perry's N. Korea Report Just Beginning of South Korea-US Policy Coordination," *Korea Herald*, 11 March 1999.

18. *Pyongyang KCNA*, 26 May 1999, as reported in FBIS, FTS19990526000626.

19. "DPRK Likely To Take Time Before Acting on Perry Proposal," *Yomiuri Shimbun*, 29 May 1999.

20. Kim Yong-nam was accompanied by a delegation of nearly 50 officials, including Premier Hong Song-nam, Foreign Minister Paek Nam-sun, Minister of People's Armed Forces Kim Il-chol, and KWP Secretary Choe Tae-pok.

21. Ibid. See also "Forum: Another China-North Korea Honeymoon'?" *Choson Ilbo*, 6 June 1999.

22. "North Korea Refuses the Comprehensive Approach During Perry's Visit," *Chungang Ilbo*, 14 June 1999.

23. Ibid. Previously, North Korea adopted the stance that if the United States provided $1 billion for three years, it would refrain from exporting missiles.

24. Ibid.

25. In an authoritative statement issued by the Committee for Peaceful Reunification of the Fatherland on May 29, Pyongyang accused the United States of preparing for war against the North by developing a new operation plan that would allow it to launch a "preemptive strike" against North Korea. Linking U.S. actions in Yugoslavia to a potential use of force against North Korea, the statement went on to call U.S. operations in the Balkans a "test war" leading up to a "second Korean war" by taking advantage of the "topographic" similarities between Korea and Yugoslavia.

26. A May 30 *Nodong Sinmun* article made the argument that North Korea must retain its missile capability to ensure its deterrence posture in the face of the U.S. threat.

27. Concurrent with the heightened militaristic rhetoric, a special joint article published by *Nodong Sinmun* and the party's theoretical journal *Kulloja* emphasized the need for an "ideological offensive" to ward off attempts by "imperialists" seeking to bring down the North's system (KCNA, 1 June). A joint article run by the party daily and theoretical monthly was highly unusual and designed to highlight an important policy or ideological position. Information provided by Open Source Center.

28. The Northern Limit Line or North Limit Line (NLL) is a disputed maritime demarcation line in the Yellow Sea between North Korea and South Korea. It acts as the de facto maritime boundary between the two Koreas.

29. During the skirmishes, several North Korean ships, including a torpedo boat and patrol boats, were either sunk or damaged.

30. "The Inside Story behind North Korea's Infiltration into the West Sea," *Chungang Ilbo*, 14 June 1999.

31. In September, the debate spilled into the public arena with the joint article from *Nodong Sinmun* and *Kulloja*, the party's theoretical journal. The article was a forceful defense of the isolationist position within the North Korean leadership, which called for adherence to the traditional socialist economic model while highlighting the need for "heightened vigilance" against "imperialist maneuvers" designed to lead countries to reform and open to the outside world. *Nodong Sinmun*, 17 September 1998, as cited in Jae Cheon-lim, *Kim Jong-il's Leadership of North Korea* (London: Routledge, 2009).

32. "North Korea Urges South to Try to Reconcile," *New York Times*, 20 February 1998; "Thawing of ROK-DPRK Relations," *Yonhap*, 20 February 1998.

33. "The Current Status of Aid to North Korea and Its Future Direction," Ministry of Unification Internet website posted on 11 May 1999.

34. "Let Us More Forcefully Carry Out the Second Great *Chollima* March," Korean Central Broadcasting Network report, 24 July 1999. The *Chollima* Movement was a state-sponsored movement in North Korea, analogous to the Chinese Great Leap Forward, intended to promote rapid economic development. It was launched in 1956. North Korea intensified the work-harder campaign by launching the "three-revolution movement" in 1973. The term *chollima* roughly translates as "speed."

35. The increasing number of commentaries on economic affairs in *Nodong Sinmun* departed from the paper's usual editorial content, which focused on political and ideological agitation. See "Propaganda on and Prospects of Economic Construction in DPRK," *Yonhap*, 26 August 1999.

36. "Propaganda on and Prospects of Economic Construction in DPRK."

37. Ibid.
38. Ibid.
39. "North Korea's New Year Message," *Choson Ilbo*, 3 January 2000.
40. Jae Cheon-lim, *Kim Jong-il's Leadership of North Korea*.
41. "DPRK Head Delegate Song Ho-kyong Profiled," *Chungang Ilbo*, 10 April 2000.
42. Pyongyang Korean Central Broadcasting Station, 1 June 2000, announced that Kim Chong-il made an unofficial (*pigongsik*) visit to China on May 29–31 at the invitation of Jiang Zemin, and that he was accompanied by Cho Myong-nok and Kim Yong-chun.
43. "DPRK Leader's Welcome of ROK President Seen as 'Highest Protocol,'" *Yonhap*, 13 June 2000.
44. In essence, the summit laid the blueprint for a cofederal form of government in a future united Korean state. The blueprint was a derivative of China's relationship with Hong Kong—one nation, two systems. The sticking point was who would lead, but the fundamental nature of the relationship was not disputed. The North would be responsible for the North and the South for the South.
45. Though the media did note Kim Tae-chung's title of president, they did not specify which country he governed.
46. Choe Won-gi and Chong Chang-hyon, *Nam-Puk chongsang hoedam 600* [Inter-Korean summit 600 days] (Seoul: Kimyongsa, 2000), as cited in Jae Cheon-lim, *Kim Jong-il's Leadership of North Korea*.
47. North Korea had long been holding fast to the position that establishing a peace system on the Korean peninsula could only come through consultations with the United States. Even during the summit talks with South Korea, North Korea avoided any discussions on military issues and the establishment of a peace system.
48. "Transforming the Armistice Agreement into a Peace Treaty," *Taehan Maeil*, 13 October 2000.
49. Madeleine Albright, with Bill Woodward, *Madame Secretary: A Memoir* (New York: Miramax Books, 2003).
50. "First North-South Defense Ministers Meeting in History," *Chugan Choson*, 12 October 2000.
51. Ibid.
52. "DPRK Military Backs Up Inter-Korean Dialogue," *Korea Times*, 27 October 2000.
53. Ri Chong-sok, researcher at Sejong Institute, as cited in "Does the North Deliberately Avoid Fulfilling the North-South Agreement or Is It Unable to Do So?" *Choson Ilbo*, 22 October 2000.
54. "Has General Secretary Kim Chong-il Stopped Visiting Military Units?" *Yonhap*, 8 November 2000. Kim Chong-il is portrayed in the North Korean media as giving "on-the-spot guidance" (*hyo'njijido*).
55. "Wind of Generational Change Emphasizing Working-Level Capabilities in North Korea's Human Resources," *Hangyore*, 18 January 2001.
56. This would mark Kim Chong-il's 60th birthday, an important event in Korean culture.
57. "DPRK's Intention Behind Setting Up State Institution for Studying Capitalism," *Foresight*, 18 November 2000. In addition, Kim Il-sung University began offering a course on "capitalist economy" in 1997.

58. North Korea actually began to show a genuine interest in capitalism after the mid-1990s, following the death of Kim Il-sung. Since dispatching 15 economic bureaucrats to Shanghai, China, in 1997, with support from the United Nations Development Program (UNDP), North Korea had been training about 200 bureaucrats in market economy by sending them to such countries as the United States, Australia, Thailand, Singapore, and Hungary.

59. At that point, Kim Kyong-hui had not been seen in public since her father's funeral in 1994. She was rumored to be shy and reluctant to take a high-profile role within the regime. Whether this had anything to do with the cancellation of the visit is not clear.

60. He was present at the farewell luncheon during the North–South summit held in Pyongyang on June 15, which was attended by several South Korean businessmen.

61. Though the exact cause for Pyongyang's backtracking is unclear, it most likely had to do with its growing concern over the politics it saw unfolding in South Korea. The popularity of the Kim Tae-chung administration had declined significantly since the summer, in large part because of a severe economic downturn. As such, the administration's focus on the Sunshine Policy appeared to wane. This meant that assumptions Kim and his economic team had made with regard to South Korea would have to be put on hold.

62. "Why Did North Korea Request for Speed Adjustment?" *Chungang Ilbo,* 26 October 2000.

63. New Year's Joint Editorial, *Nodong Sinmun,* 1 January 2001.

64. Kim Chong-il, "The Twenty-first Century Is a Century of Gigantic Change and Creation," *Nodong Sinmun,* 4 January 2001.

65. Rudiger Frank, "North Korea: 'Gigantic Change' and a Gigantic Chance," The Nautilus Institute Policy Forum, 9 May 2003.

66. Despite all its discussion of the need to reconstruct the economy, the editorial was careful to point out the continued importance of the military-first policy. As if to reinforce this notion, the editorial stressed that a "strong national economic power" and a "new era of military-first revolution" are directly linked.

67. According to some reports, Kim Chong-il's visit to Shanghai was facilitated by the existing contact between Kim's eldest son Kim Chong-nam and President Jiang Zemin's eldest son Jiang Mianheng, vice director of the Chinese Academy of Sciences. "Kim Chong-nam's Connection with Jiang Zemin's Eldest Son Behind Kim Chong-il's Visit to PRC," *Choson Ilbo,* 1 July 2001.

68. "DPRK Rush to Receive Overseas Training on 'Market Economy,'" *Hangyore,* 1 July 2001.

69. "Kim Chong-il's New Thinking and Strategy for Economic Development," *Sisa Journal,* 1 February 2001. The core economic development zones were Pyongyang, Sinuiju, Nampo, and Wonsan-Hamhung. Sinuiju was to be developed as a machine industry complex, Nampo as a light industry and processing complex. Pyongyang was to be the core of the IT and financial complex, with the Wonsan-Hamhung area set to be the science and technology complex.

70. This was the first visit to Russia by the leader of North Korea since Kim Il-sung's trip in 1984.

71. In the late 1990s, North Korea's New Year's editorials began to give increased emphasis to technological development. Characterizing science and

technology as one of the three pillars in building a powerful state, the 1999 and 2000 editorials claimed that science and technology were "powerful driving forces for the construction of a powerful state."

72. It is during this period that Kim Chong-nam's name began to surface in the international press as a possible heir apparent. "DPRK's Kim Chong-il Said Planning to Make Son, Kim Chong-nam, His Successor," *Sentaku*, 1 December 2000.

73. "North Korea's Representative Opening-Oriented Faction Kim Tal-hyon Dies," *Tong-a Ilbo*, 28 January 2001.

74. Hong Sok-hyong had served as the chairman of the State Planning Commission. The fact that he was a leading economist was taken into consideration in appointing him as chief party secretary of Hamgyong Province, where North Korea's important industrial facilities, such as the Kim Chaek Iron Complex, Songjin Steel Complex, and Ch'ongjin Shipyard, are clustered. Hong served as chairman of the State Planning Commission, which is in charge of North Korea's economic planning, from December 1993, but he turned over the chairmanship to Pak Nam-gi during the first session of the 10th Supreme People's Assembly held on September 5, 1998. "New Chief Secretary Hong Sok-hyong of the North Hamgyong Provincial Party Committee in North Korea," *Yonhap*, 24 July 2001.

75. The reshuffle of the party secretaries is notable in that it can be interpreted as an indication of strengthening policy-making functions by restructuring the party system, which had been nominal so far. In December 2001, Kim Ki-nam, former secretary for propaganda, was appointed education secretary. On a different note, the secretary for South Korean Affairs Kim Yong-sun's official activities decreased from 73 in 2000 to 35 in 2001. He only accompanied Kim Chong-il on one occasion, as opposed to 44 occasions in 2000.

76. "Entrants to Kim Il-sung University in 1960s on the Rise," *Chungang Ilbo*, 30 July 2001. Kim Chang-sik replaced Ri Ha-sop in March and Ri Chu-so replaced Ri Yon-su. It is likely that the dismissal of former Agriculture Minister Ri Ha-sop was to call him to account for unsatisfactory measures taken to increase agricultural production and for coping with natural disasters. The promotion and appointment of former vice minister Ri Chu-o was known to be a step to expand production of light industry commodities, including daily necessities, which was emphasized in 2001.

77. Andrei Lankov, one of the most insightful Pyongyang watchers, coined the phrase "de-Stalinization from below" to characterize this period. He argued that the July reforms were not top-down driven but simply a recognition by the leadership of what was taking place on the ground. See Andrei Lankov, "Pyongyang Strikes Back: North Korean Policies of 2002–08 and Attempts to Reverse 'De-Stalinization from Below,'" *Asia Policy*, No. 8 (July 2009).

78. "Report Reveals DPRK's Kim Chong-il Began Economic Reform Plan in Oct 01," *Tokyo Shimbun*, 18 August 2002.

79. It is important to note that the North Korean media never referred to the July 1st Measures as "reforms." To do so would risk undermining previous edicts laid down by Kim Il-sung and Kim Chong-il. As such, the economic reforms of July 2002, which were widely reported by the foreign press, were not explicitly mentioned at authoritative levels in North Korean media. The reform campaign was only alluded to in the media through a series of cryptic formulations that track back to a limited-dissemination of Kim Chong-il's speech to economic functionaries in October 2001.

80. Haksoon Paik, "North Korea's Choices for Survival and Prosperity since 1990s: Interplay between Politics and Economics," *Sejong Policy Studies*, Vol. 3, No. 2 (2007).

81. "North Korean [Economic] Inspection Team," *Yonhap*, 24 October 2002.

82. Though it was never made clear, Kim's strategy for these new enterprises was likely based on South Korean President Park Chung-hui's economic development plan in the 1960s. This plan was centered on giant conglomerates, known as *chaebol* (i.e., Samsung, Hyundai, and LG), to spur rapid industrialization.

83. Interview of former Russian diplomat to Pyongyang, June 2004.

84. "Kim's Explanation about Abduction Issue Lacks Credibility," *Yomiuri Shimbun*, 17 September 2002. Kim reportedly explained that those responsible for the abductions had been punished.

85. "The DPRK's Rostrum Places Importance on the Military," *Yonhap*, 28 March 2002.

86. Kim Yun-sim served in the unit named after himself in May 1977. He also served as commander of the West Sea Fleet in July 1991. He was promoted to lieutenant general in November 1996 and to colonel general in April 1997. Two months after his promotion to colonel general, he was appointed as the commander of the Navy. The fact that he was promoted to general only five years after being promoted to colonel general marked him in the minds of many Pyongyang watchers as a rising star whose experience as a field commander was highly valued inside leadership circles.

87. Kim Chong-gak was promoted to general after 10 years, following his promotion to colonel general in 1992. He was appointed vice minister of the People's Armed Forces in December 1992. Since that time, he had become one of the main spokesmen of Kim Chong-il's defense policies. In July 1994, he was listed as a member of the National Funeral Committee for late President Kim Il-sung. Two years later, he delivered a "report" address during the national report meeting to mark the 43rd anniversary of the conclusion of the Armistice Agreement. Together with Cho Myong-nok, Kim Yong-chun, and Kim Il-chol, he played a major role at the January 4, 2001, rally of the Ministry of the People's Armed Forces to discuss and explain the New Year's Joint Editorial.

88. Yo Chun-sok began his rise through the ranks in 1975 when he was promoted to major general and appointed chief of staff of the Fifth Army Corps. Nine years later, he was made commander of the Fourth Army Corps and promoted to lieutenant general. He commanded the Pyongyang–Kaesong expressway construction project in 1989 and was then promoted to colonel general in April 1992. His promotion to general came 10 years after he was promoted to colonel general.

89. The other 12 vice marshals included General Political Bureau Director Cho Myong-nok and Chief of KPA General Staff Kim Yong-chun; Paek Hak-rim, Minister of People's Security; Ri Ha-il, director of the KWP Military Affairs Department of the WPK Central Committee; Kim Ik-hyon, director of the KWP Civil Defense Department; Choe In-tok, president of Kim Il-sung Military University; Kim Il-chol, minister of the People's Armed Forces; Chon Chae-son, First Corps Commander; Pak Ki-so, commander of Pyongyang Capital Defense Command; Ri Chong-san, director of the General Bureau of Military Supplies Mobilization; Ri Yong-mu, vice chairman of the NDC; and Kim Yong-yon, president of the Mangyongdae Revolutionary Academy.

90. Chang was a member of the Central Committee and had served as a member at the Sixth Party Congress held in 1980, which had sanctioned Kim Chong-il's

status as heir apparent. He was promoted to general in April 1992. Chang had also held posts within the security apparatus and was even touted as a possible replacement for Paek Hak-rim as Minister of People's Security.

91. "Chairman Kim Chong-il's Inspection of Military Training on the Rise," *Yonhap*, 6 July 2002.

92. Four South Koreans were killed and an undetermined number of North Koreans. Hannah Fischer, *North Korean Provocative Actions, 1950–2007*, CRS Report for Congress RL30004 (20 April 2007).

93. At the time of the June 15, 1999, West Sea clash, Chairman Kim gave on-the-spot guidance in Chagang Province and then, 14 days later, he visited KPA Unit No. 409. "Chairman Kim Chong-il's Inspection of Military Training on the Rise."

94. "News from North Korea," *Hankyorye*, 5 December 2003.

95. Lankov, "Pyongyang Strikes Back: North Korean Policies of 2002–08 and Attempts to Reverse 'De-Stalinization from Below.'"

CHAPTER 3

1. North Korean General Secretary Kim Chong-il disappeared from public view for 50 days after visiting the Russian embassy in Pyongyang on February 12. He reappeared in public on April 2 after the U.S.–South Korean joint military drills ended, and the United States withdrew a group of long-range bombers that had been deployed within range of the Korean peninsula. On April 3, as if nothing had happened, Kim made a public appearance with senior officials of the North Korean Army, to show that he was still in good health.

2. This account first appeared in a book by Seiichi Ino, a former Japanese Foreign Ministry official and international analyst. See Seiichi Ino, *Kim Jong Il no Yuigon* [Kim Jong Il's Will] (Tokyo: Asahi Shimbun, 2009).

3. Ibid.

4. Ibid.

5. Ri Yong-kuk, *Nanun Kim Chong-il Kyonghowoniotta* (Seoul: Sidae Chongsin, 2002).

6. This Kim Kyong-hui biography draws on interviews with a number of senior North Korean defectors, as well as the excellent biography by Michael Madden, which can be found on his blog *North Korean Leadership Watch*.

7. "True Face of Mysterious Younger Sister Manipulating General Secretary Kim Jong Il With 'Deteriorating Heart Disease,'" *Shukan Gendai*, 30 June 2007.

8. Author's interview with North Korean defectors in Seoul, October 2010.

9. "True Face of Mysterious Younger Sister Manipulating General Secretary Kim Jong Il With 'Deteriorating Heart Disease,'" *Shukan Gendai*.

10. Paek Sung-chu, *Analysis of the Characteristics and Political Backgrounds of the Key Members of the North Korean Military Elite Group* (Seoul: KIDA, 2009).

11. "Ko Chu'n-haeng Is Not Ko Yo'ng-hu'i," *Korea International Institute*, 14 December 2007.

12. Kim Yong-suk, born in 1947, is considered by many Pyongyang watchers to be Kim Chong-il's only official wife. She gave birth to his only legitimate children recognized by Kim Il-sung—two daughters, including his beloved eldest daughter Kim Seol-song.

13. Seiichi Ino, *Kim Jong Il no Yuigon*.

14. Kim Chol-u, *Overview of North Korean Propaganda System and Key Players* (Seoul: KIDA, 2010). Although both Pak and Hyon were promoted during the 1990s, their patronage lines were more tied to Kim Chong-il than Chang Song-taek.

15. Dr. Paek Sung-chu, *Characteristics of the North Korean Succession System in the Post–Kim Jong Il Era and Prospects for the Adjustment of Its US Policy* (Seoul: KIDA, 1 April 2008).

16. ROK NIS website. See "Profiles of 34 Core Associates of Kim Chong-il," *NKnet*, 27 January 2004.

17. Kang Myong-to, *Pyongyang Dreams of Exile* (Seoul: Joongang Daily News, 1995).

18. According to a former bodyguard for Kim Chong-il, Kim referred to several members of his family as "side branches." Figures such as Kim Song-ae, Kim Pyong-il, Kim Yong-il, and Kim Yong-chu were potential rivals and if these "branches" were allowed to thrive, they would "prevent the tree from growing well." Yong-kuk, *Nanun Kim Chong-il Kyonghowoniotta*. Ri Yong-kuk, prior to defection in 1999, was allegedly a member of North Korean leader Kim Chong-il's bodyguard unit.

19. Information provided by Open Source Center, July 2007. See also "Order North Korea's Hierarchy Shows No Noticeable Change," *Yonhap*, 9 January 2003. After Kim Il-sung died, Kim Yong-chu was confined to Official Residence No. 403 where he was confined and was receiving medical care for his heart disease.

20. "The Secret Life of the Great Leader's Son in Warsaw," *Gazeta Wyborcza Online*, 25 December 2008.

21. Ibid.

22. This article underscored Kim Chong-il's leadership credentials and defined father–son succession as a North Korean "tradition." It is considered by most Pyongyang watchers to be the first indication by the Kim regime that North Korea would undergo a second hereditary succession.

23. "Rotten, Sick Society with Rampant Social Vices of All Sorts," *Nodong Sinmun*, 20 January 2002.

24. Over the course of the next four years, numerous articles would appear under the Ko Yong-hui byline, mainly lauding the exploits of the Kim family. Information provided by Open Source Center.

25. Ko Yong-hui, "Nuclear Weapons Reduction in Name Only," *Nodong Sinmun*, 23 January 2002.

26. President George W. Bush referenced the "Axis of Evil" in his State of the Union Address on January 29, 2002, and often repeated it throughout his presidency, describing governments that he accused of helping terrorism and seeking weapons of mass destruction. Bush labeled Iran, Iraq, and North Korea as the axis of evil.

27. Ko Yong-hui, "Special Treatment for Eradicating Fear of 'Terror' Syndrome," *Nodong Sinmun*, 12 March 2002.

28. The South Korean magazine *Wolgan Choson* reportedly obtained the document, which was labeled "limited to internal use," through Japanese intelligence channels.

29. Though the document failed to mention the name of the "respected mother," it was most likely a reference to Ko, given her status as Kim's wife, by

law or common law, and *Nodong Sinmun*'s proxy use of name months before. If
the intention had been to idolize Kim Yong-suk, widely believed to be Kim's legal
wife, there would have been no good reason to hide her name. "Who Is the 'Respected Mother' Who Is Destined to Become the Second Kim Chong-suk?" *Wolgan
Choson,* 1 Mar 2003.

30. In the document, the relationship of the "respected mother" to the supreme
commander is described as "the loyal subject," "guarding [*howi*] warrior," and
"number 1 aide." "Who is the 'Respected Mother' Who Is Destined To Become the
Second Kim Chong-suk?"

31. "North Korea Creates Cult around Mother of Kim Chong-il's Son," *Kyodo,*
15 February 2003. In August 2002, the Korean People's Army Publishing House reportedly published an in-house manuscript titled *The Respected Mother Who Is the
Most Faithful and Loyal 'Subject' to the Dear Leader Comrade Supreme Commander.* The
book described Ko Yong-hui as a model for all the officers and soldiers of the People's Army, like the anti-Japanese heroine Comrade Kim Chung-Suk (Kim Chong-il's
mother), who accompanied the great leader (referring to Kim Il-sung) early in the
anti-Japanese war and raised revolutionary descendants.

32. "N. Korea Intensifies Personality Cult of First Lady," *Yonhap,* 10 May
2004.

33. Kim Chong-il even attempted to appoint Chang Song-taek as the
director of the State Security Department, which is one of North Korea's most
powerful organizations, but was stopped by Kim Il-sung who felt that Chang was
becoming too powerful.

34. "Exclusive Inside Story on North Korea's Power Struggle—Kim Chong-il
Places Number Two Man Chang Song-t'aek under House Arrest," *Wolgan Choson,*
1 July 2004

35. Ken E. Gause, *Police State: North Korea's System of Control, Surveillance, and
Punishment* (Washington, DC: U.S. Committee for Human Rights in North Korea,
2011).

36. "Exclusive Inside Story on North Korea's Power Struggle, *Wolgan Choson.*

37. Seiichi Ino, *Kim Jong Il no Yuigon.* Seiichi Ino is a former Japanese Foreign
Ministry official and international analyst.

38. Toshimitsu Shigemura, *Kim Jong Il no Shotai* [The True Identity of Kim
Chong-il] (Tokyo: Kodansha, 2008). Toshimitsu Shigemura is a professor at Waseda
University.

39. Reports noted that medical teams from western countries secretly came to
treat her. In the mid-1990s, she supposedly traveled to France, and later to Switzerland in 2000, to treat her tumor and hepatic symptoms.

40. Ken E. Gause, *North Korean Military Trends: Military-First Policy to a Point*
(Carlisle, PA: Strategic Studies Center of the Army War College, 2006).

41. Won was ill with leukemia. He died in May 2004.

42. For a detailed history of the Military Security Command, see Gause, *Police
State: North Korea's System of Control, Surveillance, and Punishment.*

43. For the next five years, the Pyongyang watching community engaged in
speculation over the identity of Paek Se-bong, who seemed to appear out of no-
where. A popular theory was that Paek Se-bong's name means "three peaks of
Mt. Paektu" and was an alias for Kim Chong-chol, the presumed heir apparent.
In January 2008, it was revealed that NDC member Paek Se-bong was chairman
of the Second Economic Committee in charge of the defense industry. "Chairman

of the Second Economic Committee in Charge of Munitions Is National Defense Commission Member Paek Se-bong," *Yonhap*, 13 January 2008.

44. Ken E. Gause, *The North Korean Leadership: Evolving Regime Dynamics in the Kim Chong-il Era* (Alexandria, VA: CNA, September 2003).

45. Dick Nanto provides some sobering figures. About 40 percent of the population suffered from malnutrition, including 30 percent of the children. See his chapter in Young Whan Kihl and Hong Nack Kim, eds., *North Korea: The Politics of Regime Survival* (New York: M. E. Sharpe, 2006).

46. Pak's rapid rise among the ranks of the technocrats was probably due to his ties to former Premier Yon Hyong-muk and the so-called "Prague School" of economists at the upper echelons of the North Korean regime. Alexandre A. Mansourov, "Inside North Korea's Black Box: Reversing the Optics," in Kongdan Oh Hassig, et al., *North Korean Policy Elites* (Alexandria, VA: Institute for Defense Analyses, 2004). Alexandre A. Mansourov is a specialist in Northeastern Asian security policies and a graduate of Kim Il-sung National University. He is one of the few U.S. experts on North Korean leadership affairs.

47. Figures made available by the South Korean Ministry of Unification.

48. As a result of the July measures, many young "influential capitalists" began emerging in North Korea. These "red capitalists" were the children of government officials who had access to foreign currency, in some cases in the millions of dollars. Most of these upper-class children were involved in foreign trade ventures, through which they had come to understand the capitalist market economy and established outside contacts. By the late 1990s, the actions of these children of the elite to eschew traditional positions within the regime in favor of hard currency ventures had become problematic. Kim Chong-il even ordered a full investigation should be conducted on the status of cadre children in external organs and that cases of employment by dishonest methods should be uncovered and corrected. Despite these efforts, recent reporting in the international press suggests that a group of offspring of senior officials has been involved in a number of illicit activities. Known as *Ponghwajo* ("Torch Group"), this group is reportedly led by O Se-wan, the son of O Kuk-yol, the vice chairman of the National Defense Commission. Other members allegedly include Kim Chol-un (son of Kim Chung-il, vice director of Kim Chong-il's personal secretariat), Kang Tae-seung (son of Kang Sok-chu, vice premier), Kim Chang-hyok (son of Kim Chang-sop, deputy director of the SSD), and Kim Chol (son of Kim Won-hong, director of the Military Security Command). See "North Korea Elite Linked to Crime," *Washington Times*, 25 May 2010.

49. "North Korea Noticeably Stressing Military-First," *Yonhap*, 6 February 2003.

50. Hwang Chang-yop, *Truth and Lies about North Korea* (Seoul: Unification Policy Institute, 1998).

51. "Kim Jong-il Inspects Military Unit, His First since China Trip," *Yonhap*, 3 May 2004.

52. The train explosion encapsulated many of the problems that faced the Pyongyang watching community in 2004. Given the telltale signs emerging of a succession process, this was a year steeped in rumor regarding politics at the highest levels of the regime. See "Three Major Murderous Intentions Lurking for Kim Chong-il," *Sing Tao Jih Pao*, 4 May 2004.

53. Speculation first surfaced in the Japanese media in April 2002, and by 2003, the former South Korean Minister of Unification, Kang In-tok, enthusiastically

proclaimed that internal North Korean documents made clear that Kim Chong-chol would eventually emerge as the successor.

54. The Paek Se-bong speculation was tied to North Korea's "revolution mythology" that Kim Chong-il was born on Paekto Mountain, which was the base for the armed resistance battle against Japan. As such, a possible successor could be tied to this mythology through a cover name such as Paek Se-bong, which can loosely be deconstructed to mean "the new (*se*) peak (*pong*) of (*paekto*) Mountain." With regard to "*pong*," there are also views that it comes from the word "bud" (*pongori*).See "Kim Jong Il, 63 Years Old Today; Hereditary Succession Movement Becoming Active," *Sankei Shimbun*, 16 February 2005.

55. "With Do-or-Die Resolve—Functionaries and People's Public Security Agents in Yongch'on County People's Public Security Station," Uriminjokkkiri, 25 May 2004. Uriminjokkkiri is the Internet home page for North Korea's "By the United Efforts of Our People" movement. Its site is administered out of Shenyang, China, http://www.uriminzokkiri.com.

56. "Kim Chong-il's Wife Said Back in DPRK after Hospitalization in Paris," Kyodo World Service, 20 June 2004.

57. *Nodong Sinmun*, 7 July 2004.

58. "N.K. Paper Comments on Qualifications for Successor to Kim Jong-il," *Yonhap*, 7 July 2004.

59. "North Korea Appoints New Police Chief," *Yonhap*, 10 July 2004.

60. See Gause, *Police State: North Korea's System of Control, Surveillance, and Punishment*.

61. Established in Spain in 2000 with the approval of North Korea's Overseas Cultural Contact Committee, the KFA serves as Pyongyang's largest international contact organization, with members in over 70 countries.

62. "Disturbance in General Secretary Kim's Family—Wife Died, His Sister Received Treatment for Alcoholism, Severe Mental Illness in Paris," *Tokyo Shimbun*, 17 September 2004.

63. Many Pyongyang watchers doubted the story about Kim Kyong-hui's car accident. If the incident had occurred, one could expect that Kim's son and daughter, both of whom were studying in Europe, would have been brought back to Pyongyang. This apparently did not occur.

64. Radiopress is a Japanese agency dedicated to the monitoring of the North Korean press.

65. "North Korean Media Reportedly Drop Kim Chong-il's 'Dear Leader' Title," *Kyodo World Service*, 17 November 2004.

66. Beginning with the Sixth Party Congress in October 1980, the North Korean media began to refer to Kim Chong-il as the "Dear Leader Comrade Kim Chong-il" (*ch'inaehanu'n chidoja*). Official media use of this term continued until the death of Kim Il-sung, after which Kim Chong-il was referred to as the "Great Leader." Other North Korean media honorifics to describe Kim Chong-il include the great leader of our party and our people" (*uri tanggwa uri inminu'i widaehan ryo'ngdoja*), "the beloved and respected leader" (*kyo'ngaehanu'n ryo'ngdoja*), "the great general" (*widehan changgun*), and "the great Comrade Kim Chong-il." "DPRK Leader Status Appears Unchanged Despite Media, Portrait Anomalies," *OSC Feature*, 23 November 2004.

67. Ibid.

68. Ibid.

69. "Monolithic System of Leadership in Entire Party, Entire Army," *Choson Sinbo*, 24 November 2004.

70. The number of military-related events Kim attended surged from 38 out of 99 public appearances in 2002 to 60 out of 92 in 2004. "Kim Jong Il Used Public Appearances in 2004 to Boost Military Morale," *OSC Feature*, 24 January 2005.

71. Mansourov, "Inside North Korea's Black Box."

CHAPTER 4

1. *Nodong Sinmun*, 1 January 2005. Additional information provided by Open Source Center.

2. Meredith Jung-en Woo, "North Korea in 2005," *Asian Survey*, Vol. 46, No. 1 (January 2006).

3. Kim Yong-yun and Choe Su-yong, *Analysis of the Situation for Unification for 2005–02—The Situation of North Korea's Economic Reform* (Seoul: Institute for National Unification, 23 March 2005). Kim Yong-yun is the director of the Center for North Korean Economy and Choe Su-yong is a senior research fellow of the Center for North Korean Economy.

4. "DPRK Opens Unprecedented Military, Party Policy Meeting," *OSC Feature*, 5 February 2005.

5. It seemed ironic that Pak Pong-chu would become the principal spokesperson for the reconsolidation of control over the economy. But, as the joint editorials for 2004 and 2005 noted, the Cabinet had nominal responsibility for this sector. The 2005 editorial stated that the Cabinet's "functions and role" was to be the "organizer and executor of the country's general economic programs" and that this role should be "enhanced."

6. Ibid.

7. Jung-en Woo, "North Korea in 2005."

8. According to one source, the third meeting of the 11th Supreme People's Assembly was scheduled to be held in March 2005, but was postponed because of a conflict between the party and the government surrounding the introduction of market economy. "North Korea's 1 July [Economic] Measures, Which Adopted Market Economy, Backfired Due to Power Struggle between the Workers Party of Korea and Cabinet," *JoongAng Ilbo*, 30 December 2009.

9. "North Korean PM Says Farming, Increased Electricity, Coal Production Key in 2005," KCBS, 11 April 2005, BBC-MAPP, 13 April 2005.

10. Andrei Lankov, "Pyongyang Strikes Back: North Korean Policies of 2002–08 and Attempts to Reverse 'De-Stalinization from Below,'" *Asia Policy*, No. 8 (July 2009).

11. On July 9, KCNA announced that North Korea would return to the Six Party Talks. Under much anticipation, the talks began on July 25 in Beijing, but quickly stalled over language of how to describe North Korea's decision to give up its nuclear program. See Mike Chinoy, *Meltdown: The Inside Story of the North Korean Nuclear Crisis* (New York: St. Martin's Griffin, 2009).

12. In September, the U.S. Department of Treasury announced that North Korea had been circulating counterfeit dollar bills and laundering illegal international transaction fees through Banco Delta Asia (BDA). The United States then designated BDA as a "primary money laundering concern." In October, the United States froze assets of eight North Korean enterprises, including Haesong Trading

Corporation and Korea Pugang Trading Corporation, under charges of participating in the proliferation of WMD. In February, North Korean Foreign Minister Paek Nam-sun claimed that the resumption of the Six Party Talks was impossible as long as sanctions against his country remained in place.

13. Even North Korea's relations with China were chilled. China had endorsed the UN Security Council resolution against North Korea following the missile test.

14. KCNA, 28 January 2006.

15. "North Korea Will Also Grant General Amnesty—There Is Rumor That Chang So'ng-t'aek Will Be Included," *Kyo'nghyang Sinmun*, 13 August 2005.

16. "High Rise Residences in Pyongyang Spruced Up: Relating to Comeback of General Secretary Kim's Brother-in-Law?" JijiWeb, 8 July 2006.

17. The campaign had continued, albeit at a lower volume, for nearly two years. After Ko's death, the Ko Yong-hui byline that appeared next to stories in *Nodong Sinmun* on the Kim family was replaced by a standard "staff reporter" byline, which eventually disappeared in December 2006. Information confirmed by Open Source Center and Radiopress.

18. "North Korea Now . . . Insecurity Inside on Top of Pressure from the Outside," *JoongAng Ilbo*, 4 August 2006.

19. "Kim Jong Il Bans Succession Talks," *Dong-A Ilbo*, 5 January 2007.

20. Li Dunqiu, "DPRK's Reform and Sino-DPRK Economic Cooperation." Paper presented at the DPRK Energy Experts Working Group Meeting held on 26 and 27 June 2006 in Palo Alto, California.

21. So Chae-chin, "Significance of Chang Song-taek's Visit to China," Online Series (Seoul: Korean Institute for National Unification, 1 March 2006).

22. Jinwook Choi, "The Changing Party-State System and Outlook for Reform in North Korea," *International Journal of Korean Unification Studies,* Vol. 18, No. 1 (2009).

23. Park Hyeong Jung, "North Korean Conservative Policy Since 2006 and Chang Song-taek: Looking at 2009," Online Series (Seoul: KINU, 15 January 2009).

24. Jung-en Woo, "North Korea in 2005."

25. For this duplicity of the military-first economic line, see Kwon Yong-kyong, "The North Korean Regime's Economic Reform and Open Strategy after the 1 July Measure and Future Prospects," *North Korea Studies Newsletter*, 1 December 2008.

CHAPTER 5

1. "DPRK 2006 New Year's Joint Editorial," *OSC Analysis*, 11 January 6.

2. *Weekly Dong-A*, 27 December 2005. This harvest was no doubt a leading factor in North Korea's decision in January 2006 to cease accepting food assistance from the World Food Program.

3. "DPRK 2006 New Year's Joint Editorial."

4. In terms of disappearances within the North Korean elite, Politburo member Kye Ung-tae, former Minister of People's Security Paek Hak-nim, Director of the KWP Unification Department Rim Tong-ok, and Minister of Foreign Affairs Paek Nam-sun passed away in late 2006 and early 2007. Rumors also began to spread in July 2006 that O Se-uk, one of O Kuk-yol's sons, fled from North Korea in 2004 with the assistance of the United States.

5. "ROK Online Daily on Death of Chang So'ng-kil, Brother of Kim Jong Il's In-Law Chang So'ng-t'aek," *Daily NK,* 12 July 2006.

6. "Kim's Niece Kills Herself in Paris," *JoongAng Ilbo,* 18 September 2006. According to European sources, Chang Kum-song committed suicide after an argument with her family over her choice of boyfriend.

7. "DPRK Leader's Brother-in-Law Chang So'ng-t'aek Injured in Car Accident," *JoongAng Ilbo,* 8 October 2006.

8. "Chang So'ng-t'aek Accompanies Leader on Visits," *OSC Feature*—KCNA, 14 November 2006. A report from early 2007 noted that Chang had traveled to Russia to receive medical treatment. This report, however, was never verified. "DPRK Leader's Brother-in-Law Reportedly in Russia for Medical Treatment," *Yonhap,* 8 March 2007.

9. "The World's First Disclosure Scoop; Kim Jong Il's 'New Wife Ok Hu'i Is a 42-Year-Old Beautiful Woman'; His China Visit Was Also a Honeymoon," *Shukan Gendai,* 25 February 2006.

10. Ibid.

11. Some sources contend that she joined Kim's secretariat in the early 1980s. But, if she graduated in 1985, she most likely did not become Kim's secretary until the mid- to late 1980s.

12. Other sources argue that Kim Ok's role within Kim Chong-il's personal secretariat at this time was more wide ranging. According to one source, she belonged to the KWP Organization and Guidance Department's 5th Division (all who work near Kim Chong-il, such as guards, typists, and telephone exchangers, belong to the 5th Division) and was responsible for scheduling Chairman Kim's off-duty hours, beyond his official schedule. She also had ties to Office 39 and handled Kim's personal finances.

13. "Wedding Bells for Kim Jong Il," *Dong-A Ilbo,* 23 July 2006.

14. "Scoop Unearthed: Fourth Wife Behind Nuclear Test? Photo of North Korea's First Lady 'Kim Ok' Taken!" *Shukan Bunshun,* 19 October 2006.

15. Dr. Paek Su'ng-chu, *Characteristics of the North Korean Succession System in the Post–Kim Jong Il Era and Prospects for the Adjustment of Its US Policy* (Seoul: KIDA, 1 April 2008).

16. "The Truth about Kim Jong Il's Fourth Wife," *Shindong-A*, 1 September 2006. In North Korean parlance, the term "comrade" is used for superiors. "Friend" is used for subordinates or those of equal standing. Author's discussions with former North Korean cadre.

17. "Kim Jong Il's Chef's Inside Look at the Missile Launches, Kim's New Wife, Possible Successors, and More," *Yomiuri Weekly,* 7 September 2006.

18. Author's discussion with senior-level defector in Seoul, April 2009. See also Seiichi Ino, *Kim Jong Il no Yuigon* [Kim Jong Il's Will] (Tokyo: Asahi Shimbun, 2009). Seiichi Ino is a former Japanese Foreign Ministry official and international analyst.

19. "The Truth about Kim Jong Il's Fourth Wife," Shindong-A.

20. "Background of Kim Chong-nam's Rumored Exile into Europe," *JoongAng Ilbo,* 6 June 2010.

21. Kim Ok had a vested interest in squelching this discussion. As power centers formed around the various contenders, it could potentially undermine her position as first lady. See "The Coming on Stage of Kim Jong Il's New Wife and the Succession Picture," *Yonhap,* 23 July 2006.

22. Kim Sol-song is Kim Chong-il's oldest legitimate daughter. He has another daughter, Kim Hye-kyong, who was born to his mistress Song Hae-nim. Though her name had appeared in the international media before 2006, details about Kim Sol-song's biography were unknown. See Ken E. Gause, *The North Korean Leadership: Evolving Regime Dynamics in the Kim Chong-il Era* (Alexandria, VA: CNA, September 2003).

23. Author's interview of senior North Korean defector, who previously served in the KWP Propaganda and Agitation Department, April 2009.

24. Within the KWP Propaganda and Agitation Department, Kim Sol-song was a vice director of a department in charge of propagating party ideology, policies, and plans among the citizenry. See Kim Chol-u, *Overview of North Korean Propaganda System and Key Players* (Seoul: KIDA, 2010).

25. "Kim Jong Il's Daughter Has Control Over [Kim Jong Il's] Personal Affairs such as Schedule Arrangements," JijiWeb, 10 March 2006. Some sources claim that Kim Sol-song assumed such responsibilities in the 1990s. See *Choson Ilbo,* 18 October 2001 and 24 February 2006.

26. "Kim Jong Il's Daughter Has Control Over [Kim Jong Il's] Personal Affairs such as Schedule Arrangements."

27. "Dreams That Kim Cho'g-chol, Prince of the Kim Dynastry," *Seiron,* 1 June 2006 and 1–31 July 2006. See also Ken E. Gause, "The Rise of Kim Jong Un," *Foreign Policy Magazine* (April 2009).

28. Mike Chinoy, *Meltdown: The Inside Story of the North Korean Nuclear Crisis* (New York: St. Martin's Griffin, 2009).

29. Lee Gee-dong, "An Examination of North Korea's Power Hierarchy and Prospects for Change," *Vantage Point,* Vol. 30, No. 2 (February 2007).

30. The military's prominence on leadership rostrums had been clearly growing. Cho Myong-rok, Kim Yong-chun, Kim Il-chol, and Ri Yong-mu all featured prominently on the central report meeting rostrums commemorating the 60th founding anniversary of the party on October 9, 2005, and the 42nd anniversary of Kim Chong-il's start of party work on June 18, 2006.

31. "North Korean Military Must Be Persuaded," *OhmyNews,* 1 June 2006.

32. The North Korean media had referred to the "command post of the revolution" whenever it referred to Kim Chong-il at the center of a unified party, military, and people. By attaching the phrase "generation after generation" to this construct, the phrase took on a new meaning beyond the Kim Chong-il era, hence a hereditary succession.

33. Lee Gee-dong, "An Examination of North Korea's Power Hierarchy and Prospects for Change."

34. "A Brilliant Succession," *Nodong Sinmun,* 21 July 2001. This article defined Kim Chong-il's leadership credentials as part of the father-son succession as a North Korean tradition. The political essay noted that "we should carry forward the tradition in its purest form." The essay went on to say that a "revolution with no tradition or to which tradition is not being succeeded is dead."

35. Author's interviews with South Korean scholars with ties to the intelligence community, April 2009.

36. Ibid.

37. "By Order of North Korea: UN Halts Food Assistance There," *New York Times,* 7 January 2006.

38. Pyongyang's invitation appeared to be spurred by a U.S. invitation to Iran in June to hold nuclear talks.

39. The only other times were in September 2005, August 2000, January 2000, and January 1998. Information provided by Open Source Center, December 2006.

40. Open Source Center tracking of Kim Chong-il's cohorts, 2007.

41. "DPRK in Energy Crisis: Premier Was Ordered to Exercise Restraint in His Behavior While Minister in Charge of Power Supply Was Dismissed Over His Remarks Suggesting Limiting Power Supply," *Mainichi Shimbun*, 18 January 2007.

42. "Let Us Usher in a Great Heyday of Military-First Korea Full of Confidence in Victory," *Nodong Sinmun*, 1 January 2007. See also "Joint Editorial," KCNA, 1 January 2007.

43. "DPRK 2006 New Year's Joint Editorial."

44. "Ex-DPRK Premier Pak Pong-chu Likely Sacked for 'Capitalistic' Proposal," *Mainichi Shimbun*, 13 May 2007.

45. *Nodong Sinmun*, 3 December 2006.

46. *Monthly Choson*, 1 May 2006.

47. *Choson Sinbo*, 9 November 2006.

48. "Spokesman for DPRK Foreign Ministry on Results of DPRK-U.S. Talks," KCNA, 19 January 2007.

49. Ri Sok-chol, "Timely Appeal for Reunification and Patriotism," *Nodong Sinmun*, 19 January 2007.

50. "Secretary of WPK, C.C. Supports Joint Statement of DPRK Political Parties, Government, and Organizations," KCNA, 21 January 2007.

51. U.S. Department of State, *Initial Actions for the Implementation of the Joint Statement*, 13 February 2007.

52. "5th Session of 11th SPA of DPRK Held," KCNA, 11 April 2007.

53. Author's interviews in Seoul, April 2009.

54. "Let Us Even More Thoroughly Implement the Party's Economic Policy with the Taechon Spirit—Cabinet Enlarged at Plenary Meeting," *Minju Choson*, 18 April 2007.

55. "DPRK Premier Kim Yung-il Delivers Report Making DPRK's 59th Founding Anniversary," KCBS, 8 September 2007.

56. Patrick McEachern, *Inside the Red Box: North Koreas Post-Totalitarian Politics* (Louisiana State University Agricultural and Mechanical College, Ph.D. Dissertation, May 2009).

57. North Korean defense budget figures are not reported in raw numbers, but as percentages of the budget. Consistently, the North Korean media has claimed that defense spending ranges from 14 to 16 percent. "Gradual Increase in DPRK's Defense Budget," *Yonhap*, 25 March 2004. However, taking into consideration the characteristics of the North Korean budgetary system, ROK budget analysts believe that North Korea's actual military spending is over 30 percent of its GNP. See *ROK Defense Whitepaper* 2004.

58. Kim Chong-il, "On Becoming about a New Turnaround in Basic Construction" (conversation with chief functionaries of the party and state economic organs, 11 August 2004), *Selected Works of Kim Chong-il* (Pyongyang: Workers' Party of Korea Publishing House, 2005).

59. "Let Us Usher in a Great Heyday of Military-First Korea Full of Confidence in Victory." See also "DPRK 2006 New Year's Joint Editorial," *OSC Feature*, 12 January 2006.

60. Pyongyang Radio, 11 April 2007, as cited in Open Source Center reporting.

61. Ibid.

62. After an initial jump from 14.4 percent to 14.5 percent from 2000 to 2002 to 15.4 percent in 2003, planned allocations increased to 15.5 percent in 2004 and 15.9 percent in 2005 before leveling off at 15.9 percent in 2006. Figures provided by Open Source Center.

63. This seems to be the consensus view held by Pyongyang watchers in the United States and South Korea.

64. A cursory examination of the NDC membership in 2007 reveals that it was populated with old men, many of who were not in good health. First Vice Chairman Cho Myong-nok (81) was known to have had several treatments in foreign countries (primarily China) due to his precarious health. Ri Yong-mu at age 84 was the oldest official holding a government position among the military defense sector. His health was also rumored to be fragile.

65. VMAR Cho Myong-nok did appear at the military parade commemorating the KPA's 75th founding anniversary on April 25, 2007.

66. "The North Reshuffles High-ranking Military Leaders," *Yonhap*, 19–20 May 2007.

67. See "DPRK NDC Is Expanded, Restructured into Permanent Structure," *Yonhap*, 5 October 2007. See also "DPRK Vice Foreign Minister Kang Appointed as NDC Member," *Chosun Ilbo*, 18 June 2007. Kang's appointment has not been verified and is based on unnamed Russian sources.

68. A close confidant of Kim Chong-il, Kim Yang-gon took over a post that had been vacant since the August 2006 death of Rim Dong-ok, who also served as vice chairman of the Committee for the Peaceful Reunification of the Fatherland. The new chief of the United Front Department, a career diplomat, began his career in the KWP International Department in the 1970s. In the 1980s, he supervised activities for Eastern Europe. He became vice director of the KWP International Department in the 1990s and director in 1997. He sat alongside Kim Chong-il when he met with the South's then Unification Minister Chong Tong-yong in June 2005. He also accompanied the North's leader during his unofficial visit to China in 2001.

69. Some Pyongyang watchers ascribed the SPA appointments to a generational turnover. From their perspective, the reshuffle brought members of the so-called third generation to the fore. With the majority of North Korea's top generals in their late 60s, 70s, and even 80s, a generational shift in command was inevitable. Of the 586 generals Kim Chong-il promoted in rank since taking power in 1994, 436 were colonels being promoted to major-general. This meant that for the first time, the military was being led by officers who had no combat experience. "High-Level Personnel Reshuffle of the Korean People's Army: Hard-Line Policy Remains Unchanged," *Feng Huang Wang*, 8 May 2007. This assertion of a generational turnover was challenged by other Pyongyang watchers. In terms of age difference, there was a six-year difference between Director of the KWP United Front Department Kim Yang-kon (born in 1942) and his predecessor Im Tong-ok (born in 1936). There was a nine-year age difference between Chief of the General Staff Kim Kyok-sik (born in 1944) and his predecessor NDC Vice Chairman Kim Yong-chun (born in 1935), and a five-year difference between Premier Kim Yong-il (born in 1944) and the former Premier Pak Pong-chu (born in 1939). Likewise, the age difference, from five years at minimum to nine years at maximum, falls far short of the criterion for generation change based on age.

70. While reporting the names of 19 high-ranking generals who attended the April 2007 parade, the Korean Central News Agency placed Kim Kyok-sik at the fifth position, following Kim Chong-il, President Kim Yong-nam of the Supreme People's Assembly, Cho Myong Rok, and newly appointed Premier Kim Yong-il.

71. Dr. Pak Yong-taek, *Enhanced Position of the North Korean Military and Its Influence on Policymaking* (Seoul: KIDA, 2008).

72. "Commander of DPRK's 108th Mechanized Corps Kim Myong-guk Profiled," National Intelligence Service Database, 13 March 2003.

73. "DPRK's Vice Director of KPA General Political Department Propaganda Bureau Pak Chae-kyong Profiled," National Intelligence Service Database, 23 April 2003.

74. "The North Reshuffles High-ranking Military Leaders," *Yonhap,* 19–20 May 2007.

75. "The Longest Night in Pyongyang: General Secretary Kim Jong Il Hospitalized Urgently for Cardiac Infarction," *Shukan Gendai,* 23 June 2007.

76. According to South Korean sources interviewed by the author, Kim may have undergone surgery in May for a heart condition. There were also rumors that a Chinese medical team was dispatched to Pyongyang in June to care for Kim. Despite these health issues, Kim was able to conduct the affairs of state. Interviews in South Korea, April 2009. See also "The Longest Night in Pyongyang: General Secretary Kim Jong Il Hospitalized Urgently for Cardiac Infarction," *Shukan Gendai.*

77. "NIS: There Is No Symptom of Kim Jong Il's Chronic Illness Getting Worse," *Yonhap,* 11 June 2007.

78. "Kim Jong Il Enjoys Art Performance Given by Russian Art Troupe," KCNA, 25 June 2007.

79. North Korea had pledged in February to disable its Yongbyon reactor, but it missed an April deadline because of a dispute over $25 million in North Korean–linked funds that had been frozen because of a Treasury Department investigation. North Korea demanded a wire transfer, but for months no bank would agree to accept the money because about half of it appeared linked to North Korean money laundering and other illicit activities.

80. "Foreign Ministry Spokesman Emphasizes We, Too, Will Enter Into 13 February Agreement Implementation Under Condition Where the Frozen Funds Issue Has Been Resolved," KCNA, 25 June 2007.

81. "South Korean Visits North, Offering Aid for Arms Cuts," *New York Times,* 3 October 2007.

82. "DPRK KPA P'anmunjo'm Mission Chief Proposes DPRK-US Military Talks," *OSC Feature*—Korean Central Broadcasting Station, 13 July 2007.

83. "U.S. and S. Korean Bellicose Forces' War Exercises against DPRK Assailed," *Nodong Sinmun,* 3 September 2007; "Lesson of History," *Nodong Sinmun,* 6 September 2007.

84. Statement by Robert Carlin in Chinoy, *Meltdown: The Inside Story of the North Korean Nuclear Crisis.*

85. Ibid.

86. North Korean media, however, did not indicate Chang's new status until December 7, when it referred to him as a "department director of the Workers' Party of Korea Central Committee" in a news report on Kim Chong-il's inspection of Korean People's Army production units.

87. Until the early 1990s, the Central Committee contained an Administrative Department. It was headed by Kim Si-hak, a figure who along with Chang Song-taek built the foundation for establishing the succession structure in the Three Revolutions Team Movement. Hyon Song-il, *Pukhan-u'i Kukkajo'llyak-kwa P'awo' Ellit'u'* [North Korea's National Strategy and Power Elite] (Seoul: Sunin Publishing, 2006).

88. As part of Pak Pong-chu's effort to secure the Cabinet's control over the economy, he had engineered the so-called June 9th Directive, which established the National Economic Cooperation Committee (NECC). This committee became the primary entity for doing business with South Korea's private sector.

89. *Dong-A Ilbo*, 11 February 2008.

90. According to South Korean reporting, the KWP Organization Guidance Department and the Central Prosecutor's Office launched an investigation in 2006 centered on organizations dealing with South Korean affairs, including the KWP United Front Department. Chon Hyon-chun, *Analysis of Recent Changes in North Korean Power Elites* (Seoul: Korea Institute for National Unification, April 2008). At the same time as the NEC/NECF affair, the KWP Organization Guidance Department was also investigating a high-ranking official of Office 39, an office closely tied to Kim Chong-il's personal secretariat. Choe Chong-son was "dismissed" as director of the Taesong General Bureau for embezzlement of government funds in the amount of $1.4 million (approximately 150 million yen). Lee Yong-hwa, "Massive Purge of Officials for Embezzlement of Government Funds Effected Repeatedly," *Sapio*, 9 April 2008.

91. "Chang Song-taek of the North Leading the Party's Administrative Department and the Social Cleanup Drive," *Yonhap*, 17 March 2008.

92. Pak Hyong-chung, *North Korea's Conservative Domestic Policies Since 2006 and Chang Song-taek; Looking Ahead to North Korea in 2009* (Seoul: Korea Institute for National Unification, December 2008).

93. Chinoy, *Meltdown: The Inside Story of the North Korean Nuclear Crisis.*

94. Stephen Haggard and Marcus Noland, "North Korea in 2008," *Asian Survey*, Vol. 49, No. 1 (January/February 2009).

95. "Repeated Babble About 'Alliance' which Calls for the Era of Confrontation," *Nodong Sinmun*, 17 March 2008.

96. Pyongyang radio, 11 April 2008.

97. Pyongyang radio, 9 April 2008.

98. Haggard and Noland, "North Korea in 2008."

99. According to one source, North Korea faced a food shortage of 1.8 million metric tons and 200,000 to 300,000 lives could be lost in 2008 due to renewed famine. This was disputed by other sources that claimed that the situation was not that serious. "North Korean National Defense Commission Orders Distribution of Wartime Food Reserves to the Army," *DailyNK*, 27 May 2008.

100. The regime described rising world food prices as a "global trend" not specific to North Korea. The implicit message was that as with other countries, North Korea faces severe challenges to feed its people. *Nodong Sinmun*, 10 May 2008.

101. Pyongyang radio, 9 April 2008.

102. According to one source, North Korea acknowledged possessing 38 kilograms of plutonium. Chinoy, *Meltdown: The Inside Story of the North Korean Nuclear Crisis.*

103. Up to the day of the parade, signals were coming from the regime that this would be the largest parade review "in this generation." The program for the parade was set at the beginning of the year and drills and exercises related to the event had been taking place for six months. Most North Korea ceremonial reviews take one hour. 60th anniversary reviews have taken longer; the parade commemorating the 60th anniversary of the founding of the KPA (April 25, 2002) took two and a half hours. "Examination of a Very Atypical Military Parade Unattended by Kim Jong Il," *Sapio*, 8 October 2008.

104. "DPRK Leader 'Collapsed' in August," *Chosun Ilbo*, 8 September 2008.

105. "Detailed Information on Theories about Death and Serious Illness of Kim Jong Il," *Seiron*, 1–30 November 2008.

106. It was his 13th inspection in August, which was in keeping with his recent schedule of public events (11 occasions in June and 16 in July).

107. Seiichi Ino, *Kim Jong Il no Yuigon* [Kim Jong Il's Will] (Tokyo: Asahi Shimbun, 2009).

108. "Detailed Information on Theories about Death and Serious Illness of Kim Jong Il."

109. There is much debate about this Chinese medical team. Some sources contend that China sent a team of three doctors and two nurses, led by a neurosurgeon, from the People's Liberation Army General Hospital (commonly known as the 301 Hospital) in Beijing. Other sources are more specific, saying China sent a neurologist from the so-called 301 Military Hospital, the general hospital under the People's Liberation Army; a traditional Chinese medicine doctor; and lastly an expert in adult diseases from the 305 Military Hospital. The 301 Military Hospital is renowned as China's state-of-the-art general hospital. Deng Xiaping was hospitalized there until shortly before he died. The 305 Hospital is a luxury medical complex exclusively for government leaders, located near Zhongnanhai. However, when the Chinese medical team arrived in Pyongyang, they were only given limited access to the patient. "Confession of Kim Cho'ng-nam, 37, Eldest Son: 'Father Jong Il's Present Condition and Successor,'" *Shukan Gendai*, 22 November 2008.

110. "China's Secret Report on X-Day for Kim Jong Il," *Bungei Shunju*, 1 December, 31 December 2008.

111. Ibid.

112. "DPRK Diplomat Dismisses Reports of Leader's Ill Health as 'Conspiracy,'" *Kyodo World Service*, 10 September 2008. See also "DPRK's No. 2 Leader Denies Kim Jong Il Sick," *Yonhap*, 10 September 2008.

CHAPTER 6

1. According to South Korean sources, on or around January 8, 2009, Kim Chong-il informed the KWP Organization Guidance Department that he had chosen Kim Chong-un as his successor. This unleashed a flurry of activity within leadership circles as first deputy director Ri Che-kang began to communicate this decision to cadre above the division level. "N. Korean Leader Names Third Son as Successor: Sources," *Yonhap*, 15 January 2009. Osamu Eya, a long-time Japanese Pyongyang watcher, however, contends that Kim in fact designated his successor in the months after his stroke in 2008. As evidence, he notes that Kim Chong-un appeared in a December 20 photograph of one of Kim Chong-il's first guidance

inspections (at the Huichon Youth Electrical Appliance Complex) since returning from his illness. The photograph, however, was not made public by KCNA
until 2010. In the background of the photograph, a red sign is visible that reads:
"Our automobile assembly plant was inspected on 20 December 2008 by venerable
comrade General Kim Chong-un." See Osamu Eya, "Photo Analysis Shows That
'Successor' Process Began for Kim Chong-un Just Four Months after Kim Jong-il's
Stroke," *Sapio*, 9–29 March 2011.

2. Words by Choe Chun-kyong, music by Ri Chong-o: "Let Us Raise a Toast,"
Nodong Sinmun, 8 January 2009.

3. Information provided by the Open Source Center.

4. In the song, references are made to "General Kim" (*uri kim taejang*).
According to North Korean defectors interviewed by the author, in early 2009,
Kim Chong-un was referred to as *kim taejang* or *ch'o'ngnyo'n taejang* ("young
general").

5. In June 2009, *Mainichi Shimbun* obtained a group photo of Kim Chong-un
and his classmates.

6. Interview of Kenji Fujimoto in *Yomiuri Weekly*, 17 September 2006.

7. According to one prominent Pyongyang watcher, Kim Chong-un was receiving "private lessons" from Kim Il-sung Military University professors. Various military officers have been identified as the third son's tutors, including Ri
Yong-ho and Kim Yong-chol.

8. The prominent Pyongyang watcher, Chong Song-chang, claimed that Kim
Chong-un held the position of a section chief (*kwajang*) at the Organization and
Guidance Department (*Dong-A Ilbo*, 28 May 2007). Open Radio for North Korea, a
South Korean radio service that relies heavily for its reporting on sources based
in North Korea and North Korean escapees, contended that Kim Chong-un was
assigned to the KPA General Political Department (*Yollin Pukhan Pangsong*, 23 February 2009).

9. Kim Chong-un's profile began to rise at the end of 2004 and picked up
around 2006 with media reports that his older brother, Kim Chong-chol was not
a contender. South Korean intelligence officials were on the record by 2007 as be-
lieving that Kim Chong-chol had been "excluded from the group of potential successors long ago due to his physical frailty and non-political nature." See *Monthly
Chosun*, 1 October 2004; *Dong-A Ilbo*, 16 February 2006 and 28 May 2007.

10. *Monthly Chosun*, 1 October 2004; *Yonhap*, 6 October 2005 and 6 September
2006.

11. *Chosun Ilbo*, 23 June 2003; *Dong-A Ilbo*, 28 May 2007. One high-ranking
South Korean intelligence official noted as early as 2004 that Kim Chong-un was
"very involved with various activities and has leadership skills." *Chosun Ilbo*,
1 September 2004.

12. The South Korean media reported that Kim Chong-un has high blood pressure and diabetes (*Yonhap*, 15 January 2009). Several media sources reported that
in August or September of 2008 he had sustained a "serious physical problem" in
a traffic accident and was in a "critical condition" (*JoongAng Ilbo*, 11 September
2008; *Shukan Gendai*, 13 December 2008). These rumors soon disappeared and have
not resurfaced in subsequent reporting.

13. *Yonhap*, 1 June 2008; *Kungmin Ilbo*, 10 September 2008.

14. "Power Struggle May Be Intensifying in North Korea over [Kim Jong Il's]
Successor," *JijiWeb*, 3 May 2009.

15. "Kim's brother-in-law said to mastermind N. Korea's leadership succession," *Yonhap*, 15 February 2009.

16. The first benefit Chang might have accrued from this agreement may have been to undermine Kim Ok's position within Kim Chong-il's inner circle. In March, reports began to seep out of North Korea about a new rumor that Kim Ok was behind an assassination attempt on Ko Yong-hui in 2003. "Rumor of Kim Ok Engineering Traffic Accident of Kim Cho'ng-un's Biological Mother Spreads," *Yonhap*, 3 March 2009.

17. Kim Kyok-sik had only served in the post of Chief of the General Staff for two years, having been appointed in 2007. This, of course, led to widespread speculation over the reason for his removal and whether it was a demotion based on merit. Some have speculated that Kim Chong-il decided he needed Kim Kyok-sik's operational expertise in this sensitive military region, which borders the West Sea, where skirmishes with South Korea have occurred in the past.

18. The SPA also made the first changes to the constitution since 1998, elevating military-first policy to a level equal to *Chuche*. "North Korea Modifies Its Constitution to Reflect Kim Jong-il System," *Hankyoreh Online*, 29 September 2009. The SPA also made revisions seemingly aimed at a return to economic orthodoxy. The State Planning Commission was elevated and removed from the Cabinet's direct oversight—ostensibly to expand its ability to centrally plan economic activity. Consistent with the renewed emphasis on heavy industry, the SPA sanctioned a restructuring of the Cabinet wherein each industry had its own dedicated ministry. This move was hinted at by the splitting up of the ministries dedicated to heavy industry. The Ministry of Coal and Power was divided into a Ministry of Coal and a Ministry of Power. A new Ministry of Crude Oil was created out of the old Ministry of Extractive Industries, and the Ministry of Metal and Machine Building was split into a Ministry of Metal Industries and a Ministry for Machine Building. The Capital City Construction Department, which had ties to Chang Song-taek, was elevated to ministry status.

19. The decision to enhance the powers of the NDC was reflected in the 11 February announcement of the major military leadership shakeup. Kim Chong-il signed the order first as head of the NDC and second as the chairman of the KWP Central Military Committee (CMC), a subtle reversal of the normal order for Kim's titles and the institutions associated with him. "Formulation of Kim Cho'ng-un Succession Appears to Be through Form of First Vice Chairman of National Defense Commission," *Yo'llin Pukhan Pangsong*, 28 September 2009.

20. "(Viewpoint) North's Photos Tell a Hidden Story," *JoongAng Daily*, 21 April 2009.

21. "A Strategic Move toward a Collective Leadership System for Post Kim Chong-il Era," *Facta*, 1 May 2009. Author's discussions with North Korean defectors and South Korean, Japanese, and Chinese Pyongyang watchers, March–April 2009.

22. Author's discussions with South Korean Pyongyang watchers, April 2009. See also "North Korea Conducted a Large-Scale Reshuffle of Organizations Dealing with South Korean Affairs," *JoongAng Ilbo*, 21 April 2009.

23. "Seoul, Washington Focus on N. Korean Spymaster," *Chosun Ilbo*, 5 June 2009. See Also "DPRK Official's Alleged Involvement in Making Supernotes," *Chosun Ilbo*, 4 June 2009.

24. Kim Yong-chol oversaw the inspection of the Kaesong Industrial Complex in December 2008 and has been the primary spokesman regarding the expulsion of foreign personnel from the complex. See "DPRK Military Gains Upper Edge in Power Struggle," *JoongAng Ilbo*, 20 January 2009. Another source contends that Pak Myong-chol, a councilor within the NDC, also plays an important reporting role with regard to this espionage apparatus. Pak Myong-chol was purged in 2004 for his involvement in a luxury wedding where many high-ranking party cadres gathered in violation of rules laid down by Kim Chong-il in an effort to prevent possible conspiracies. A former chairman of the Physical Culture and Sports Guidance Committee, Pak is rumored to be a protégé of Chang Song-taek. The resurrection of his political fortunes has tracked closely with Chang's own resurrection. See "North Korea Integrates Maneuvering Organs Targeting the South and Overseas into Reconnaissance General Bureau," *Yonhap*, 10 May 2009.

25. Office 35 (headed by Ho Myong-uk) is the KWP's investigation department in charge of collecting information on foreign countries and South Korea.

26. The KWP's External Liaison Department (headed by Kang Kwan-chu) is in charge of educating and dispatching agents. "North Korea Integrates Maneuvering Organs Targeting the South and Overseas into Reconnaissance General Bureau."

27. Ibid.

28. According to North Korean defector sources, the SSD director's responsibilities in recent years have been assumed by one of the KWP Administration Department's deputy directors. Author's discussions in South Korea, April 2009. More recent reporting from 2010 and 2011 suggests the possibility that Kim Chong-un has assumed this post.

29. In 2009, there were questions about whether competition still existed between the Chang apparatus and the party elements of regime security and monitoring that remained outside his control, such as the Organization Guidance Department and the Guard Command. Though Kim may have wanted to maintain control over these entities as a check on Chang's growing power and influence, Chang's role in the NDC would ensure his ability to play a role in issuing guidance and instructions to those parts of the security apparatus that currently exist outside his direct control. Author's discussion with a senior North Korean defector, May 2009.

30. Though the shift in leadership dynamics may have reduced the number of reporting chains to Kim Chong-il and reined in his proclivity toward divide and rule politics, he has maintained certain levers of control that ensure his dominant role within the regime. For example, he maintains personal control over the Guard Command and the KWP's Organization Guidance Department.

31. Economic affairs are another area where the reporting links appeared to have been strengthened. Until 2009, economic policy was spread across numerous ministries and committees within the KWP, Cabinet, and SPA apparatuses. Most of the responsibility for economic planning now seems to be centered on the State Planning Commission (SPC). The SPC, which used to report as a ministry to the Cabinet, now appears to have semi-autonomous status under new SPC Chairman and Vice Premier Ro Tu-chol, outside of the Cabinet organization. It is unclear, however, whether Ro reports directly to Kim Chong-il or a point of contact within the NDC, such as Chang Song-taek.

32. Author's discussions with South Korean Pyongyang watchers, April 2009.

33. See Andrei Lankov, "North Korea: Attempt at Counter-reforms," *Sluchaynyye Zametki Andreya Lankova*, 16 March 2009.

34. "Three Red-Crowned Crane Propagandized as Possible Sign of Hereditary Succession—Chang Song-taek to Mentor Successor," *Sankei Shimbun*, 5 May 2009. At least one source contends that O Kuk-yol, Kim Yong-chun, and Choe Ik-kyu (director of the KWP Propaganda Department) have led efforts to pave the way for the Kim Chong-un succession. See "Sources: Kim Chooses Third Son as Heir," *JoongAng Ilbo*, 2 June 2009.

35. Author's discussions with senior North Korean defectors and South Korean Pyongyang watchers, April 2009.

36. See for example "Brother-in-Law Gains Real Power in Kim Dynasty: Will Kim Chong-un or Kim Hyon Become the Successor?" *AERA*, 20 April 2009; "The North's Chang Song-taek Line Emerging to Center of Power," *Yonhap*, 13 February 2009.

37. See "Power Struggle May Be Intensifying in North Korea Over Successor," *JijiWeb*, 3 May 2009; "DPRK Military Gains Upper Edge in Power Struggle," *JoongAng Ilbo*, 20 January 2009; "North Korea Puts Spy Agencies Under Military Control in Major Shakeup," *Yonhap*, 10 May 2009; "Power Struggle Behind DPRK's Nuclear Test," *Sapio*, 2 June 2009.

38. The North Korean media did not publicly announce the state date of the 150-Day Battle. On May 4, 2009, *Nodong Sinmun* stated for the first time that North Korea was in the midst of the battle.

39. "Let Us Accomplish Brilliant Victory in 150-Day Battle With Might of Single-Hearted Unity," *Nodong Sinmun*, 7 May 2009.

40. "Kim's Heir Apparent Increasingly Visible in N. Korea: Sources," *Yonhap*, 11 May 2009.

41. Subsequent speed campaigns took place once in the 1980s, 1990s, and (a 100-day battle) in 2005.

42. "DPRK Party Organ Reviews Kim Chong-il Initiated 70-Day Battle, 200-Day Battle," *Nodong Sinmun*, 5 May 2009.

43. The North Korean military press was quiet on the succession in 2009, waiting until 2010 to begin its loyalty campaign around the successor. In January, *Choson Inmingun*, the military daily, began to use expressions such as "nerve center of the military-first revolution" (*so'ngunhyo'ngmyo'ngsunoebu*) and "comrade of the military-first revolution" (*so'ngunhyo'ngmyo'ngdongji*) in its coverage.

44. "Morning Star General to Turn Water into Wine," *Daily NK*, 15 May 2009. South Korean media alleged that the late Ko Yong-hui had asked high-ranking party and army officials to call Kim Chong-un by the name of "Morning Star General"—reminiscent of Kim Chong-il's nickname "lodestar" when he was inheriting power from Kim Il-sung—in an effort to make him the successor. *Monthly Chosun*, 1 February 2004; *Munhwa Ilbo*, 30 August 2004.

45. "Sole Successor, Sagacious General Kim Chong-un," *NK Chisigin Yo'ndae*, 12 May 2009.

46. According to a North Korean party source in North Hamgyong Province, the KWP Propaganda and Agitation Department on 9 July issued a decree titled "The Direction for Propaganda and Agitation in August" to each provincial and municipal party department clearly specifying: "Stop sending out propaganda regarding Captain Kim in lecture meetings or on Third Broadcasting Network (TBN) [an internal North Korean cable broadcast that began to identify Kim

Chong-un by name in July], and refrain from using the expression 'Young General of Mt. Paektu.'" This action was taken by Kim Chong-il out of concern for international criticism of the third-generation succession system, not an order to halt the succession process itself. The North Korean authorities actually ceased propaganda activities starting July 28. "Kim Cho'ng-un Propaganda Comes to a Halt," *Daily NK*, 27 August 2009.

47. "DPRK's Kim Yong-nam Calls for 'Fruitful Relations' with New Japan Gov't," *Kyodo World Service*, 10 September 2009.

48. According to a South Korean intelligence official, there were unconfirmed reports that Kim Chong-il's health had recovered and he had given orders that the succession issue was not to be discussed within the country.

49. "Great Change Seen in North Korean Power Succession," *Foresight*, 19 September–16 October 2009.

50. Even though it does not necessarily reflect the hierarchy of real power as it is, the rostrum hierarchy serves as the most important criterion by which to grasp key power groups in North Korea.

51. CNC refers to a new initiative to computerize industrial facilities, which began in August 2009.

52. One indication that the poster was authentic is that its spelling of Kim Chong-un's name corresponded to the revised spelling highlighted in a South Korean NIS report in October. According to the report, the new spelling was discovered in September.

53. The Chinese media also suggested that China was seeking to stabilize bilateral ties, strained in recent years by North Korea's two nuclear tests and missile tests. "PRC FM Yang Jiechi Discusses Premier Wen Jiabao's Visit to DPRK," New China News Agency, 6 October 2009.

54. The Chinese press was more reserved on the issue of economic aid, noting that the two countries signed unspecified "economic and technological cooperation agreements" and agreed to build a new bridge over the Yalu River. The website of a Hong Kong television station with ties to the PLA reported that the assistance may have included oil shipments to North Korea and increased food aid. See *Feng Huang Wang*, 5 October 2009.

55. The New Year's Joint Editorial had bluntly touted the superiority of the socialist planned economy as the best approach for ensuring economic order.

56. James Lister, "Currency Reform in North Korea," *Korea Times Online*, 8 January 2010.

57. In fact, this apparently was the first-ever publicized visit by Kim to a headquarters of any ministry. See "Leader Inspects Headquarters of People's Security Ministry," DPRK Radio, 22 November 2009. Though the details of the ministry's apparent elevation are not currently known, some Pyongyang watchers believe that Kim has taken steps to reestablish the balance of power that existed within the internal security apparatus before the Ministry of People's Security's demotion in the late 1990s.

58. "Cabinet Decision on Currency Reform Issued," *Chou'n Po'ttu'l*, 2 December 2009.

59. The time window for the exchange was six days.

60. "N. Korea Revalues Currency for First Time in 17 Yrs," *Yonhap*, 1 December 2009. See also "Key Dates in North Korea's Currency Reforms," *Yonhap*, 1 December 2009.

61. "Militant Banner Which Calls to a New Victory," *Nodong Sinmun*, 9 January 2010.

62. Ibid.

63. The conference, which was held in Wonson, was reportedly overseen by Chang Song-taek. "Impacts of the Major Blunder of 'Currency Re-Denomination' That Is Shaking North Korea," *Foresight*, 1 March–31 March 2010.

64. Pak's failure to appear with Kim Chong-il at a number of guidance inspections of economic facilities in January marked the first public indication that his standing in the leadership was possibly in jeopardy. He was last mentioned in the North Korean media on 4 January in a report on Kim's visit to a construction site. By March, it was apparent that Pak was being expunged from the record when images of him were removed from a reshowing of a television documentary. The original broadcast—first aired on February 24—included eight scenes showing Pak with Kim Chong-il. Information provided by the Open Source Center, March 2010. Around this time, rumors began to surface that Pak Nam-gi had been publicly executed.

65. Kim reiterated his laments about the economy at the beginning of February. He said that his immediate ambition was to end his people's dependence on corn for subsistence and feed them rice and wheat products. "I'm the most heartbroken by the fact that our people are still living on corn. What I must do now is to feed them white rice, bread and noodles generously." *Nodong Sinmun*, 1 February 2010.

66. Premier Kim Yong-il's direct apology to village chiefs, who are representatives of the people of each region, was tantamount to an apology to the people themselves. "N. Korea Climbs Down Over Anti-market Reforms," *Chosun Ilbo Online*, 11 February 2010.

67. Chong Kwang-min, *Political and Economic Implications of North Korea's Currency Reform* (Seoul: Institute for National Security Strategy, 2010). After Kim's apology, most money changers and traders who had been arrested were reportedly freed.

68. Rice prices rose 30 times from 20 won per kilogram at the end of 2009 to 600 won at the beginning of January 2010. The black-market exchange rate soared from 30 won per U.S. dollar in early December to 530 won at the end of January.

69. This statement overlapped with the promotion to the Cabinet of technocrats well versed in running a planned economy. One such person was Yun Gi-cheong. One defector explained, "Yun Gi-cheong is a person who Kim Il-sung was in favor of. After he died, she stepped back from the economic field." Many believed she was charged with resolving the crisis in the chaotic people's economy.

70. In an interesting move, Kim replaced his own fund manager, Kim Dong-un, the director of Office 39, with Chon Il-chun. Kim Dong-Un, one of Kim Chong-il's confidantes, was among a number of North Korean officials blacklisted by the European Union in 2009, thus making it difficult for him to continue in his position. "N. Korea Leader Replaces Personal Fund Manager: Report," *AFP*, 4 February 2010. Around the same time, Ri Chol, the North Korean ambassador to Switzerland and the point man for Kim Chong-il's finances in European banks (rumored to be $4 billion), was recalled to Pyongyang. Ri had been the ambassador to Switzerland since 1980, during which time he oversaw the welfare of Kim's sons when

they were studying abroad. Rumors are that he was recalled to take part in the succession process. "N. Korean Ambassador to Geneva Expected to Leave Office," *Yonhap,* 10 March 2010.

71. The power and reach of the internal security apparatus had been growing for several years. In April 2010, the Ministry of People's Security was elevated in status, which was reflected in its new Korean name (*inminboanso'ng*), and removed from the Cabinet and placed under the National Defense Commission alongside the State Security Department (*kukkaanjo'nbowibu*). This move seemed to be part of the strategy to strengthen the control over the population to ensure that it did not waver in the face of the deepening economic crisis.

72. With the spread of cell phones in North Korea, information on North Korea's domestic situation by 2009 was becoming increasingly communicated to South Korea and the rest of the outside world in nearly real time. South Korea's Internet-based media, human rights groups, and other organizations are in regular contact with North Korean citizens through cell phones. According to Orascom Telecom Holding, an Egyptian cell phone provider operating in the country, by September 2010, cell phone usage in North Korea had risen to 300,000.

73. Following the decree, North Korea's security organs in the border areas were placed on around-the-clock alert status. A high-ranking escapee from the North said, "Security organs' house searches are based on the instructions from higher echelons, but the searches are also for the purpose of making money on the pretext of the crackdown." "DPRK's Stricter 'Suppression' of People after Currency Reform," *Chosun Ilbo Online,* 27 February 2010.

74. *Daily NK,* 5 March 2010.

75. "Fallout from Currency Redenomination—Kim Jong Il Attends Mass Rally, Omens of Crisis for Regime," JijiWeb, 13 March 2010.

76. KCNA, 29 December 2009.

77. A case in point was the arrest of two journalists, Euna Lee and Laura Ling, in March 2009. Their detention and the trial that followed raised the tensions on the Korean Peninsula. Both were subsequently returned to the United States following an unannounced visit to North Korea by former U.S. President Bill Clinton on August 4, 2009.

78. "KPA General Staff Spokesman's Press Statement on ROK-US Joint Exercises," Korean Central Broadcasting Station, 25 February 2010.

79. Information provided by Open Source Center, March 2010.

80. "Text of DPRK Foreign Ministry Statement Proposing Talks for 'Peace Agreement'," KCBS, 11 January 2010.

81. "Spa Presidium President Speaks at National Meeting to Mark Kim Chong-il's Birthday," Korean Central Broadcasting Station, 16 February 2010.

82. Author's interviews with Pyongyang watchers in South Korea and China, June 2010.

83. Author's interview with a senior North Korean defector, January 2011.

84. "N. Korean Officer Says North Sank the *Cheonan,*" *Chosun Ilbo Online,* 20 April 2010.

85. For a detailed discussion of North Korean covert maritime operations, see Ken E. Gause, "A Maritime Perspective of North Korean WMD," paper presented at the 4th Annual CNA-KIMS Conference, Seoul (October 2010) and printed in *The Republic of Korea's Security & the Role of the ROK-US Navies* (Seoul: Korean Institute for Maritime Studies, 2010).

86. KBS 1 TV, 8 April 2010.

87. "DPRK Finance Minister at SPA Session Reports on 2009, 2010 State Budget," KCBS, 9 April 2010.

88. U Tong-chuk's promotion, his second in two years, suggested his continued rise within the leadership. According to one defector interviewed by the author, U Tong-chuk, who had for a long time been tied to Chang Song-taek, was moving closer to Kim Chong-un and would become the spearhead of the heir apparent's attempts at power consolidation.

89. In January, North Korea merged two northern cities, Rajin and adjacent Sonbong, to form its first "special city," known as Rason. It later lowered corporate tax rates and simplified administrative procedures to help speed development and attract more foreign investment. In March, China acquired a 10-year lease of Rajin Port on North Korea's east coast, potentially increasing shipping access to the Sea of Japan. Lee Kwang-ho "Kim Jong-il's Five Day Trip to China," *Vantage Point*, Vol. 33, No. 6 (June 2010).

90. Kim's delegation was the largest ever to accompany him to China. It included figures from the party, military, and Cabinet.

91. Approximately 100 small Chinese companies out of 150 that have investments in North Korea are based in Jilin and Liaoning provinces near the northeastern border with the North.

92. "Top Leaders of China, DPRK Hold Talks in Beijing," *China Daily*, 7 May 2010.

93. "N. Korea and China Agree to Strengthen Economic Ties," *Hankyoreh Online*, 8 May 2010.

94. It is unclear whether the aid reportedly promised by Wen Jiabao in October was also taken off the table. According to Chinese sources, in his meeting with Chinese Premier Wen Jiabao, Kim asked for around $10 billion in investment to repair the infrastructure in the border region. Although Wen agreed with the importance of infrastructure repairs, he reportedly avoided giving a direct response about the scale of any investment. China reportedly did agree to an outlay of 500,000 tons of food. "Kim Jong Il Requested Much, Received Little From China," *Daily NK*, 13 August 2010.

95. "Beijing's Rebuff Made Kim Cut China Trip Short," *JoongAng Daily*, 17 May 2010.

96. Widespread speculation leading up to the visit and during the visit was that Kim was going to discuss the succession with the Chinese leadership. Much of this was driven by a Xinhua report that Kim stated that the Sino-North Korean friendship "has stood the test of time and will not change due to the change of time and the *alteration of generations.*" Subsequent reporting suggests that in fact the subject was not broached.

97. "Jang Song-taek Seen as Powerful Figure Behind N. Korean Throne," *Chosun Ilbo*, 11 May 2010.

98. Author's discussion with several of China's Pyongyang watchers, June 2009, May 2010, and January 2011.

99. According to South Korean intelligence, several of North Korea's trading enterprises that operate in China receive their political backing from Chang Song-taek. "Jang at the Fulcrum of Regime Future," *Daily NK*, 26 January 2011.

100. *KCBS*, 2 June 2010.

101. Over the previous year, Chang and Ri had frequently appeared in public together, suggesting an effort to eschew any speculation of remaining differences among Kim's key aides.

102. KCNA, 13 May 2010.

103. The SPA typically meets only once a year to approve legislation put forth by the party. It had not met twice in one year since 2003.

104. Choe Yong-rim was born in 1930 and served as a Central Committee department director before becoming chief secretary of the Secretaries Office of the Kumsusan Assembly Hall, which handled Kim Il-sung's personal affairs. Later he held posts as vice premier of the Administrative Council, director of the Public Prosecutor's Office, and secretary general of the SPA Presidium. In 2009, he was appointed chief secretary of the KWP's Pyongyang City Committee.

105. Lee Kwang-ho, "Paving the Way for Power Succession," *Vantage Point*, Vol. 33, No. 7 (July 2010).

106. In the reshuffle, Kang Nung-su, Kim Rak-hui, Ri Thae-nam, and Chon Ha-chol were appointed vice premiers. Other vice premiers, who concurrently held ministerial posts, included Cho Pyong-chu (minister of the Machine Building Industry) and Han Kwang-bok (minister of Electronics Industry). An Chong-su became minister of light industry, and Cho Yong-chol and Pak Myong-chol became the ministers of food stuff and daily necessities and physical culture and sports, respectively. Pak was a protégé of Chang Song-taek, who was purged along with his patron in 2004.

107. Given the proximity of the SPA meeting to Kim's trip to China, some Pyongyang watchers speculated that the Chinese leadership may have expressed its wish that Chang Song-taek be given a more prominent role within the regime. Author's interview with South Korean Pyongyang watchers, October 2010.

108. "Workers Party of Korea Central Committee Political Bureau Decision," KCBS, 23 June 2010.

109. The "August Incident" took place in 1956. While Kim Il-sung was in Moscow, elements of the Yanan and Soviet factions devised a plan to undermine his authority at an upcoming plenum of the Central Committee. This would be done through an orchestrated criticism of Kim for not "correcting" his leadership methods, developing a personality cult, distorting the "Leninist principle of collective leadership." Kim became aware of the plot upon his return and was able to delay the plenum and foil the coup. This plot gave Kim the impetus he needed to carry out a significant purge of the party. See Andrei Lankov, *From Stalin to Kim Il-sung: The Formation of North Korea 1945–1960* (New York: Hurst & Company, 2002).

110. For a more thorough discussion of Kim Chong-il's decision-making and leadership style, see Appendix B ("Decision Making at the Center of the Hub and Spoke").

111. Chang Seong-chang, "Significance of the Third WPK Conference and Its Predicted Outcome," *Vantage Point*, Vol. 33, No. 9 (September 2010).

112. South Korean reporting suggested the presence of Kim Chong-un on the trip for three reasons. First, China did not deny that Kim Chong-un was present, as it had done during Kim's visit in May, but merely stated he was "not on the guest list." Second, Kim Chong-il kept his activities thoroughly under wraps compared to his higher profile in May. Third, Kim's armored train had 17 cars in May but 26 in late August. "Seoul Believes Kim Jong Il's Heir Came Along on China Trip," *Chosun Ilbo Online*, 9 September 2010.

113. These reports were later confirmed.

114. KCNA, 30 August 2010.

115.   For months, the North Korean media had consistently reported that the conference would be held "in early September," which was interpreted by foreign observers, as well as North Koreans themselves, to mean as late as the 15th.

116.   "Kim's Poor Health Said to Delay Opening of KWP Meeting," *Kyodo World Service*, 13 September 2010. Won Sei-hoon, director of South Korea's National Intelligence Service, however, told the South Korean National Assembly that Kim's health was not a factor behind the delay.

117.   "DPRK Delays Key Party Meeting Due to Floods," *AFP*, 15 September 2010.

118.   According to one senior North Korean defector, this line of reasoning reflected an inaccurate understanding of leadership dynamics in Pyongyang. The relationship between Chang Song-taek and O Kuk-yol was quite close, spanning several decades. Both realized that the other was critical for regime stability. In addition, Kim Chong-il needed both to ensure that the succession process went smoothly. Author's interview in Seoul, January 2011.

119.   "Speculation on N. Korea Mushrooms," *Korea Times*, 19 September 2010.

120.   "Delegates' Conference to Begin Next Week," *Daily NK*, 21 September 2010.

121.   Kang Sok-chu had been a first vice foreign minister for 24 years. As the former chief nuclear envoy, he negotiated the 1994 Agreed Framework between North Korea and the United States, an achievement that earned him the honor of "national hero," and confirmed his position within Kim Chong-il's inner circle. Kim Kye-hwan was the chief North Korean representative to the Six Party Talks when the parties agreed on the Joint Statement of 19 September 2005, which laid the framework whereby North Korea would drop its nuclear ambitions in exchange for financial aid from the negotiating partners and diplomatic recognition. Ri Yong-ho had been a core member of North Korean delegations in negotiations with the United States on such issues as nuclear weapons, missiles, disarmament, and human rights. He had also been ambassador to the United Kingdom, Belgium, Luxembourg, and Ireland before returning to the foreign ministry in 2007 to become the deputy negotiator on the nuclear talks.

122.   Thirty-three other officers were also promoted, including one to colonel general (Ryu Kyong) and six (Ro Hung-se, Ri Tu-song, Chon Kyong-hak, Kim Kuk-ryong, Hwang Pyong-so, and O Il-chong) to lieutenant general. Within hours, in a separate order, Ri Yong-ho, the chief of the General Staff, was promoted to vice marshal by virtue of NDC Order No. 7.

123.   Choe's family ties to the Kim family explain his political rise. He is the second son of Choe Hyon, one of Kim Il-sung's closest comrades. He is also known to have maintained a close friendship with Kim Chong-il since childhood and to have a good relationship with Chang Song-taek. Benefiting from his father's political patronage, Choe has served in several key posts. In 1996, he was named the first secretary for the Kim Il-sung Socialist Youth League, the second largest organization in the North after the Korean Workers' Party. He was demoted in 1998 for involvement in a corruption scandal. In 2003, he made a political comeback as a vice director of the KWP General Department. In 2007, he was named secretary in charge of North Hwanghae Province. His political strength was reflected when he came to the inter-Korean border to greet then-South Korean President Roh Moo-hyun for the 2007 summit. He also accompanied Kim Chong-il on trips to China and other public activities.

124. Korean Central Broadcasting Station, 30 September 2010.

125. The last revisions to the Party Charter took place at the Sixth Party Congress in 1980. According to one source, the timing of the revisions was tied to the succession. As long as Kim Chong-il's health holds out, the Party Charter means little. However, when he passes from the scene, this document sets out the rules governing the negotiation and compromise involved in creating a new ruling order. See Kim Jin Ha, "The North Korean Workers' Party Charter: Revisions and Their Political Dynamics," *Online Series*, CO 11–08 (Seoul: KINU, 2011).

126. However, the description of the party itself was changed from a "Marxist-Leninist Party" to a "Kim Il-sung Party."

127. Korean Workers' Party (KWP) Charter [*choso'n rodongdang kyuyak*], 28 September 2010, as published in *North Korea Tech*, 21 January 2011.

128. The number of Central Committee departments was reduced in number; however, it seems that directors of special offices (e.g., Chon Il-chu, Office 39) were not included in the North Korean reporting. Those named included Kim Ki-nam (Propaganda and Agitation), Chang Song-taek (Administrative Affairs), Kim Yong-il (International), Kim Pyong-hae (Cadres), Ri Yong-su (Working Organization and Capitol Construction), Chu Kyu-chang (Munitions Industry), Hong Sok-hyong (Finance and Planning), Kim Kyong-hui (Light Industry), Choe Hui-chong (Science and Education), O Il-chong (Military Affairs), Kim Yang-gon (United Front), Kim Chong-im (Party History Institute), and Thae Chong-su (General Affairs). No director was designated director of the Organization Guidance Department, leading to the assumption that Kim Chong-il still held this post.

129. The Central Auditing Commission's new chairman was Kim Chang-su, who was assisted by vice chairman Pak Myong-sun. The membership included Choe Pae-chin, Kim Chol, Sim Chol-ho, O Ryong-il, Kye Yong-sam, Ryu Hyon-sik, Ko Myong-hui, Pang Yong-uk, Chang Chong-chu, Ho Kwang-uk, Chi Tong-sik, Chong Pong-sok, and Choe Kwon-su.

130. The Control Commission was headed by Kim Kuk-tae, the former KWP Secretary for Cadres. He was assisted by first vice chairman Chong Myong-hak and vice chairman Ri Tuk-nam. The membership included Cha Kwan-sok, Pak Tok-man, Cha Sun-kil, and Kim Yong-son.

131. Ri Yong-ho is a descendant of one of the founding families of the regime. His father, Ri Pong-su, was a member of the Partisan Guerrilla Faction who enjoyed a close relationship with Kim Il-sung. Some Pyongyang watchers predicted that Ri Yong-ho will in the future replace Kim Yong-chun as Minister of People's Armed Forces.

132. Most noticeably, O Kuk-yol was only appointed to the Central Committee, but not the Politburo, raising speculation that his power had been diminished. According to some Pyongyang watchers, O was kept out of the Politburo because he did not fully support the succession. Other Pyongyang watchers contended that his power remained intact along informal channels based on his long-time relationship with Kim Chong-il.

133. According to Article 27 of the party constitution, the Central Military Committee oversees implementation of the party's military policies, guides development and production of munitions, and has command and control over North Korea's armed forces. Established in 1962, the KWP Central Military Committee also has a ceremonial role. It sponsors the armed forces day celebrations. Since 1995, the CMC has supplanted the party in issuing congratulatory messages

to all military events. See Hyeong Jung Park and Kyo Duk Lee, *Continuities and Changes in the Power Structure and the Role of Party Organizations Under Kim Jong Il's Reign,* Studies Series 05–05 (Seoul: Korea Institute for National Unification May 2005).

134.   The KWP Munitions Industry Department is referred to in the North Korean media as the KWP Machine Industry Department.

135.   Notably, Kim Chong-il also debuted in the fifth spot in the power rankings after the Sixth Party Congress in 1980.

136.   Since his public debut, Kim Chong-un in public appearances typically is listed immediately after the top layer of the Political Bureau and before its main membership. The photograph taken after the Party Conference showed Kim Chong-un sitting two spots to the left of Kim Chong-il. Because North Korean ranking emanates side to side from the senior most official beginning from the right, this would place Kim Chong-un in the fifth spot. The photograph also revealed other important succession-related clues. Kim Ok (Kim Chong-il's mistress) and Kim Yo-chun (Kim Chong-un's younger sister) stood just behind Pak Chong-sun, the first vice director of the KWP Organization Guidance Department, indicating their informal roles within the power hierarchy.

CHAPTER 7

1.   Merle Fainsod, *How Russia Is Ruled* (Cambridge, MA: Harvard University Press, 1965).

2.   This is increasingly the view among China's Pyongyang watchers. Over the last few years, concern in Beijing has shifted from a failed succession to economic decay as the driver for future instability in North Korea. Author's interviews in Beijing, May 2011.

APPENDIX A

1.   After Kim Il-sung's unitary ruling system was established in the late 1960s, the Political Bureau ceased to be a collective consultation body. It became a rubber stamp where only the voices of Kim's loyal supporters were heard. Nevertheless, it remained a body where "constructive opinions" (i.e., those that fit within the boundries of Kim's own thinking) often broadened Kim's own thinking. Hyon Song-il, *North Korea's National Strategy and Power Elite* (Seoul: Sunin Publishing, 2006).

2.   Toward the end of the Kim Il-sung period, policy consultation within formal leadership circles became perfunctory, replaced by a reporting mechanism whereby policy drafts were drawn up by each ministry and department and passed directly to Kim Chong-il's office where they were prioritized and if deemed worthy passed to Kim Il-sung. The Political Bureau would be convened only to ratify decisions that had already been made by the Kim duopoly.

3.   The banquet for close aides was a method originally designed by Kim Chong-il for the purpose of winning cadres over to his side prior to his successor designation, but, after he was designated as the successor, it was used mainly for managing close aides and realizing closed-door politics. In addition, the number of banquet participants increased and the composition of participants also became

more diverse, along with the consolidation of the Kim's succession structure. The number of banquet participants, which was less than 20 in early 1970s, more than doubled to around 40 in 1977 and amounted to more than 100 people at times according to the occasion and character of the event in the 1980s. The banquet scale reportedly reached a peak in the 1980s and has been gradually decreasing since the 1990s. Ri Han-hyong, *Taedonggang Royal Family's 14-Year Travel in Disguise* (Seoul: Dong-A Ilbo, 1996); Hwang Chang-yop, *I Saw the Truth of History* (Seoul: Book Publisher Hanul, 1999).

4. "Analysis of the DPRK Power Group," *JoongAng Ilbo,* 4 January 2007. Kim's remarks at close aide gatherings and on-the-spot inspections are all recorded, summarized as official documents, and then conveyed as instructions or made into works such as *Selected Writings of Kim Chong-il.* Hwang Chang-yop, *Truth and Lies about North Korea* (Seoul: Unification Policy Institute, 1998).

5. Rumors began to appear in 2010 and 2011 that Kim Chong-un is the director of the SSD. At the time of this writing, these rumors can not be verified.

6. KWP Number 1 office building originally served as Kim Il-sung's primary party office. In 1976, Kim Il-sung moved into the presidential palace built in Pyongyang's Hyongjesan District and Kim Chong-il took up residence in the party headquarters. As for the building itself, it is hundreds of meters long and three stories high, built out of steel and concrete and decorated with natural granite outer walls and marble relief carvings. Each wall in the building is about 80 centimeters thick. It consists of rooms assigned to senior party vice directors, as well as a section devoted to Kim Chong-il's personal typists and operators. Approximately 10 security officers of the Guard Command's First Division are on duty inside the headquarters where Kim Chong-il works; officers of the Second Division stand guard at the reception post controlling access from outside; a company of bodyguards are deployed around the fence; and officers of the Sixth Division are on duty in areas surrounding the fence. In addition, bodyguards of the Eighth Division stand guard in emergency underground tunnels. Ri Yong-kuk, *Nanun Kim Chong-il Kyonghowoniotta* [I Was Kim Chong-il's Former Bodyguard] (Seoul: Sidae Chongsin, 2002). Ri Yong-kuk, prior to his defection in 1999, was reportedly a member of Kim Chong-il's bodyguard unit.

7. According to some sources, the secretariat was created in the mid-1980s, when Kim Chong-il carved out its responsibilities from the KWP Central Committee, most likely from several departments, including the General Affairs Department, which oversees a variety of housekeeping functions for the party leadership.

8. "Kim Chong-il Secretariat, at the Center of Power Although Not Listed as an Official Organization," *Choson Ilbo,* 15 April 2001.

9. Ibid.

10. "Kang Sang-ch'un, New Director of the Secretariat for General Secretary Kim Chong-il," *Yonhap,* 25 April 2002.

11. "DPRK Leader's 'Closest Aide' Reportedly Arrested in Macau; Release Speculated," OSC Feature, 31 January 2006.

12. "DPRK Defector on Kim Chong-il's Family, Close Aides," *Gendai,* 1 August 2003.

13. The name comes from the location of this office, which is on the third floor of Office Complex Number 1, where Kim Chong-il's offices are located.

14. U Chong-ch'ang, "ROK Monthly on DPRK Kim Chong-il's Slush Fund Deposits in Swiss Banks," *Seoul Wolgan Choson*, 1 November 2000, FBIS translation KPP20001019000046.

APPENDIX B

1. This personal decision-making system replaced the one that existed during the Kim Il-sung era in which the party oversaw the policy-making process. During this period, the flow of decision making consisted of a bottom-up component in addition to the top-down instructions from Kim Il-sung and Kim Chong-il. New policy proposals in a department or ministry went to that institution's party guidance committee, where it was reviewed and submitted to the relevant Central Committee department. A section chief would determine whether the policy proposal fit within established party guidelines before sending it up to senior leadership (deputy director, first deputy director, or secretary) for approval. The department director (or party secretary, if there is one for the department) would submit the policy proposal to the party Secretariat to be placed on the agenda for an upcoming meeting, which would be chaired by the General Secretary. Once the General Secretary approved the policy proposal, it would be sent back to the appropriate Central Committee department, which would pass it back to the originating institution for implementation. Dr. Pak Yong-taek, *Enhanced Position of the North Korean Military and Its Influence on Policymaking* (Seoul: Korean Institute for Defense Analysis, 2008).

2. In most cases, Kim's instruction comes in the form of a document requesting that a department to draw up a policy or investigate the implications of a particular policy line. It is not unusual, however, for such a request to come via a telephone conversation between Kim and one of his close aides.

3. For example, Kim Chong-il's instructions given to the Ministry of Foreign Affairs are mostly in the form of "remarks addressed to First Vice Minister Kang Sok-chu." Hyon Song-il, *North Korea's National Strategy and Power Elite* (Seoul: Sunin Publishing, 2006).

4. Every ministry and department throughout the government and party have councilors. These are people, normally with close ties to Kim or his personal secretariat, who have a clear understanding of his policy intentions. It is their job to draft correspondence between their home ministry or department and the Kim apparatus. Author's discussion with senior North Korean defectors residing in Seoul, April 2009.

5. These reports are registered at the party's Confidential Documents Bureau after receiving the final approval of the department or ministry's leadership. They are then sent to the Kim Chong-il personal secretariat where they are prepared for his approval. Hyon Song-il, *North Korea's National Strategy and Power Elite*.

6. Kim's secretariat is not authorized to reject any document without first receiving his approval. Hyon Song-il, *North Korea's National Strategy and Power Elite*.

7. According to Kim's former chef, Kenji Fujimoto, Kim no longer relies only on fax machines to respond to urgent reports. He also receives reports and conveys

his instructions through a private internal computer network. Kenji Fujimoto, *Kim Jong Il's Chef* (Seoul: Wo'lganchoso'nsa, 2003).

8. Whether this block of time still exists for Kim to read and respond to document reports in the aftermath of his stroke is not known.

9. A distinction was made between a "handwritten instruction" and a "handwritten document" in early 1990s as the volume of guidance from Kim's office increased dramatically leading to laxity in interpretation during the implementation process. Hyon Song-il, *North Korea's National Strategy and Power Elite.*

10. Hyon Song-il, *North Korea's National Strategy and Power Elite.*

11. Ibid.

Index

About the Author

KEN E. GAUSE is a senior research analyst with CNA, a not-for-profit, federally funded research and development center for the Navy and Marine Corps located in Alexandria, Virginia. He also created and oversees CNA's Foreign Leadership Studies Program. Based on methodologies and analytical techniques he helped develop during the 1980s with his work on the Soviet Union, the FLSP specializes in studies of the world's opaque regimes—their leaderships and decision-making dynamics. In the public domain, Mr. Gause has published numerous articles on the North Korean leadership for such publications as the *Korean Journal for Defense Analysis, Foreign Policy Magazine*, and *Jane's Intelligence Review*. He is also the author of *North Korean Civil-Military Trends: Military-First Politics to a Point* (Carlisle, PA: Strategic Studies Institute of the U.S. Army War College, 2006) and *Police State: North Korea's System of Control, Surveillance, and Punishment* (Washington, DC: Committee for Human Rights in North Korea, 2011).